30 SHORT PLAYS

FOR PASSIONATE ACTORS

30 SHORT PLAYS
FOR PASSIONATE ACTORS

Edited by Lisa Soland

Foreword by Lawrence Harbison

30 SHORT PLAYS FOR PASSIONATE ACTORS
Edited by Lisa Soland, with a foreword by Lawrence Harbison

Published in 2016 by All Original Play Publishing
P.O. Box 32381
Knoxville, TN 37930
AllOriginalPlays@gmail.com

First Edition: December 2016
Printed in the United States of America
Book Design by Zachary Hodges
Logo Design by Charlotte Widen
Cover photo by Steve Wilson: Tiffany Tallent in *Hooray for Hollywood!* produced along
    with a collection of plays by Lisa Soland entitled, *The Ladder Plays*.

ISBN 978-0-9965721-3-2
Library of Congress Control Number 2016909207

CONTENTS

PLAYS FOR TWO MEN

PLAYS FOR TWO WOMEN & ONE MAN

PLAYS FOR TWO MEN & ONE WOMAN

PLAYS FOR THREE WOMEN

PLAYS FOR THREE MEN

PLAYS FOR FOUR OR MORE ACTORS

• • • • • • • • • • • •

RIGHTS AND PERMISSIONS

FOREWORD

Lisa Soland, teacher, actress and a fine playwright herself, has here assembled a wonderful collection of short plays. Some are comic (laughs), some are dramatic (no laughs), some are somewhere in between. A few of the playwrights whose work is represented here are ones whose work I have published in the anthologies I have edited for Smith and Kraus and Applause Theatre and Cinema Books, such as Don Nigro, Debbie Lamedman, Stephanie Hutchinson, Gary Garrison and Craig Pospisil and Ms. Soland herself, but most are new to me. It never ceases to amaze me when I contemplate the huge number of really fine playwrights. I don't think there has ever been such a wealth of writing for the theater.

If you're a passionate actor, a teacher or a director looking for a play to do, you won't find a better place to start looking than this book.

— Lawrence Harbison

About Lawrence Harbison

For over thirty years, Lawrence Harbison was in charge of new play acquisition for Samuel French, Inc., during which time he was responsible for the publication of hundreds of plays, by playwrights such as Jane Martin, Don Nigro, Tina Howe, Theresa Rebeck, William Mastrosimone, Charles Fuller and Ken Ludwig among many others; and the acquisition of musicals such as *Smoke on the Mountain, A…My Name Is Alice* and *Little Shop of Horrors*. He is a now a free-lance editor for Smith and Kraus, Inc., for whom he edits annual anthologies of ten-minute plays and monologues for men and for women, and for several years edited their annual New Playwrights and Women Playwrights anthologies (for a complete list of his Smith & Kraus books, click on the Writers tab at www.smithandkraus.com); and for Applause Theatre & Cinema Books, for whom he has edited several monologue, scene, full-length, 10-minute and 5-minute play anthologies. His column, "On the Aisle with Larry," is a regular feature at www.smithandkraus.com as well as on his blog at www.playfixer. com and on www.doollee.com, the international playwrights database. He is a member of two NYC press organizations, the Outer Critics Circle and the Drama Desk, and was a member of the Drama Desk Awards Nominating Committee for the 2010-2011 and 2011-2012 seasons.

He works with individual playwrights to help them develop their plays (see his website, www.playfixer.com). He has also served as literary manager or literary consultant for several theatres, such as Urban Stages and American Jewish Theatre. He has served many times over the years as a commentator for various M.F.A. programs and as a judge for play contests and lectures occasionally at colleges and universities. He taught in the Theatre Dept. of the University of Michigan in the winter semester of 2016. He holds a B.A. from Kenyon College and an M.A. from the University of Michigan.

His book, *How I Did It: Establishing a Playwriting Career*, a collection of interviews with playwrights, was published by Applause Theatre & Cinema Books in March, 2015. *The Best 10-Minute Plays of 2016* and *The Best Stage Monologues for Men* and *The Best Stage Monologues for Women* were published by Smith and Kraus, Inc. in 2016. *Best Plays 2015*, the latest installment in an annual series he edits for Applause, will be published in the fall of 2016.

SENSIBLE LOW-HEELED BROWN PUMPS

A commentary on
The All Original Playwright Workshop

My first AOPW experience was as an *actor*. At least it started out that way. I had previously worked with Lisa, as an *actor*, so she knew that I was an *actor*. I was very excited to participate in the workshop, because, as an *actor*, I have always loved supporting new work. New work is critical to the survival of theater, and, as an *actor*, it thrilled me to be the first person to say a playwright's words aloud. It has always been important to me to help a playwright distill a character's thoughts, words, emotions, to the very essence of its being. It is an honor and a privilege and a sacred, intimate trust that must exist between an actor and a playwright. And, as an *actor*, I understood (and understand) this trust deeply.

So, I showed up on the first day of the eight-week thrill fest of embodying characters that were fresh out of someone's imagination, early and ready to go. It was a Saturday morning. Lisa dressed in a pantsuit and wore sensible, low-heeled, brown pumps. For those of us who were new to the workshop, she made introductions. And there I was, scrubbed, rosy, enthusiastic, and very, very naïve.

It was all going swimmingly. Plays were being developed, scenes were being created, feedback was given, rewrites were happening. It was very, very exciting! Every Saturday morning, there I was, scrubbed, rosy, enthusiastic, and very, very naïve, but facilitating the work of playwrights.

Until week five. Because on week five, after a very satisfying read-through of a scene, a suggestion was made.

Now, as previously noted, I am an *actor*, and I am an *actor* who is open to suggestions. I will go so far as to say that I welcome suggestions. It is one of the ways in which I hone my *acting* craft. But this suggestion that was made, caused me to stop breathing momentarily. In fact, to this day, I cannot recall the scene I had just read. I remember only that it felt good to read it.

It was suggested by Lisa, to me (an *actor*, participating in the workshop as an *actor*, to facilitate the playwrights' work) that I, an *actor*, should "write something."

"I'm not a writer. I'm an *actor*. I'm here to facilitate the playwrights' work," I naïvely responded to Lisa.

"Well," she said. "That's like going to a potluck and not bringing a dish."

"Uhhhhhhhhhhh," I said. Now, one would think that this response would be sufficient to convince Lisa that I was unable to string even two words together. But Lisa is… Well, Lisa is many wonderful things, but the appropriate word here is, tenacious.

"I'll tell you what," she said. "You go home and write something really bad. I mean, crappy. In fact, I challenge you to write the worst piece of crap ever to be written."

"I…uhhhhhhhh," I said. *Well, lookee there. I strung two words together*, I thought.

"And you come back next week, and you're going to read it to the rest of us. Whatever it is. And truthfully? It's not going to matter what it is. And, I bet you surprise yourself."

Even though Lisa was nowhere near me, I could feel one of her sensible, low-heeled, brown pumps resting firmly against my bum, pushing me forward.

I waited until the morning before the next Saturday workshop to start. Not that I didn't try earlier, but I already had writer's block and I hadn't even started yet. Fearing that Lisa would actually exert force on my bum with that sensible, low-heeled, brown pump, I took that Friday morning off from work and sat in the UCLA-adjacent Starbucks on Wilshire and put my pen to the paper. I wrote a ten page or so, stream of consciousness monologue, I guess. Very sloppy. Big cursive strokes.

The next morning, week six, I showed up with a blotchy face and dark circles under my eyes. I hoped that either Lisa had forgotten, or that there wouldn't be sufficient time for me to read what I had written. After all, the playwrights who had worked since day one were preparing their final scenes for the performance – the public performance that happened on week eight. Which was only two weeks away. That would take priority, surely. Everyone settled in to their little theatrical seats, long depleted of any satisfactory padding.

Typically I am not nervous on stage. One time I showed up to see a play, and was whisked backstage, put in costume, and performed with script in hand. I had not seen the show. I had not attended a rehearsal. I thought that would be the most terrifying moment of my career. But then, Lisa called my name.

Somehow I made it onto the stage and sat in a chair. I read my stream of consciousness piece of crap. I finished. Silence. No applause, polite or otherwise. No comments, whispers, coughs, or clearing of throats. Just dead silence.

So I sat there. Waiting. Finally, Lisa said, "Well." She turned to the group, sitting in the audience chairs. "What do you think, guys?" Lisa asked. Not a word from anyone. Lisa turned back to me. "I tell ya, you've got about five plays there, Melanie. Pick one and start writing it. I'll need a ten-minute scene by next week."

That scene led to a play. That play got a reading at the Pasadena Playhouse. I am still an *actor*. But I'm now also a *playwright*. And I hope that Lisa never, ever, throws away those sensible, low-heeled, brown pumps.

Today, my short play *Old School* is being published alongside brilliantly crafted plays in an anthology by a person who inspires the best work out of her students by letting them off the "perfection" hook and instructing them to write crap. So thank you, Lisa! Thank you for training us how to craft really tight short plays and otherwise. Thank you for always encouraging your students to write – to just put pen to paper, or fingers to keyboard, and write. Do the work. Keep doing the hard work and stop worrying about the outcome. The outcome will always take care of itself. See!

– Melanie Ewbank, actor *and* playwright

Biography

Lisa Soland's plays *Waiting, Cabo San Lucas, The Name Game, Truth Be Told*, and *The Man in the Gray Suit & Other Plays* have been published by Samuel French Inc. With over 40 publications, Ms. Soland's work can also be found in "best of" anthologies by Samuel French Inc., Smith & Kraus, Applause Books, and Dramatic Publishing. She has produced and/or directed over 80 productions and play readings, 55 of which have been original. Ms. Soland has taught playwriting at Florida State University, Pellissippi State College, Lincoln Memorial University, and Maryville College. She created and led The All Original Playwright Workshop in Los Angeles for ten years, and continues to teach workshops throughout the country.

Hooray For Hollywood!

Lisa Soland

Hooray for Hollywood! was first produced in a collection of short plays entitled, *The Ladder Plays* at the Clayton Performing Arts Center at Pellissippi State College on March 23, 2012. The performance was directed by Lisa Soland and starred Tiffany Tallent in the role of Peg. The collection was then produced at Muskingum University Theatre and opened November 29, 2012, with J. Webb taking on the role of Peg. *The Ladder Plays* then opened at the Hermosa Beach Playhouse, October 7, 2016, in Hermosa Beach, California, produced by Geraldine Athas and directed by Julie Vasquez Nunis.

CHARACTERS

    PEG ENTWHISTLE: A talented, tortured soul, age 24. Wears gardenia perfume. Suffering intense mental anguish. [Based on the true story.]

SETTING

    Atop the letter "H" in the Hollywoodland sign, on top of Mount Lee in Griffith Park in Tinseltown, Hollywood, California.

TIME

    September 16, Friday night, 1932.

• • • • • • • • • • • •

The stage is empty but for an 11 feet wide, by six feet high block of white corrugated metal in the shape of an "H," with a ladder standing up behind it, unseen. (If in full view, the "H" would stand 50 feet high.) Peg, a 24 year old blonde woman with a short flapper hair cut and out of breath, appears over the back of the "H" and climbs over one of the two peaks of the letter. She is dressed in 1930's period clothes – a coat, hat, and carries a small purse.

PEG: Oh to be Ophelia and without thought or deed, simply fall into a body of water and make the decision , while floating, that when I go under, I will not struggle. I will not fight. I will choose instead to sink, like the heavy psychological weight I am, to the bottom of the lake. Lake Hollywood. Where is…? (Looks to her right, offstage.) There she is. The moon illuminates her for me, calling me to her, but I am finished with treading through the thorny primrose path. Here shall be my final destination.

(Peg sits, dangling her legs over the top of the "H," opens her purse and extracts a note pad and a pen, and begins to write her note.)

"Dear Uncle Harold, I hope that this will not prove an embarrassment to you in any way, or to my brothers, but I could no longer continue clawing my way through this treacherous experience called life." I would really like to know why in God's name I would be worried about him. My brothers? – yes. But him…?!

(She tears up the paper and throws it to the ground, then talks to God.)

PEG: God in heaven, are you there? I'm sitting here, before you, torn and broken. My heart permanently wounded. *(Beat.)* "The attractive good-hearted ingénue." My roles of conviction have vanished into a dreadful thin air, and I am left here with no character but a poor, leftover rendition of myself – Peg Entwhistle, actress extraordinaire, "attractive in the manner of a number of other fresh ingénues."Yip pee for me. I'm just like every other Tom, Dick and Harriet. What a death sentence that is – to be just like everyone else. *(Beat.)* To play any kind of an emotional scene I must work myself up to a certain, fevered pitch. If I am able to reach this with my first word, the rest of the words and lines take care of themselves. But if I fail, I have to build up the balance of the speeches, and in doing this, the whole characterization falls flat. For my characters, this applies, and now…for me.

(She stands to survey the situation.)

PEG: I must work myself up into some unnatural fevered pitch. Because what I am about to do here this evening, is not natural. It is unnatural to dive headfirst into the cold, hard ground. And not becoming of a young lady, either. Not becoming of my…special upbringing. *(Beat.)* Dear God, why me? "Peg, is that all you have for me on such a night as this? Such a dull uninteresting question for one such as you – a learned actress with style and talent and charisma." Well, look at where my talent has gotten me. Take a good, hard look, God! I never was much of a writer. Wish I had been. Seems like a much more balanced and sane sort of existence. But I must write now.

(Peg returns to sitting and the writing of the note.)

Pen something of interest in this last of notes.

(An idea, she writes.)

"I am leaving this mortal coil due to a long life of secret keeping; the pain of keeping a secret that must never be told, from one blackened heart to the next" – a dirty rotten thing, repeated, despite my admitting the wrong done unto myself. Despite that I am aware of it and recall every last perpetration. Evil repeats itself, it is in its unique design to do so, and I do not have the key to break the horrific cycle.

(To escape the pain, she becomes the dramatic actress.)

"There must be another way, she tells herself, but no proper escape is found." I have not one cent to my name. If I just had the funds to return to New York. If I just had train fare…I could get out of this Hollywood hell. Thanks, RKO! Thank you for ending my measly worthless life for me!

(Peg looks down and to her left, reading the letters beneath her.)

PEG: H, O, L, L… "Hollywoodland." A nightmarish place where starlets
shrivel and dreams die a slow and miserable death. *(Beat.)* "In a play
we must tell nothing that is not revealed by the spoken words; you
must find out all you want to know from the characters in the play.
There can be no rummaging in the past for us to show what sort of
people our characters are; we are allowed only to present them as they
toe the mark; then the handkerchief falls, and off they go."
(She drops her handkerchief and watches the manner in which it falls to the ground.)
Shuffling off this mortal coil. Act three, scene one.
(She stands to deliver the famous lines from Hamlet, as Hamlet.)
"Whether 'tis nobler in the mind to suffer the slings and arrows of
outrageous fortune, or to take arms against a sea of troubles, and by
opposing end them: to die, to sleep no more; and by a sleep, to say
we end the heart-ache, and the thousand natural shocks that flesh is
heir to? The fair Ophelia."
*(Peg bows as Hamlet, welcoming Ophelia, and then using her notepad as a fan
to fan herself.)*
"O! woe is me, to have seen what I have seen, see what I see!"
Woe is me.
(An idea occurs to her and she sits again, to write.)
"To whom finds this note amongst my things, had I been given the
chance, I would have played Ophelia much more effectively than that
ol' stuffed shirt Ethel Barrymore!" *(Crumples the paper and throws.)* "To
whom discovers my purse and coat, tell my uncle politely that he can
go to hell." *(Tears and throws paper, with sarcasm.)* A charming picture of
youth, I am. "In the cast Peg Entwistle and Humphrey Bogart hold
first place in supporting the star, Billie Burke, and both give fine and
serious performances. Miss Entwhistle presents a charming picture
of youth." Charming indeed. I haven't a good word to say about anyone
I have ever met. I wonder what Will Rogers would say to that!
(Peg removes mirror and lipstick from purse and applies.)
If my mother hadn't died, leaving me to my father to raise, with no
other woman at his disposal…but me. If my mother hadn't died…
Well, maybe then I would have stood a chance. Maybe I would be
like Will Rogers. But when one is so dismantled, one cannot face a
dismantled world. It's like broken glass trying to see itself in the
reflection of broken glass. *(Beat.)* People will ponder, they will ask,
"Why did she do it?" I must consider this when I write the note. I must
keep them pondering over it; mystery is what makes the play. Not all

Lisa Soland

answers should be revealed. I must maintain the mystery…and as a good woman, take the weight of sin with me.

(Reading aloud as she writes.)

PEG: "I am afraid I am a coward. I am sorry for everything." Everything? Am I sure I want to say that? After all, I did charm my father, right? It was my doing. My coy attitude and behavior, but…at such a young age. I, the great Broadway actress – coy at such a very young age. *(Stands.)* Who in their right mind would name their daughter "Millicent?" What were you thinking, Robert and Emily? You, with such normal names. *(Crumples paper and throws.)* I'll use Peg. Peg Entwhistle will do just fine in this wonderful world of entertainment. And what a movie debut I had! "David O. Selznick's Thirteen Women starring Irene Dunne, Myrna Loy and Peg Entwhistle." A disaster, like everything I touch. Tell me now Swami, what swift doom do you see happening here this evening? Maybe I should write to you instead. You are real, aren't you? If you exist in a movie, you must be real. Was it you who planted this unthinkable thought into my mind? Jump. Jump. Stop talking yourself to death and jump. *(Beat.)* Movies may make you famous but it's the theatre that makes you good. The only acting that challenges – my one remaining hope – shattered. If they'd only responded in some way positive to my audition, the Beverly Hills Playhouse. Hell, I'm a shoe-in for the role of a woman who commits suicide, don't you think? *(Looks up to God.)* You who created me like this – tainted! Don't you think?! That part was mine and they did nothing but sit there with those two-faced-looks on their Beverly Hills faces, saying how much they loved me, but did I receive a notice? Any form of communication whatsoever? No. This town isn't meant for soft souls. How does Will Rogers do it? "I never met a man I didn't like." Liar! Just like everyone else in this town, says one thing but means something else entirely. *(Beat.)* This city – all glitz and glamour, but when you take away the lights, all you have is the cold, hard metallic letters that do nothing to sooth the dark and lonely emptiness of failure. I'd get the hell out but I won't ask Harry for the money. He'll ask for another…favor, in a long line of favors. And I'd rather die.

(Realizing what she has said.)

PEG: Well…why not? Why not?! *(She writes, standing.)* "I am afriad I am a coward. I am sorry for everything. If I had done this a long time ago it would have saved a lot of pain."

PEG: Including my own. "P.E."

(Peg carefully folds the piece of paper and places it into her purse. She removes her coat, folds it and places it carefully, with the purse beside it. She then looks up into the sky.)

Forgive me.

(Having prepared herself, she is now ready to jump. Peg places her arms above her head, as if to dive and then…lights out.)

END OF PLAY

Biography

Don Nigro is one of the most widely published and produced playwrights in the world. Of his more than 400 plays, Samuel French has published 194 in 57 volumes, and those not yet published are available in manuscript at the Samuel French website. Three new volumes, *Nights At The Stray Dog Café*, *A Snowfall In Berlin* and *Traven And Other Plays* were published in the summer of 2016. His work has been translated into many languages and produced all over the world. Recent productions include *The Chaplin Plays: A Double Feature*, in New York; *Don Giovanni* in Moscow; *City Of Dreadful Night* in Los Angeles; *Animal Tales* in Ukraine; *A History Of The Devil* in Mexico City; and a film of *The Weird Sisters*, produced in Berlin.

Jezebel

Don Nigro

Jezebel was first presented in February of 2002 by Shadowbox Cabaret at 2Co's Cabaret in Columbus, Ohio, with Chris Lynch as Jimmy Prophet. Directed by Matthew Hahn.

(Playwright's note: This play is for my friends Anna Theresa Cascio and Pat Skipper, who sent me an old newspaper clipping, and let me sleep on the couch.)

        JAMES PROPHET: A theatre critic.

SETTING
        A bar in New York.

TIME
        1930s.

• • • • • • • • • • • •

There is one character, James Prophet, a theatre critic. He speaks to the audience from a bar in New York in the 1930s.

PROPHET: A lot of people think critics have no heart, but take it from me, that'sbullshit. We have feelings, too. We can bleed, we need love, we like to feel important, just like anybody else. We just have a job to do. Don't you go check and see what it says in the paper before you waste your time and money going to see a movie that's too stupid for your dog? I perform an important public service. And what do I get for it? Does anybody ever say thank you? Fat chance. But I'm proud of my work. That's why I want to explain to you exactly how all this Jezebel crap happened, so you'll understand how it was.

It started when McGonigle assigns me to this dance concert, a one-woman show by a dancer who is, shall we say, to be kind, a few decades past her prime. I didn't want to go. I don't do this dance crap much any more, but it was my regular beat once. Hell, everything was my beat once. I've written everything from gardening to homicide for this rag. But I was especially anxious to avoid this one because I used to know the lady in question, back in Chicago, when she was a lot younger and a pretty hot little number, and I saw her do this same program, called "Jezebel," and I didn't like it much then, so how good are the chances I'm going to like it now that she's got enough lard in her ass to bake two years' worth of gingerbread? Besides, the damned slut wouldn't sleep with me. Everybody else in Chicago who wore pants, and a couple who didn't, but not me. I could picture what it would be like: old lard ass out there bounding around with this stupid grin on her white, pasty face, impersonating a woman half her age, wobbling around like a swan on drugs and trying not to fart. And the poor jerks all around me pretending to each other that it's wonderful, so as not to let on to anybody that they're bored out of their minds and only here to impress somebody or other with how cultured they are. God, what a joke.

Still, I was going to go. I really was. I mean, it's a job—a dirty job, in this case, but something that had to be done—so I stopped at Rico's for a couple of drinks before curtain time, and that son of a bitch John Rhys Pendragon was there. Christ, I hate that guy. The bastard gets to go all over the world, always in the middle of this war or that scandal, interviewing everybody from Henry James to Joan Crawford and all the life forms in between. And the son of a bitch hates me, too. I mean, he thinks I'm the lowest.

—Where the hell did you crawl out from, Jimmy? says Pendragon. Getting your gallon of wine so you can go sleep through Shakespeare?

I told him to go perform an indecent act with a sheep, but he just laughed. He was sitting there with a blonde, a brunette and a redhead, and as usual getting along real well with them. The guy's always had the most incredible luck with women. I don't know how the hell he does it, or what they see in him. I know he's got to be seventy if he's a day, but the brunette, who's the cutest of the three, seems to be giving me the eye, but Pendragon is talking to them, and they're looking at me and laughing, so I know he's poisoning their minds about me. So I figure if I want to make any time with this brunette I better get my ass the hell over there, which I do. And these are three extremely fine looking women, so I says, Are you ladies by any chance actresses? And of course they all are. Well, show girls, out of work, naturally. So I tell them I'm James Prophet, the famous theatre critic, and they seem pretty impressed by this. They ask me if I'm going to the theatre tonight, so I tell them I've got to go see this dance concert by this old claw-footed has-been, and Pendragon looks at his watch and says, Shouldn't you be staggering over to the theatre about now, pal? The show's about to start. But the more wine I drink, the better the brunette starts to look to me, and the other two look pretty damned good, too, so I say, Hell, Pendragon, I don't even have to go to know what it's going to be like. And I describe for them how old lard ass will lumber out and stumble around like the Queen of the Ostriches, and then in the end get thrown head first from the tower, which is my favorite part because there's always the chance she'll miss the mattresses and break her scrawny neck, and the girls are laughing so hard they're almost peeing themselves, giggling and touching me and getting their hair near my face. God, they smell great. And Pendragon points to his watch and I say, Don't try to get rid of me, Johnny. Hell, I could write this damned review without even going. And he says I could never get away with that, so I bet him twenty bucks I could, and he says, You're on.

I'm feeling so damned good by this point that nothing bothers me, but Pendragon says, The dogs are going to lick your blood, Jimmy. The dogs are going to lick your blood.

But I'm on a roll. I'm composing the review in my head, and the girls are laughing, and it seems to me I'm making a great impression, but when I go to the john I come back and they're gone. The bartender tells me Pendragon left with the brunette and the blonde left with the redhead. I am pretty depressed by this turn of events, so I have a couple more glasses of wine, and then I happen to look at my watch and see that it's ten-thirty, so I get a cab over to the newspaper and sit down and write my review and hand it in, and then I go home and go to bed. It was one of my better reviews, if I do say so myself. I was really proud of it.

So the next morning I stagger down to the paper with this incredible hangover, and somebody from the theatre calls the paper, and they're furious about this bad review I've given old lard ass, and McGonigle is on the phone with them saying Uh uh, uh huh, uh huh, like he always does, and then he gives them this little speech of his about Freedom of the Press and the First Amendment and all that crap, and then he gets quiet again and starts in with the Uh huh, uh huh, I see, I see. I'll look into it and get back to you, he says. Then he comes over to my desk with this grim look on his face, and he says, Jimmy, they're a little ticked off down there at the nasty review you did for the dance concert last night.

—Listen, Mac, I says. My heart is breaking for them, but if they can't stand the heat, they should get their butts off the damned radiator.

Lisa Soland

And Mac says, Well, maybe, Jimmy, but the thing is, the star wasn't feeling well last night, and she couldn't go on, so they had to put somebody on in her place. So old bucket bottom, as I believe you refer to her in your sensitive review, didn't go on at all.

Now my head is killing me, but I don't panic. I says, Look, Mac, it's no big deal. I wasn't feeling too well myself last night. Maybe it was something I ate. I must have missed the announcement about the replacement. What's the difference? So it was a different lard ass doing that crap. It was still crap.

—But Jimmy, says McGonigle, when old lard ass couldn't go on, they didn't replace her with another woman. She's got no understudy. She's the only one who does this Jezebel thing, so they put on these two guys doing some goddamned Fric and Frac, Cain and Abel thing.

—Two guys? I said. It was two guys?

—That's what they tell me, says Mac.

—Well, I says, I guess I didn't have my bifocals on last night.

—You didn't go, did you, Jimmy? says Mac.

—Of course I went, I says. What do you take me for?

—Jimmy, he says, how the hell could you mistake two big fucking pansies doing Cain and Abel for one old broad doing Jezebel?

—Well, I says. Hell, Mac. Old lard ass is as big as two men.

But I knew that wasn't going to fly.

—You are in deep, deep shit, my friend, says Mac. I don't know if I can get you out of this one.

—Ah, worry, worry, I says. It'll all blow over. Nobody really gives a shit.

But it doesn't. There's this really big stink about it in the other papers, several of which I have left employment at various times in the past, having burned a few bridges rather spectacularly in departing. Some of these assholes have been looking to get me for a long time, so they play it up with a lot of pleasure. Plus, the whole damned theatre community has got a big wad up their collective artsy fartsy butt about it, partly because I may have been a shade rough on some of them over the years, in my capacity as the world's greatest authority. And to make it worse, somebody digs up the blonde and the redhead, who swear they heard me bragging I didn't need to be there to write a review. So the Old Man calls McGonigle into his office and gives him the royal what for, screaming and throwing things around and using some pretty colorful language, and McGonigle comes out looking full of woe and says, I'm sorry, Jimmy, but the Old Man says I got to can you. I got no choice. Clean out your desk.

So I do what any responsible journalist would do. I go to the nearest bar and get as drunk as I can. And in walks John Rhys Pendragon, since the nearest bar happens to be Rico's, and that is where he drinks. And he comes over and says, Jimmy, I want to tell you how sorry I am about what happened. Now where's my twenty bucks?

So I tell him what he can do with his twenty bucks, and suggest a few things about his ancestry, but he just laughs and buys me a drink. Then Eddie Quinn from the Union comes in, and sits down beside me, and puts his arm around me, and says, Don't worry, Jimmy. The Union is going to take care of you.

So I suggest that he go screw his sister, because the Union never in the past did much for me but take my money, but it turns out, to my surprise, that old Eddie can spot an opportunity to turn shit into gold when he sees it, and damned if the Union don't actually come through for me. They make an even bigger stink than there was before. They tell the Old Man that I have toiled mightily in the vineyards for many years on his arse-wipe of a paper, shamefully overworked and grossly underpaid, and now that I've been involved in one little misunderstanding, the cold, greedy management has jumped at the chance to put me and my children out in the street—this last is a nice touch, given that I haven't seen my children in eight years and wouldn't know

Lisa Soland

them if they mugged me on the subway—and that every Union member on the whole damned paper is going out on strike tomorrow morning if he doesn't reinstate me immediately.

Now, I am not personally so sure that's what would happen, because frankly half these guys don't know me from Myrtle McTurtle, and the other half hates my guts, and I haven't exactly been a great Union man in my time, but Eddie Quinn can smell a great excuse for a major league power play when he stumbles over one, and the Old Man, after a lot of yelling and screaming and extremely creative neo-Elizabethan cussing I really wish I had written down, finally grits his teeth and agrees to take me back, because, as he puts it, what the hell does he care what a bunch of artsy fartsy damned tinker bells think, anyhow? So not only do I get hired back, but I get back pay for the time I was fired, and a nice raise to boot. That'll teach those artsy fartsy shitheads to mess with James Prophet. And the next night, John Rhys Pendragon comes up to me at the bar and gives me the twenty bucks and says, Okay, Jimmy, here's your money. You win. I want you to know, he says, it wasn't that I ever underestimated your remarkable ability to land on your feet. I simply overestimated the intelligence of the dogs. One of my persistent faults.

So actually it turned out to be a real career boost for me. In fact, to tell you the truth, I haven't been to a performance of anything in three months, and I think I'm doing some of the best reviews of my life, now that I don't have to waste so much time sitting in those damned drafty or overheated, cramped, filthy old theatres, inhaling the stench of the general populace, my cretinous loyal readership, and looking at crap every night. I'm telling you, this is great. The problem with most reviewers is, they go to the theatre way too much, and it rots their brains. Don't get me wrong. Broadway is my beat, and New York is the greatest city in the world, and I love the theatre, but, Christ, give me a break. It's like my ex-wife. I like her a hell of a lot better now that I don't have to sleep with her any more. So listen, sweetheart. The show doesn't let out for another twenty minutes or so. You want to buy me a drink?
(Lights out.)

END OF PLAY

Biography

With multiple ten-minute play productions, Ms. Athas is most proud of her recent production of her full-length play, *The Ten Year Plan*, also developed as part of The All Original Playwright Workshop. She enjoys helping other playwrights see their work come to life as a producer of Hermosa Beach's Ten-Minute Play Festivals. Gerry thanks Lisa Soland, and her sons, Nick, Alex and Andrew, for their unwavering support.

The Golf Lesson

Geraldine Athas

The Golf Lesson was written in The All Original Playwright Workshop and first produced for AOPW's production of "Wind and Tide" on October 11, 2009, at Theatre Encino, Encino, California. It was directed by Lisa Soland and starred Todd Covert in the role of RJ and Shannon Kennedy in the role of JoJo. *The Golf Lesson* was then produced at the Second Story Theatre in Hermosa Beach, California, on June 4, 2011 as part of "Take Two," an evening of ten-minute plays. There it was directed by Geraldine Athas, JoJo was played by Elizabeth Sandy, and RJ was play by Greg Abbott. *The Golf Lesson* was then produced at the Brick House Theatre, North Hollywood, California on July 30 to August 21, 2016 as part of "Near-Life Experiences," an evening of one-act plays presented by the Write Act Repertory. There it was directed by Susan C. Hunter, JoJo was played by Kay Capasso, and RJ was play by Frank Amiack.

CHARACTERS

JO JO: 30-35ish female – very beautiful woman with a sexy quality – she's, in a word, "hot" and "out of his league" – with a pleasant smile. She's wearing a short, white golf skirt and white golf shirt, with a bag of golf clubs, ideally a golf bag carrying cart.

RJ: 30-35ish, male – average looking with average physique – wearing a bright, solid colored golf shirt and obnoxious, plaid golf pants, with a bag of golf clubs, ideally with a golf bag-carrying cart.

SETTING

Golf driving range.

• • • • • • • • • • • •

Jo Jo, with beautiful form, swings and hits golf ball. RJ arrives pulling golf clubs behind him on a cart and carrying a bucket of balls. He is stunned by Jo Jo's beauty and her beautiful swing. [Swinging clubs can be real or mimed.]

JO JO: Are you my lesson?

RJ: *(Fumbling slightly.)* Lesson?

JO JO: My eight a.m. lesson with the golf pro?

RJ: I'd like to think I was a pro, but no... I'm not a pro.

JO JO: Oh sorry, the guy in the shop told me to come out to this booth and Bill would be there for my lesson.

RJ: Oh Bill, he's always late. He'll be here.

JO JO: Oh.

(Jo Jo puts on her white golf glove, chooses a different club, stretches out her arms then places her ball on the tee. RJ chooses a club also. Jo Jo is just about to swing when RJ swings with a grunt. Jo Jo, bothered by his grunt, stops mid-swing. Jo Jo swings. Jo Jo takes out a "ball" places it on the tee and just as she lines up for her next swing, RJ swings again with a grunt. Jo Jo backs off her ball and stares at RJ.)

RJ: Something wrong?

JO JO: Yes.

RJ: My swing, my club, my plaid pants?

JO JO: No. No. No. The noise.

RJ: What noise?

JO JO: The noise you make when you swing. It's like a grunt.

Lisa Soland

RJ: I don't make any noise when I swing.

(Jo Jo motions for him to swing. He obliges and grunts.)

RJ: I don't hear anything.

JO JO: Grunt. Are you listening for it?

(RJ swings again with a grunt.)

JO JO: It's like a... *(Imitates the noise.)*

RJ: I don't do that.

(Jo Jo waves her hand to RJ, inviting him to swing. RJ lines up to swing. She waits. He swings. Grunt.)

RJ: It's not really a grunt. It's more like a huff.

JO JO: So you do hear it?

RJ: Okay, I hear it. I guess I do that when I'm really comfortable with my swing.

JO JO: Well, it's disturbing to the player next to you.

RJ: No one has ever told me that before.

JO JO: Well they may not have told you, but it is. If I wasn't waiting for my lesson I'd move to another tee.

RJ : Sorry. I'll try to keep it down.

(They both line up for a new shot. RJ notices her and he swings with no grunt. He "watches" his ball curves way off to the left. He's not happy. RJ backs off from his ball and stares at Jo Jo.)

JO JO: Something wrong?

RJ: Yes, I was so worried about not grunting that I can't concentrate on my swing.

(Jo Jo stares in amazement.)

RJ: *(Complaining.)* What now?

JO JO: It's just that...you're considerate.

RJ: Considerate?

JO JO: Yes. That you would change your routine because I asked.

RJ: Well, yes. I guess that was considerate.

(Jo Jo takes off her golf gloves, reaches out her hand for a handshake.)

JO JO: I'm Jo Jo. Jo Jo Barnes.

(RJ shakes her hand. They stare.)

RJ: Robert James Armstrong. My friends call me RJ.

JO: Nice to meet you, RJ.

RJ: Oh. You'll be friends with a grunter then?

JO JO: I'll be friends with a guy who stops grunting for me.

RJ: Ok.

(They both hit the ball again.)

JO JO: You must be a very considerate husband.

RJ: I'm not married.

JO JO: Oh. Very considerate boyfriend, then.

RJ: No. I'm not a boyfriend either.

JO JO: Oh.

(They both hit the ball again.)

RJ: You mean your husband doesn't compensate for you?

JO JO: No.

RJ: Oh.

JO JO: No. No. No husband.

RJ: Boyfriend?

JO JO: No.

RJ: Oh.

JO JO: Oh.

RJ: You know, I was thinking.

JO JO: Yes.

RJ: I was thinking you have a really nice…swing.

JO JO: Oh really?

RJ: Yes. It's very…fluid.

JO JO: What do you mean?

(RJ demonstrates.)

RJ: It flows.

JO JO: Oh. Thank you.

RJ: I have an idea.

JO JO: Oh?

RJ: How about we line up for a shot, then you just go first and you won't have to worry about my grunt?

JO JO: That's really very sweet. And considerate.

(They both hit the ball. Both smiling ear-to-ear. Jo Jo all excited then suddenly...)

JO JO: You know, I was thinking…

RJ: Oh?

(The each hit a ball.)

JO JO: I must confess. Why I really took up golf.

RJ: Oh?

JO JO: I took up golf to meet men.

(Both smiling. They hit the balls again.)

RJ : Well, then, you know I really must confess something, too.

JO JO: Oh?

RJ: I'm filling in for Bill today.

JO JO: What?

Lisa Soland

RJ: I am your lesson.

JO JO: You're the pro?

RJ: Yes.

JO JO: *(Kinda annoyed.)* Why didn't you say?

RJ: Well, this is kind of embarrassing.

JO JO: Worse than the grunt?

RJ: Much worse.

JO JO: Oh.

RJ: I...uh... You know, when I saw you I thought, "I can't give a lesson to this beautiful woman with that beautiful swing."

JO JO: Oh.

RJ: Yep.

JO JO: Thank you, I guess.

RJ: Wait. It gets worse.

JO JO: Oh?

RJ: I thought, "A woman that beautiful is going to be difficult. The beautiful ones always are."

JO JO: Oh.

RJ: I'm so sorry. You're actually very nice.

JO JO: Thank you, I guess.

(They go back to hitting the balls – her first, then him.)

JO JO: Okay, okay, I thought something, too. About you.

RJ: Really?

JO JO: I thought you looked ridiculous in those plaid pants. And I was hoping you weren't the pro.

RJ: Oh.

JO JO: Wait it gets worse.

RJ: Oh.

JO JO: I thought that any guy who wears plaid pants like that must be a real jerk.

RJ: Oh.

JO JO: But, you're not.

RJ: Thank you, I guess.

(They go back to hitting the golf balls.)

RJ: Fascinating.

JO JO: What?

RJ: Well, I always substitute for Bill because he always teaches the women golfers. I thought that would be a great way to meet women.

JO JO: Oh.

RJ: Isn't that great?

JO JO: How so?

RJ: We're both trying to meet someone.

JO JO: I guess.

>> *(They go back to hitting balls.)*

RJ: Meet any nice guys playing golf?

JO JO: Not any nice ones.

RJ: Not any?

JO JO: *(Smirking.)* Not until today. *(Hits a shot.)*

RJ: Oh really.

>> *(RJ hits a great shot with a loud grunt.)*

JO JO: And you?

RJ: Today's a first for me, too. I mean. Meeting a beautiful. And nice. Woman. Playing golf.

>> *(Pause.)*

JO JO: I have an idea.

RJ: Yes.

JO JO: Would you like to hit a bucket of balls together someday?

RJ: Sure.

JO JO: How about today?

RJ: That's a very nice idea.

>> *(He motions for her to hit the ball first. She swings, hits the ball with a loud grunt.)*

END OF PLAY

Biography

At the age of sixteen, Christina Martinez joined the All Original Playwright Workshop in Los Angeles, and wrote her first play, *Love Chaines* as her High School senior thesis. Christina continues to write and work on perfecting the one-act play. She can be found most days, working behind a desk or walking her dog, Diego.

My Little Big Brother

Christina Martinez

My Little Big Brother was written in The All Original Playwright Workshop's Four-Day Intensive in Los Angeles, California, where it was then included as part of the final workshop reading presentation, "Everything But The Kitchen Scene," on July 13, 2014.

CHARACTERS
> LYDIA: Female in her early twenties. She's a self-sufficient,
> hard-working, intelligent young woman. She is a year
> and a half younger than her brother.
> DAVID: Male in his early twenties. He's an overweight, hard-
> working, depressed young man. He is the older
> brother.

SETTING
> David's bedroom.

· · · · · · · · · · · ·

*David is asleep on the bed, without a bed sheet, facing upstage. The room is a
mess. There is a TV and two computer monitors on a desk that is too big for the
space. There is an oversized office chair in between the mattress and the desk.
Books, magazines, empty beer cans stashed in various areas. There are a few
different sized empty bottles and brands of whiskey on the desk and strewn across
the room. A tattered blanket blocks the sun from the only window in the room.
The door to the bedroom is stage left. The overall feel of the space is disheveled
and depressing.*

LYDIA: *(Offstage, loudly knocking on the bedroom door.)* David! David! What the hell
David?!? I'm coming in. You better have pants on.
*(Enters the room and can immediately smell the alcohol. Looking around the room,
she is hesitant to walk further than a foot or two into the room.)*
David, wake up.
(No response. Louder.)
Wake up!
*(David stirs. Turning slowly to face her, the audience can see for the first time that
David is hung-over with dark circles under his eyes.)*
LYDIA: What are you doing? Why aren't you at work? David!
DAVID: *(Dazed. Annoyed.)* What?
LYDIA: I said why aren't you at work? Gary called me. They're looking for
you. Are you still drunk?
DAVID: What do you want?
LYDIA: They are looking for you. Gary called me and asked me to come
and check on you. You haven't answered your phone. Mom and Dad
have been calling you. They are both freaking out, saying they'll drive
back from the ranch if they have to. Jesus, David, have you even slept?

Lisa Soland

DAVID: No.

LYDIA: What the hell is wrong with you? Gary said you better show up today or they're going to fire you.

DAVID: *(Rolling over.)* So what?

LYDIA: David, I'm serious. *(Quivering.)* I don't need this shit right now. I had to drop everything . I literally left James at the house with the U-Haul. I'm supposed to be moving today and instead I'm here checking on your ass. I don't need this shit right now.

DAVID: *(Turning to yell at her.)* Then go! *(Winces.)*

LYDIA: DAVID! I'M SERIOUS! THEY'RE GOING TO FIRE YOU! Do you understand? This isn't a game. They are serious this time. Whatever stunt you pulled this time has them fuming. Gary said that if you don't go in today they are going to fire you no questions asked. No more chances. *(Beat.)* I drove all the way here. Just get up. I'll drive you. Come on, David. What happened?

DAVID: Nothing.

LYDIA: What do you mean? This is *not* nothing. What happened?

DAVID: Nothing! I'm just sick of their shit. They don't care about me. They're just like everybody else... I'm not a human to them. I'm another number. Why should I work there?

LYDIA: Look, we all hate our jobs, okay? But now is not the time to pull this crap. Seriously. You want another job? Great. We'll find you another job. But you cannot do this right now. Not like this.

DAVID: I can't go back.

LYDIA: Well, you have to. They're looking for you.

DAVID: Probably so they can fire me.

LYDIA: Okay! Great! Maybe you can get severance or something. But you have to get up. I mean it. I don't have time for this. You're supposed to be the big brother, David. I can't just drop everything like this. You have GOT TO GET YOUR SHIT TOGETHER!

DAVID: *(Starting to sob.)* I can't. I can't go back there. I can't do this.

LYDIA: David… What happened?

DAVID: They are fucking assholes! All they do is make me feel worthless. And they don't even know how much I do for them. I don't even know why I stay... I put my heart into this insane work and for what? So I can kill myself? I can't keep showing up day after day just so they can piss on me. Piss on everyone. It's not worth it.

LYDIA: I get it. Don't you think I get it? But this is not new. This is life. It's not perfect. But sometimes we have to just deal. I'm not saying sell your soul for them but please…please…don't give up like this. Not today. Let's just get you to work and see what happens. Maybe it won't be that bad. So you didn't show up today, no biggie.

DAVID: I didn't show up yesterday either.

LYDIA: David. What the hell —

DAVID: I got drunk. Monday night. I posted something on Facebook and they saw it.

LYDIA: What do you mean?

DAVID: I was just venting. But I was drunk. So it was pretty brutal. I called out the executives. Called them all life sucking demons that don't know their head from their assholes.

LYDIA: David.

DAVID: I know. My phone started blowing up like seconds later. Gary kept calling me. But it was too late. It was already out there and I just didn't care.

LYDIA: So you kept drinking?

DAVID: *(Ashamed.)* Yeah.

LYDIA: Jesus. Since Monday night? David. It isn't supposed to work like this. You can't lose your job. Not now. Not with Dad out of work.

DAVID: Fuck Dad.

LYDIA: David. Dad just doesn't get you.

DAVID: No, Lydia, Dad doesn't even see me. I'm just a shadow to him – a shadow that helps with the bills.

LYDIA: They need you to keep your job. We all need you to keep your job. I can't help. I'm already stretched as it is. You know that.

DAVID: Yeah.

(Pause.)

LYDIA: How does this happen?

DAVID: What?

LYDIA: How do two kids grow up at the same time, in the same family, with the same parents, and end up so completely different? How does that happen? I know it wasn't always great, but we had it good compared to most. You know that. How does it happen that I have to drive here in the middle of the day, in the middle of the week, in the middle of my life, to scrape up the remnants of your life? This isn't right.

DAVID: I'm sorry.

LYDIA: *(Getting mean.)* No you're not. You're not sorry. You're pathetic! You're supposed to be my big brother! I'm supposed to be able to go to you when I need help. I'm supposed to look up to you. What the hell is wrong with you?!

DAVID: I'M A FUCKING ALCOHOLIC! *(Beat. Crying.)* Can't you see that? Can't ANYBODY see that? No. No... Nobody sees it. No one really cares do they? *(Silence.)* I've never admitted it until just now but it's true. All I want to do is drink. I don't want to think. I don't want to hurt. I don't want to live.

LYDIA: Don't say that. David. You're not an alcoholic.

DAVID: LYDIA! Yes I am! Don't tell me that I'm not! I'm a fucking alcoholic. Don't try and sweep this under the rug with the rest of my life. I'm trying to tell you something important here. Please. Please don't ignore that. I'm an alcoholic, just like Dad was. You have to know that.

LYDIA: So what now? So now you're just going to lie there and wallow?

DAVID: So what.

LYDIA: Look, I want to help. Any way I can. Just tell me. But please... Please, I'm begging you. Just get up. Take a shower. I'll take you to work myself.

DAVID: Do you remember...in third grade...? You were in third grade. I was in fourth. Do you remember when they sent me to your class?

LYDIA: No.

DAVID: Really? You don't remember me being sent to your class?

LYDIA: No.

DAVID: I'd really messed up. I don't even remember what I did anymore. Something bad, I don't know... Whatever it was my teacher was furious with me. She yelled at me in front of the whole class. Then she wrote me a pink slip and sent me to your class... She said, "If you want to act like a third grader then you can go be with the third graders. Like your little sister." And she sent me away. *(Beat.)* I started to cry. I remember walking down the hallway to the third grade classrooms. I was so humiliated. And I knew you'd be embarrassed. I knew you'd pretend like you didn't know me. *(Beat.)* And you did. You pretended like you didn't know me.

LYDIA: David. I honestly don't remember that.

DAVID: My whole life, Lydia... My whole life has felt like one long walk down that humiliating hallway.

LYDIA: *(Beat.)* I'm sorry. For ignoring you. I shouldn't have done that.

DAVID: We were little. And it was so long ago. *(Silence.)* What am I supposed to do now?

LYDIA: I don't know. But we'll figure it out. I promise. *(Beat.)* Maybe for

now we just take it one day at a time? Isn't that what they say? In AA
or whatever? I don't know. Maybe you should look into it...

DAVID: AA...? Yeah, maybe...

LYDIA: I don't know, David... You really don't think you can make it in today?

DAVID: I feel like shit.

LYDIA: *(Smiling.)* You look like shit.

DAVID: *(Smiling.)* Thanks.

LYDIA: Maybe your first step should be a shower.

DAVID: Yeah, okay.

LYDIA: Then I'll drive you?

DAVID: *(Considering.)* Yeah, okay.

LYDIA: Good. *(Beat.)* David? I'm really sorry for ignoring you. I know we
were just kids, but that's no excuse. I've done some shitty things. I'm
not proud of myself sometimes. But you are my brother... I'm sorry.

DAVID: Thanks.

LYDIA: Is it okay if I call Mom and Dad and let them know you're all right?

DAVID: Not yet. Let them worry a bit.

LYDIA: *(Smiling.)* All right. But I am calling Gary.

*(David stands and crosses to door. He stops in the entryway to listen. Lydia speaks
into the phone with her back to David.)*

LYDIA: Gary? Yeah, he's okay. He's in the shower now. *(Annoyed.)* Listen,
everything is going to be fine. He's agreed to let me drive him. He
doesn't need you to lecture him right now, okay...? Good. You'll have
to bring him home... Okay. Bye.

(She hangs up the phone and looks up to see that David has been watching her.)

DAVID: Thanks.

(Lydia shrugs "you're welcome." Lights out.)

END OF PLAY

Lisa Soland

Biography

Bette Smith began writing in The All Original Playwright Workshop in the Spring of 2003. Her first piece, *The Executor*, was produced at that time. Since then she has written several shorts, a children's play and a full-length play. Her one-woman show, *Days of Dilemma*, won the AOPW Fellowship Award and was produced at the Whitefire Theatre in February 2015 at the Solo Fest.

Self Check Out

Bette Smith

Self Check Out was written in The All Original Playwright Workshop and first produced for AOPW's production of "Have Pen Will Travel" on Feb 23, 2006. It was directed by Nina Sallinen, with Bette Smith playing Mary and Nina Sallinen as the Voice. It was since produced by the Whitefire Theatre in Sherman Oaks, California, in the Spring of 2014 for their production of "Spring Shorts." Subsequently, it was chosen as one of the "Best of Shorts" at the Whitefire and was presented again, opening in October of 2016.

CHARACTERS
> MARY: Frustrated shopper. Adult female.
> VOICE: Sensual, sweet, or robotic voice. Should be read with the same inflection. May increase volume, but keep the same rhythm.

SETTING
> Supermarket at the checkout.

TIME
> Present day. Late afternoon.

• • • • • • • • • • • •

Supermarket at checkout area. Center stage has a table with a scanner screen. Other checkout areas are beyond the fourth wall. A sign is hanging which reads "Self Check Out." Mary enters from offstage, laden down with items from the store, talking on her cell phone.

MARY: Are you sure you want me to get these now…? But the lines are unbelievable. How much time do you have…? Forget it then! I can't possibly be out of here in five minutes. I'll be lucky if I even see the clerk in five minutes. There are only two lines open and each one has at least twenty people… There is no express line, at least if there is, it's not open… Self check out? It's right here… I don't know, I've never done it before… If it's that easy, how come everyone's standing in those lines…? No, there's no attendant, they must be short of help…! All right, I'll try. I just hope it's not too complicated… No! Don't leave. How will I get home…? I'm not going to take the bus. I don't have time for that. Besides, I'll be carrying all of these groceries, and most of them are for you. Well, just sit there! A parking space will open up… Then drive around the block, for God's sakes, but don't leave! *(She places the items on the table. A loud objectionable sound is heard.)*
VOICE: Unidentified item in bagging area.
MARY: What? *(Looks at items.)* Oh, sorry! *(Grabs them.)* Where am I supposed to put…? I knew I should have taken a cart. *(Puts stuff on the floor.)* Now what do I do? Let's see. Begin! *(Touches screen.)*
VOICE: BEEP.
MARY: That was easy.

35

Lisa Soland

VOICE: Scan first item.

(Mary picks up an item and tries to scan it in many directions.)

VOICE: *(Repeats until next line.)* Scan first item.

MARY: I'm trying to. Where's the scanner? Where's the little beam of light —

VOICE: BEEP.

MARY: Finally! $2.99! That's right! Hey, this is cool! People have got to be crazy to wait in those long lines.

VOICE: Place item in bag in bagging area.

(Mary places the item in her purse.)

VOICE: Place item in bag in bagging area.

MARY: Oh. Right! Sorry!

(She takes the item out of her purse and places it in a plastic bag next to the scanner.)

VOICE: Scan next item. *(Voice repeats several times.)*

(Mary tries several times before —)

VOICE: BEEP.

MARY: $6.99? Right! I'll be out of here in five minutes, no problem.

VOICE: Place item in bag in bagging area.

MARY: OK! *(She does.)* How's that? I'm getting good at this!

VOICE: Scan next item. *(Voice repeats.)*

(Mary picks up a large bag and has trouble maneuvering it.)

VOICE: Scan next item.

MARY: I'm trying, I'm trying. This is heavy and I'm having trou—

VOICE: Scan next item.

MARY: Give me a break! Shit!!

VOICE: Do not use profanity.

MARY: *(She stops and looks around, startled.)* Where the fu— ? Sorry! Where are you?

VOICE: Scan next item. *(Voice may repeat.)*

(Mary obediently scans again.)

VOICE: BEEP. Place item in bag in bagging area. *(Voice repeats.)*

(Mary tries to obey, but the item is too big for the bag, so she places it on the table away from the other bags. A loud objectionable sound is heard.)

VOICE: Unidentified item in bagging area. *(Voice repeats.)*

MARY: This is not an unidentified item. This is my kitty litter and I already scanned it. Look! $8.99! Right there!!!

(A loud objectionable sound is heard.)

VOICE: Unidentified item in bagging area.

MARY: Fine! *(She grabs the bag and puts it on the floor.)*
VOICE: Place item in bag in bagging area. *(Voice repeats.)*
MARY: It won't fit! How am I supposed to place it in that little bag?
VOICE: Place item in bag in bagging area.

> *(Mary grabs a bag from the table and tears it open. She places it on the table next to the other items and puts the bag of litter on top of it.)*

MARY: There! Nya, nya, nya, nya, nya — nya — !
VOICE: Scan next item. *(Voice repeats.)*

> *(Mary takes a bottle of wine and scans it.)*

VOICE: BEEP.

> *(Mary picks up the wine.)*

VOICE: Please present I.D. to attendant before purchasing alcoholic beverages.
MARY: Are you kidding? I'm si... I'm way over twenty-one.
VOICE: Please present I.D. to attendant before purchasing alcoholic beverages.
MARY: There's no attendant! Where is the attendant?
VOICE: Please present I.D. to attendant before purchasing alcoholic beverages.
MARY: Look! I've got white hair! See? *(Mary scans her hair and notices the price on the scanner.)* $99.90? You gotta be kidding?
VOICE: Please present I.D. to attendant before purchasing alcoholic beverages.
MARY: No! That wine was $9.99, not $99.90!
VOICE: Please present I.D. to attendant before purchasing alcoholic beverages.
MARY: I am not paying $100 for a bottle of wine!!!
VOICE: CHEAP.
MARY: Where the hell are you?
VOICE: Do not use profanity.
MARY: I'll use any language I please!
VOICE: CREEP.
MARY: This is getting ridiculous! Take the wine off the bill!
VOICE: This transaction is being taped for your protection.
MARY: I don't care. I never pay that much for wine. I usually go to Trader Joe's and pay $5.99.
VOICE: Please present ID to attendant before purchasing alcoholic beverages.
MARY: I will not. I don't want your fucking wine!

VOICE: Do not use profanity.

MARY: I don't want the wine or any of this. You can kiss my...

(She empties the bag onto the table, and scoots her ass up onto the scanner.) Here, scan this!!! *(Hops off and storms out.)*

VOICE: Do not recognize barcode. Please try again. Do not recognize barcode. Please try again.

(Lights fade out.)

END OF PLAY

Biography

Kim Miller grew up in Illinois and studied creative writing at Knox College in Galesburg, Illinois. She began her college career as an English major, but could not help visualizing everything she read and telling everyone around her about it, so studying theatre was the next logical step. She is currently an Associate Professor of Theatre at the University of the Cumberlands in Williamsburg, Kentucky, where she teaches acting and directing. *Standby* is her second published short play.

Standby

Kim Miller

Standby was written during a playwright workshop sponsored by Arts in the Gap, a summer art program of Lincoln Memorial University. *Standby* was then given a public reading in "What Our Hands Wrote," in Cumberland Gap, Tennessee, June of 2016.

CHARACTERS
>BETH: Young woman engaged to Oscar.
>OSCAR: Young man engaged to Beth.

SETTING
>TSA check area at an airport.

• • • • • • • • • • • •

Beth stands center, admiring the engagement ring on her finger. There is a table for containers of cleared personal items upstage, where Beth's purse and carry-on luggage rest. There are two chairs stage right. Oscar stands stage left with his arms over his head, as if he is in a body-scanning machine.

BETH: Oscar, I love it! I never want to take it off! You know, if TSA would have made me take it off to go through security, I would have refused to come one step further. I've heard that these containers can get knocked over and what's inside them ends up inside the conveyor belt never to be found again.
>*(Beth removes her purse and carry-on from the inspection table. Oscar lowers his arms and closes his legs while Beth begins to put on her jewelry that she did have to remove. Oscar crosses to Beth and hugs and kisses her.)*
OSCAR: And I don't ever want you to take it off, Beth! *(Begins to put on his personal items from the table, shoes last.)* But if you weren't here, there's no way we could get married in Vegas tonight, could we?
>*(Beth kisses Oscar even as he is putting on his shoe.)*
BETH: You are so romantic! First the ring and now Vegas! I love you so much! I can't believe you did all this without me knowing about it.
>*(She takes a selfie of the two of them. Oscar balances on one foot, trying to put on his shoe.)*
BETH: I want to record every single minute of our life together.
OSCAR: *(All dressed.)* Come on, darling, we can do better than that!
>*(He grabs Beth to pose for another photo.)*
BETH: Wait! Let's post a pic with our tickets in hand, so everyone knows our news. The two of us are at the gate on our way to Vegas and I'm wearing this ring!
OSCAR: Let's wait until we have the marriage license —
BETH: No, hold up the tickets —
OSCAR: — with the lights of Vegas as a background to our officially,

newly-wedded bliss!

BETH: No, this way when we land in Vegas and driving between the airport and the chapel, we can read everyone's reactions online. It will be like our friends are there with us.

OSCAR: *(Touched.)* I love you.

(Oscar and Beth take another selfie showing off the ring.)

BETH: Wait! Get the tickets. We need to show everyone where we're going.

OSCAR: *(Beat.)* We don't have the tickets yet. We're on standby.

BETH: What?

OSCAR: The name's on a list, a standby list. *(Beat.)* Since we're already at the gate, there's a good chance we'll get on board. *(Reassuringly.)* It's Vegas! There's always another flight to Vegas. If we don't make this one, we'll get the next one.

BETH: I think it's the last flight tonight. I don't want to spend my wedding night in an airport. What will people think?

OSCAR: People don't need to think anything. It's not their wedding.

BETH: Our friends will post their congrats to this photo and we'll have to respond that we are enjoying the bright lights of Gate 23 on the B Concourse here at home.

OSCAR: What does it matter if we're here or in Vegas, as long as we are happy? We can't wait for everything to be perfect.

BETH: *(This statement strikes Beth and she begins typing into her cell phone.)* "So this happened to me today. I am so happy." *(She finishes typing and looks at Oscar.)* And now it's sent.

OSCAR: Really?

BETH: Really.

OSCAR: We're gonna make this flight.

BETH: We're getting married.

OSCAR: In Vegas.

BETH: Tonight.

OSCAR: Tonight! It will happen.

(Oscar and Beth hug and kiss again. They look around. Smile at each other. They look around some more.)

VOICEOVER: Welcome to United flight 3933 with direct service to Las Vegas, Nevada. We will begin boarding shortly. Would standby passengers C. Thompkins and F. Snell come to the desk at Gate 23 on the B Concourse, please? C. Thompkins and F. Snell, we have tickets for you.

(Oscar and Beth cross to chairs and sit.)

OSCAR: We won't have to wait long. I'm sure of it.

BETH: Vegas is going to be great. We are going to have so much fun!

OSCAR: The guys at work will be shocked.

BETH: My friends are going to lose it!

VOICEOVER: I'd again like to welcome passengers to United Flight 3933 to Las Vegas, Nevada. Just remember what you do there, stays there. We will begin boarding shortly. Would standby passengers C. Thompkins and F. Snell come to the Gate 23 Desk on the B Concourse, please?

OSCAR: I'll be Snell if you want to be Thompkins.

BETH: Funny. Do you think those are the only two extra seats available? I really do not want to spend my wedding night here. *(Pause.)* Oscar, why didn't you get the tickets ahead of time, like you did the ring?

OSCAR: *(Shrugs.)* It'll be OK. We'll get this flight. You'll see. Maybe Thompkins and Snell are the first names on the list and the gate agent doesn't want to deal with a crowd.

(Beth stares at Oscar.)

OSCAR: It can be very intimidating – crowds. We're fine.

BETH: *(Uncomfortable pause.)* Did you think I wouldn't come?

OSCAR: Well, if TSA would have made you take your ring off —

BETH: No! You know I was just joking. Did you think I wouldn't elope, or fly with you to Vegas… *(Pause.)* …or say yes?

OSCAR: *(This is painful.)* Well, after the last time…

BETH: You said you forgave me. You said you were over it.

OSCAR: I thought so. I think so. I love you and I need to be with you, yet I couldn't go through that again.

BETH: You know what happened. I can't believe you don't trust me now.

OSCAR: No, listen to me. This is what life is. Making the next step is never guaranteed, so why not take each one as it comes and be happy where we're at? So we only make it through TSA but get stopped at the gate? Fine. We're together. We make standby work. Thompkins and Snell get their seats and then we get seats? And then five other random people get seats. Great. We are on our way to Vegas. Either way we are together.

BETH: It was just so stressful last time. Your mother —

OSCAR: *My* mother? *My* mother! You never listen to anyone except *your* mother.

BETH: OK, my mother and your mother and everyone else. No one was happy — least of all me, us.

OSCAR: But it was supposed to be *our* marriage.

BETH: I know. I ruined it. There was so much to think about. Mom tried to help, which is more than your mother did.

OSCAR: You left me standing at the altar. Well, in the minister's room behind the altar.

BETH: I've said I'm sorry.

OSCAR: Because your mother told you to say that to me?

BETH: No. No! I am sorry because I screwed up. I should have stood up to her, but I didn't. She kept telling me what it would be like to be married, what I needed to do, how I needed to be, and I just got overwhelmed. I couldn't see us as she was telling me it would be.

OSCAR: She doesn't know. How it was for her doesn't mean it will be that way for us. I stood in the minister's office, and I waited in that office about 15 minutes. Seemed a lot longer. So this time, standby just seemed to be the best option.

BETH: OK. I need to stand up to her, but I don't know if I can. Eloping is the right idea. I love you that you thought of it.

OSCAR: We are going to be great together.

VOICEOVER: Hello again, and again welcome to Flight 3933 to Viva Las Vegas, still-in Nevada. It feels like it's been a long wait, but don't worry, we are going to begin boarding this flight soon. At this time, would the Gold Club members step up to the gate and would standby passenger B. Tinton come to the Gate 23 Desk on Concourse B. B. Tinton, we have a ticket for you.

(Oscar and Beth look at each other, then off-stage right.)

BETH: Did they just say my name? Did you hear that? Did you put the tickets in my name?

OSCAR: Just go to the counter and find out what they have to say.

BETH: But —

OSCAR: Just go.

(Beth exits and Oscar pulls out his phone and smiles at what he sees there. He puts the phone away. He rubs his face with his hands and then rests his head in his hands. Beth returns.)

BETH: *(Angry.)* What's going on, Oscar? There's a ticket for me if I want it. I asked the gate agent about a ticket for you, because your name should on the list too. *(Pause.)* The ticket agent said no one named Oscar Phillips is on the standby list. *(Pause.)* Is this some kind of payback? Are you going to walk out on me now? *(Beth looks around.)* Are you recording this? Or when we don't get on the plane, and we walk back into the terminal, will everyone be there to see you dump me? What is this, Oscar?

(Oscar pulls a ticket out of his back pocket. Beth stares at him and the ticket.)

BETH: Would you have left me here? If there were no other tickets? If Thompkins and Snell had taken the last two seats? If you had to? Or maybe if you wanted to?

OSCAR: *(Sincerely.)* I would never leave you. But I also won't stay, if you won't be with me. It's you and me. I am asking you to make a break from your family and start one of your own, because it's what we want, not what our parents want.

VOICEOVER: We will now begin general boarding for Flight 3933 to Las Vegas, Nevada.

OSCAR: Beth, you should know before you get on that plane that I don't intend to return. I want you to come with me and marry me, but if you decide not to, I won't be around for another try. And I want you to know how much I love you, but I won't stay in this holding pattern anymore. At every point this afternoon, I've been preparin myself, mentally steeling myself, for the moment you back out on me, because I know you might. You don't have to take the ticket, but I am getting on that plane. And I'm not returning.

BETH: Standby.

OSCAR: Yes. Standby. Eventually —

BETH: I will deal with my mother. But today is the day I move to Vegas.

VOICEOVER: Attention, please. Passengers of Flight 3933 with service to Las Vegas, Nevada, I regret to inform you that the plane you were to take has an engine malfunction. Flight 3933 is cancelled. Another flight is rescheduled for 7 am tomorrow. There is a regularly scheduled flight at 5 am. Please come to the desk if you would like to be placed on standby for the 5 am flight. We will begin boarding the replacement flight at 6:30 am.

(Oscar carefully watches Beth. Beth grabs her carry-on but sets it at her feet. She unzips it and pulls out a pillow. Beth carefully fluffs the pillow and lays it on Oscar's lap. She pleasantly lays her head on the pillow and gets settled in for the night. Beth then gets an idea, looks mischievously at Oscar, then pulls out her camera and they take a selfie.)

END OF PLAY

Biography

Mona Deutsch Miller has had several plays produced in southern California, including the 60-minute absurdist play, *The Beating*, short comedies *Receipts*, *The End of the Line*, and *I'Rock Around the Campfire*, and short drama *The Photograph*. Two of her plays received The All Original Playwright Workshop Fellowship Award.

Strangers on a Train

Mona Deutsch Miller

Strangers on a Train was written in The All Original Playwright Workshop, where it received its first performance on June 26, 2008, at The Actor's Group in North Hollywood. The play starred Lauren N. Kidd (who was incredibly adept at making a noose) and Michael Ring, with direction by Mona Deutsch Miller. It was produced under the title *The End of the Line* in the Hollywood Fringe Festival at the Open Fish Theatre, June 7 to 22, 2012, as part of Fierce Interventions, a program of short plays produced by Fierce Backbone. That production was directed by Herb Isaacs and starred Ann Ryerson and Ashley McGee. The play received its first publication in Journal 13 of Sin Fronteras/ Writers Without Borders (2009).

CHARACTERS

> LOUISE: A woman, casually dressed, same age as Phillip, with a sort of manic energy, carrying a boxy, sharp-edge suitcase. (British accent required)
>
> PHILLIP: Fastidiously dressed man, same age or a little younger than Louise, wearing an elegant coat, gloves and scarf, intent on committing suicide. (British accent required)

SETTING

> Train compartment, with window facing audience.

• • • • • • • • • • • •

The stage is dark. There is a sound of a train screeching to a halt followed by a sickening loud thud and a horrendous scream. Lights immediately come up brightly, revealing a train compartment with Phillip, an exceptionally neat, well dressed man, and Louise, normal-looking but with a certain manic energy. She carries a boxy, sharp-edged suitcase or briefcase. They sit opposite each other and react to the loud noises in uncomfortable silence. Louise looks particularly disturbed. Each wants to look out the window and see what happened, but does not want the other to think ill of him. Finally, Louise gets up and stares downstage out the "window." She stands transfixed with voyeuristic horror.

(This sequence and the following dialogue are performed quickly.)

LOUISE: No one got to him in time. A shame.

> *(Phillip politely but insistently tries to cough his way into Louise giving up her spot at the window. After she does not respond, he gently nudges her to get her to share the space. Acting as if she is being very gracious, Louise offers him a place at the window so he can see.)*

PHILLIP: Thank you. Oh.

> *(Staring out the window, he's profoundly upset but holds it in. Finds he can't help himself. He has to look, and does so sometimes through his fingers.)*

PHILLIP: My, my. My God.

> *(Louise watches Phillip. There are moments when he seems overcome by the horror outside and about to yield the space back to her, but then, at the last minute, he stares out once again. Louise clears her throat to signal her desire to have her spot back. Phillip finally gets the hint.)*

49

LOUISE: Thank you. Well.

PHILLIP: Messy.

LOUISE: Maybe it'll rain, wash away the blood, and his…foot.

PHILLIP: His foot?

LOUISE: *(Gingerly points out the window.)* Up there.

PHILLIP: *(Taken aback.)* Didn't see that. Frightfully messy.

(Phillip fastidiously arranges himself on his seat, carefully removing and folding his coat, scarf, etc.)

LOUISE: The rain will perhaps, uh, remove all traces of…what happened. I do hope the train starts soon. He's delayed us. Now we won't move for hours. Must get to my next appointment. This one did not work out.

PHILLIP: He's delayed us? How very thoughtless. I'm on a schedule.

LOUISE: Maybe not thoughtless. No doubt depressed. Poor bloke. He made it to where he's going, though. I do believe it's starting to rain. Well, that will clear up some of the blood. I don't know about the pieces, though.

PHILLIP: Oh no! Not more rain! Then there will be mud in the garden!

(Phillip looks at his shoes with loathing and scrapes them on the floor. Louise observes him carefully.)

LOUISE: Are you going far?

PHILLIP: An eternity away.

LOUISE: The last stop you mean?

PHILLIP: Yes, you could put it that way. But this rain – oh, I loathe messes of any sort.

LOUISE: *(Reassuringly.)* Of course, it may turn sunny. In fact, it's looking quite sunny now. A lot of sun just arrived. Fancy that. I should have brought my sunglasses.

PHILLIP: Oh then, what did he do it for? Who kills himself on a *sunny* day? He's ruined it for me, he's ruined it for me.

LOUISE: You were counting on the rain, then?

PHILLIP: No – but he ruined it for me.

LOUISE: By delaying the train, you mean.

PHILLIP: No, not that. Well, a little. I wanted it to happen at tea time. Precisely. Mum would just be putting the kettle on, that shabby chipped enamel thing…

LOUISE: He's slowing me down, I can tell you that. And I really did try this morning. So many delays, you know. Quite a sight, though. *(She moves back to the window and is exhilarated by her view. She becomes disappointed.)*

Oh, they're cleaning it up now. Well, we'll be going soon. Good thing, too. I've got so much to do today. So many things to finish off.

PHILLIP: *(Completely dejected.)* I'm finished. Just finished.

LOUISE: No, I've been watching you. You're just an obsessive compulsive. They're rarely finished with anything. Always another little inch to clean, another tile to scrub. My first husband was like that. I realized the way to get him really, well, randy, was to clean every surface in the house. If I'd just kept the newspapers off the kitchen table we'd have had a much better sex life...

PHILLIP *(Mortified.)* Please, I can't. I'm sorry, but I can't listen to this. It's so – personal.

LOUISE: You don't even know me.

PHILLIP: That's rather the point.

LOUISE: Well, it can hardly matter what I tell you. Once the train gets moving, we're just strangers on a train, and anyway, I'm certainly not going to the end of the line. You'll be rid of me long before then.

PHILLIP: It seems to me we're strangers on a train whether or not it is moving.

LOUISE: *(Returning to the window.)* Oh, the coppers are there now. They've covered up the...various pieces... Hmmm, that must be his head down there...but they're having trouble getting to that one severed foot.

PHILLIP: Oh please! That's enough. Do get away from the window. Someone might see you – looking. And then what would people think!

LOUISE: Oh, I'm sorry. I had thought you were interested.

PHILLIP: He really did ruin it for me.

(Louise studies Phillip carefully.)

LOUISE: By jumping?

PHILLIP: Indeed. Now everyone will think I'm a copycat. Not that I was intending to start from so high up. Stupid idea that.

LOUISE: Stupid?

PHILLIP: Too messy by far. I was going to step down between the cars when the train stopped at Croydon.

LOUISE: Croydon.

PHILLIP: *(To himself.)* Very neat, nothing to clean up. Mind the gap. I'll show them all how to mind the gap. *(To Louise.)* I had it all worked out, put my note inside the tea cozy, that horrible gingham rag, and then... this.

LOUISE: *(Nodding knowingly.)* You could fool them.

PHILLIP: How?

LOUISE: Poison.

PHILLIP: Too slow.

(Louise removes a medicinal-looking bottle from her suitcase. Phillip is involuntarily fascinated by Louise's bottle. He reaches for it and reluctantly, she lets him hold it. He treats it like a precious jewel.)

PHILLIP: Did you get that at the chemist?

(Louise pointedly takes it back.)

LOUISE: *(Very proud.)* No. Homemade. And I haven't got very much. *(Beat.)* Have you thought of a gun?

PHILLIP: Absolutely not. They're far too noisy. And terribly dangerous. I don't own one anyway.

LOUISE: Oh, you could borrow mine. I'm done with it.

(Louise removes a small gun from underneath her skirt.)

PHILLIP: You've used this gun of yours? You mean, it's used. *(Looking at her skirt.)* Not fresh.

LOUISE: Only a few times. Practically brand new. I keep it spanking clean. Even Harold approved of the finish.

PHILLIP: It's just some sort of target practice gun, right? One of those replica thingies? Yes? Just filled with blanks, that sort of thing?

LOUISE: No. I've got loads of bullets too, in case you miss the first time.

PHILLIP: *(Increasingly nervous.)* Oh, home security then?

LOUISE: Well, it has helped my peace of mind. I don't know if "home security" is really the right word for it. Perhaps "personal security." A device suitable for "persuasive advice." Ooh, I quite like that. It rhymes.

PHILLIP: The police do advise against having guns at home. Can lead to horrific consequences.

LOUISE: *(Delighted.)* Oh yes, I know. They're the best.

(Phillip is becoming more and more unnerved.)

PHILLIP: The rain, that man out there, with his foot and…nothing else up on that wire…and now you, with your used implements! This is not proper at all. *(He starts to get up.)*

LOUISE *(Blocking his exit and pointing the gun at him.)* So soon? We were just getting acquainted.

PHILLIP: Ssstttop! Someone will get hurt!

LOUISE: I thought you wanted to get hurt.

PHILLIP: Not like this! So…so messy!

LOUISE: *(Still blocking the exit, miffed.)* Well, I'm sure we can come up with something else. I'll put it away, if it bothers you so much.

(In a ladylike way, Louise puts the gun back under her skirt. Still blocking the

door, Louise reaches into her suitcase and pulls out a rope, already knotted into a noose. Phillip is horrified and tries to exit the compartment, but Louise is in the way. After they constantly block each other in very polite fashion, each moving to the same side as the other, Phillip wearies and sits down.)

PHILLIP: *(After a pause.)* You carry rope with you?

LOUISE: I like to be prepared. And I had my eye on you on the platform. Your poor posture rather gave away your intentions.
(Phillip immediately straightens up.)

LOUISE: Of course, I have something of a talent for sniffing out these things. Didn't get to the poor bloke outside in time, though.
(Louise looks around the compartment, at the ceiling in particular, gently swinging the noose.)

PHILLIP: You like to assist?

LOUISE: Not exactly. But I am experienced in these matters. I'm sorry. I just don't see any hooks up there. Do you? I should put my glasses on, I suppose.

PHILLIP: No hooks. Absolutely no hooks. There are no hooks in the ceiling on the train.

LOUISE: Of course, I should have realized that. It's not as if people put up hanging plants to keep them company. And the conductor and those other men have far too much to do to go around watering plants, even if there were hooks in the ceiling.

PHILLIP: Exactly. That's undoubtedly why they don't have those hooks.

LOUISE: Don't you think the compartments would be much homier if there were hanging plants? It would make travel more relaxing. Cozy. I love fuchsia.

PHILLIP: Hanging plants are quite untidy. Hardly worth the trouble. To do it properly you've got to take each one down, move it to the sink, water, wait until that drip drip drip stops. I've taken care of Mum's for years. And you think train conductors would do that? Regularly? No, there would be dead plants, fallen leaves, and all kinds of dreadful untidiness.

LOUISE: I was only trying to be helpful. It's not my fault that they don't have any hooks in the ceiling.

PHILLIP: How can it be that we're still not moving? This is unbearable.

LOUISE: You probably could slip the end of the rope through the top of the window, and jump down from an upper berth.

PHILLIP: This isn't a sleeping compartment.

LOUISE: Well, I know that, but you could if you got yourself a sleeping compartment. I'd give you the rope. Are you too cheap to get a sleeping compartment?

PHILLIP: Certainly not. Did you see this coat? Burberry.

LOUISE: Well, problem solved then. Get yourself a sleeping compartment.

PHILLIP: I wasn't planning an overnight journey.

LOUISE: No, I suppose the trip you're planning is considerably longer. You know, on second thought, since you won't get yourself a sleeping compartment, and you don't want any mess, I suppose I could let you have some of my drink.

(Louise goes to fetch the bottle from her suitcase.)

PHILLIP: That's really not necessary. It's probably quite bitter.

LOUISE: You could be a little more appreciative. You're so critical.

PHILLIP: No, no. I'm not. You're very generous. Really. But this is something I have to do...alone.

LOUISE: And I can tell, you're a micro-manager. Just like Harold. You didn't want to use a gun that had been used, even if it was spanking clean – and I do clean it regularly – and then, even though there aren't any hanging plants you've already decided that they would be messy and drip water or dead leaves or something like that...

PHILLIP: I have experience with hanging plants! And anyway, I said no such thing!

LOUISE: I suppose you didn't like the quality of my knot. I haven't perfected it yet. I'm working on it.

PHILLIP: That's not it at all. It's a beautiful knot. It's just that...

LOUISE: You are massively unappreciative!

PHILLIP: No, no, really, I am most grateful for your offer. And I think I'm reconsidering now that doing it by teatime is out of the question... but, I...

LOUISE: You've got to do it your way, I suppose. *(Beat.)* Do you like to dance?

PHILLIP: What?

LOUISE: Do you like dancing?

PHILLIP: This really isn't the time or place...

LOUISE: We're stuck here, the train isn't moving, and I'm afraid I'm forgetting my bossa nova. I could show you the basic step. It would help me practice. I've been taking lessons, you see, but I need a male partner.

PHILLIP: Really.

LOUISE: Anyway, I could help you out with your goal, because, well, if I take my suitcase and put it here...*(Moving the suitcase to a downstage corner.)* ...and then we dance a little, and you trip and fall over, and hit the edge of the suitcase, you'll probably break your neck. Almost everyone who dances with me tends to fall at some point.

PHILLIP: I'm having second thoughts, actually. *(Getting up. He begins to beat violently on the walls of the compartment.)* Someone, please, someone, anyone! Help! Help! *(He makes a dash for it, evading Louise, and exits, screaming.)* Oh, thank God! I'm still alive!

LOUISE: And they say I don't help anyone with my methods. I knew it was going to be a productive day.

(Louise pats the gun and her vial of poison appreciatively, and then practices making the right knot for a noose.)

END OF PLAY

Biography

Haley Sullivan is a Maryville College graduate (class of 2016) with a Bachelor of Arts in Theatre Studies with Licensure. Her passion for theatre is matched only by her passion for learning and education. Sullivan is from Franklin, Tennessee.

Turn Out The Lights?

Haley Sullivan

Turn Out The Lights? was written as part of the playwriting course at Maryville College in Maryville, Tennessee, in spring of 2014. The play was then given a public reading in "8 X 10," in the Haslam Family Flex Theatre in the Clayton Center for the Arts on the campus of Maryville College on May 4, 2014.

CHARACTERS

> ALLISON: A 16-year old virgin, who has been dating her boyfriend Seth for four months. She has decided she has to sleep with him or he will leave her. She is well groomed and dresses 'popular' but classy: think 'pretty in pink.'
>
> SETH: A 16-year old virgin who thinks his girlfriend is expecting him to sleep with her. He's dressed 'typical' for a somewhat popular guy, wearing a hoodie with a zipper.

SETTING

> The living room at Allison's parent's house.

TIME

> Present day.

• • • • • • • • • • • •

A sofa with pillows is center stage, with a side table with a lamp. Allison and Seth are sitting on the sofa holding hands. Seth lets go of Allison's hand and awkwardly puts his arm around her.

ALLISON: *(Tense.)* What are you...?

SETH: Oh, do you want me to stop? *(He starts to remove his arm.)*

ALLISON: No...it's okay.

SETH: Great.

> *(Pause. He kisses her cheek, she turns to him, they kiss lightly on the lips.)*

SETH: Allison... *(Shyly.)* So, should we go upstairs?

ALLISON: *(Moving out from under his arm.)* Upstairs? Why?

SETH: Well, I just thought that maybe you would want to be in your bed when we... We would have more room that way.

ALLISON: *(Quickly.)* No we wouldn't. *(Pause.)* I mean, I have a twin so...and we're already... Let's just stay here.

SETH: *(Almost relieved.)* Okay.

ALLISON: Do you...have something? *(Realizing she is not being clear.)* I mean, do you have a... Well, you know —

SETH: *(Realizing.)* Oh! Yeah. *(He reaches for his wallet in his pocket.)* I've got it right here. *(Pulls out a condom.)*

ALLISON: Great, what kind...?

SETH: Huh?

Lisa Soland

ALLISON: I mean, it looks different than mine. I mean the ones I have...
(She pulls out from behind her a small box of condoms like you would buy at a gas station.)

SETH: You bought some?

ALLISON: *(She starts to say yes and then stops.)* Actually, no... Brittany —

SETH: Brittany?!

ALLISON: ...got them...for me. She heard my parents are out of town this weekend and she thought we might need them. *(She fidgets with the box and then stops awkwardly.)* I told her I thought you would probably bring something, but she told me *I* better, too. She said she never goes out without a pack of these. *(She shakes the box.)*

ALLISON: Um...yeah.

SETH: *(Takes the box from her.)* Thanks. *(He looks at the box, studying it.)* They are different, aren't they? *(He compares the pack to his single condom, he holds up his single condom.)* This one is...normal? I guess. I mean...there isn't anything special about it. I don't think there is, at least. It doesn't say there is, anyways. *(Shifting his attention to the box.)* This is... Well, it says, "For her pleasure." So it —

ALLISON: What does that...? *(She stops, embarrassed she has to ask.)*

SETH: It means... I guess it means it has stuff that is made to make you... Well, it is made so that you get the best... *(Too embarrassed to go on.)*

ALLISON: *(Realizing what he means, she tries to hide her surprise.)* Oh. Right.

SETH: So...which one do you want to use?

ALLISON: I... Which one is better? I mean, is yours better?

SETH: It's not mi... A guy on the team, Rex, gave me this. So I don't... *(He looks down at the two kinds of condoms in his hands.)*

ALLISON: Rex?

SETH: Allison, I don't really —

ALLISON: I guess we... The one you bought. *(She picks up the box.)* That way I can just give Brittany hers back. *(Realizing what she is implying.)* I mean, if you...if we don't use them all.

SETH: *(He tries to smile.)* Right.

ALLISON: *(Getting up to hide the box again.)* So, I guess you should...make yourself comfortable.
(Allison looks around and then stuffs the box behind the sofa pillow while Seth awkwardly unzips his hoodie and leans back on the sofa. Allison turns her attention back to him.)

ALLISON: Comfortable?

SETH: Yeah. *(Looking at her sweater.)* You?

ALLISON: *(Looking down, she starts to take her sweater off shyly, but stops.)* I'm fine.
(They both stay there for a second and then Allison sits on the edge of the sofa.)
ALLISON: Seth —
SETH: You want to…?
(He gestures for her to sit closer, after a second she does. They sit awkwardly for a second and then he gets up.)
SETH: Turn out the lights?
ALLISON: What?
SETH: Do you want to…? Or I can…turn out the lights?
ALLISON: Do we need to? I mean, do you…?
SETH: I just thought it would make things eas… More romantic.
ALLISON: Sure. If you think we should.
(Neither of them moves for a second.)
SETH: We can wait a minute if you want.
(Allison gives him a look that he cannot read; she is wondering if he means wait for lights or sex.)
SETH: To turn out the lights…
ALLISON: *(Slightest hint of disappointment.)* Oh. *(Pause.)* Yeah. Let's…let's wait a minute for that.
(Seth sits back down. Pause.)
ALLISON: I guess we should…
(Pause, then she cautiously kisses him.)
SETH: Allison —
(Allison kisses him a little stronger now. He leans into her kiss then breaks away.)
SETH: Should we? *(He motions to the condom.)*
ALLISON: I… *(She slides away a little.)* Seth, I just… I —
SETH: *(Looking at the condom then back at her.)* I…don't think we should do this. We just aren't ready yet. Is that OK, babe?
ALLISON: *(Truly smiling.)* Of course!
SETH: I'm so sorry, honey.
ALLISON: *(Relieved.)* Don't be.
SETH: OK. Great. *(Pause.)* So I guess I should go now?
ALLISON: You don't have to. I mean, just because we aren't going to have… doesn't mean you can't stay a while. We could watch a movie?
SETH: I don't know, Allison. Maybe I should go before someone thinks that we are… I mean my car is right outside and it's late. Brittany lives right down the street, if she sees it…
ALLISON: So? What does it matter what she thinks? What does it matter

Lisa Soland

what anyone at school thinks? *(She turns towards him comfortably.)* I mean, think about it. We've been together for about four months now. Everyone at school thinks that we are going to do it this weekend. I thought we were going to.

SETH: Yeah, but we agreed that we —

ALLISON: I know. But don't you think it's going to be weird if we go into school Monday and people start talking about it and we have to tell them nothing happened? And then they start asking why and we have to explain that we didn't want it right now and then they start talking about us and how it's weird that we don't want it right now. Is it weird that we don't want it right now?

SETH: No, it's not.

ALLISON: I don't think so either, but they might. And then it will be weird for us explaining it all, don't you think?

SETH: I guess.

ALLISON: I mean, what about Rex and the other guys on the team? They all think you and I are going to...well...you know.

SETH: Yeah, they do.

ALLISON: I don't want to have that conversation with anyone and I know you don't either.

SETH: So what? Am I supposed to go around telling people we did it? You want me to lie about it?

ALLISON: No. Not lie about it, just don't correct them. If someone thinks we did, there is no harm in letting them think it. Right?

SETH: *(Smiling.)* Right. That way they are happy and we are happy. Everyone wins.

ALLISON: Exactly. *(Smile.)* So it's agreed? We let them think we did it?

SETH: Yes. If they think we had sex, then we had sex.

(Blackout.)

END OF PLAY

Biography

Isaac Price is a senior English major at Lincoln Memorial University. As an actor, he began performing in high school as part of the cast of *Zombie Wedding*. During his freshman year of college he performed in *Daddy's Dyin': Who's Got the Will?* in the role of Buford Turnover. In September of 2016, he performed in Lorraine Furtner's *Rules of Rock Creek*. He co-wrote an Appalachian dialect version of Shakespeare's *Taming of the Shrew*. *When Life Gives You Lemons* is his first original play.

When Life Gives You Lemons

Isaac Price

When Life Gives You Lemons was written in June of 2016 during a playwright workshop sponsored by Arts in the Gap, a summer art program of Lincoln Memorial University. The play was then given a public reading in "What Our Hands Wrote," in the town of Cumberland Gap, Tennessee, that same month.

CHARACTERS
>   GIRL: 6 to 12 years old.
>   MAN: Any age, homeless.

SETTING
>   A lemonade stand on a street corner with little traffic.

. . . .

A homemade lemonade stand with a table and chair sits center stage, containing plastic cups and a pitcher. A young girl sits, calmly waiting for customers. A man enters in ragged clothes and a dirty coat, and crawls toward the stand, obviously exhausted.

MAN: Water...please...

GIRL: *(Politely.)* I'm sorry, sir. This company doesn't sell water. I have lemonade, if you would like a cup.

MAN: Yes, anything. Just please, something to drink.
>   *(Girl pours a cup of lemonade from the pitcher. Man watches her, eagerly licking his parched lips.)*

GIRL: All right, sir. That will be one dollar.

MAN: I don't have any money, but...
>   *(Man reaches toward the cup, but the girl pulls it away.)*

GIRL: Sorry, sir. It's one dollar per cup. No free samples.

MAN: *(Desperately.)* Please, it's so hot and I'm so thirsty. Just one cup...
>   *(The man reaches for the cup again, but the girl taps his hand away.)*

GIRL: Sir, I can't afford to be giving away free lemonade. If I give you one, then you might go and tell someone else that they can get a free drink if they just ask sadly enough. Soon I'll have more sob stories than lemonade.

MAN: Please, little girl, I...

GIRL: *(Interrupting.)* It's Ms. Starr.

MAN: Ms. Starr, please. I haven't had anything to drink all day. It's just one cup of lemonade.

GIRL: *(Insulted.)* Sir, I'll have you know that this isn't some cheap store-brand lemonade. I use only the finest organic lemons and hand-squeezed them myself this morning. This is a quality product. I can't just give it away for free.
>   *(Man goes into a brief coughing fit, but Girl doesn't seem to buy it.)*

Lisa Soland

MAN: Little girl, have pitty…

GIRL: *(Interrupting.)* Ms. Starr.

MAN: Have a heart!

GIRL: Look, sir, I'd be happy to give you a sample if I could. It's just that I'm still trying to get my business off the ground and I can't afford to just give away the product. I'm still in the red from buying ingredients and making this stand.

(Man groans and leans against the stand in defeat.)

GIRL: Sir, no loitering. You're disrupting traffic.

(Man looks around, exasperated, but there are no other customers. He looks back to Girl, who continues to give him a stern stare.)

MAN: All right, fine. Just give me a minute to catch my breath.

(The two have a brief silence between them. The man opens up his dirty coat and begins fanning himself with his hands while breathing heavily. The girl looks at him in confusion.)

GIRL: Sir, if you're so hot, why don't you just take your coat off?

(Man stares at Girl and clutches his coat tightly, almost fearfully.)

MAN: *(Shouting.)* No!

(His strong reaction startles Girl, and he takes a deep breath to calm himself.)

MAN: No, I… I think I'll leave it on. Don't want to have to carry it around, you know?

GIRL: *(Uneasy.)* Whatever you say, sir.

(Another awkward silence passes between them. Man begins fanning himself again with one hand, although the other hand remains tightly clung to the coat.)

MAN: Why's a kid like you sweating out here in the sun trying to sell lemonade, anyway? You have something in mind you're saving up for?

GIRL: As a matter of fact, yes. I'm going to buy a new bike.

MAN: A bike, huh? Couldn't you just ask your parents to buy you one?

(The man starts slowly reaching for the lemonade again, careful not to catch the girl's attention.)

GIRL: Mom says you don't understand the value of money until you work for it yourself. She's a real hard worker, and I want to earn the bike on my own so that she doesn't have to waste her money on me. I'm going to be a self-made success, just like her.

(Man slowly reaches for the lemonade again, but Girl notices and taps his hand away yet again.)

GIRL: I just wish she would have let me built the stand by myself, but she said I'm too young to use the power saw. I agreed to compensate her once I start turning a profit.

MAN: Huh. So tell me about this bike you want.

GIRL: Well, it's a real pretty red one with a bell and a white basket on the front.

MAN: Sounds nice.

GIRL: It is. It matches my wagon. Once I have them both, I can use them to take my lemonade stand on the go. I'll make much more money as a mobile vendor.

MAN: Now, wait a minute. I thought you said you were running the stand so you could buy the bike? You're going to keep selling lemonade after you get it?

GIRL: Of course. The bike is just the first in a series of financial investments to expand the company. Starr Lemonade will be at the top of the market by the end of the fiscal year.

(Girl pulls out a spreadsheet from behind the stand and hands it to the man.)

GIRL: Here, this is my timetable.

MAN: *(Amazed.)* I'm impressed, kid – I mean, Ms. Starr. This is really well thought out. You'll be a business mogul in no time. *(Looking over document.)* Now it says here that you plan on closing from November through March. Why's that?

GIRL: Well, duh. It's winter. Nobody wants ice-cold lemonade when it's cold outside.

MAN: Fair enough, but why not try branching out into other drinks? Hot chocolate isn't hard to make, and it would sure help expand your clientele. Plus you wouldn't have to miss out on the holiday rush.

GIRL: *(Stunned.)* That's a really good idea, Mister. How'd you come up with that so fast?

MAN: *(Man smiles and hands back the spreadsheet.)* Oh, I'm full of ideas, some of them better than others. In fact, I used to be an entrepreneur just like you.

GIRL: Really?

MAN: *(Nodding.)* Mm-hmm. I was always coming up with ideas that I'd try and sell to people. For example, I once tried to make a biodegradable shoe that could be used as fertilizer when it wore out.

GIRL: Wow! I never would have thought of something like that! So what happened?

MAN: Well, I couldn't get the idea to work. I couldn't find a good material that would be both durable enough for a shoe and able to decompose. So I eventually had to give up on it.

GIRL: Huh. That stinks.

MAN: Yeah, well, they can't all be winners.

GIRL: *(Notices Man still holding tight to coat.)* So what about that coat? It seems pretty important to you.

MAN: *(Smiles weakly.)* I guess you could say that.

GIRL: *(Excited.)* Is it another one of your ideas? Does it have an air condition built into it? Is there a pocket that warms up food, like a tiney microwave? Is there a battery in it that lets you shock anybody who tries to touch it?

MAN: *(Chuckles and releases his grip on coat.)* No, nothing like that. It's just the only thing I can really call my own.

GIRL: What do you mean?

MAN: I wasn't as smart with money as you are. I had to pay out of my own pocket to try out my ideas, and I ended up putting more money into my projects than I got out of them. That didn't bother me too much until I got laid off at my job, and I started building up debt to try and keep my projects going. I sold everything I owned, and I now have to focus on just making it day-to-day. *(Beat.)* Once you get this low, it's hard to pick yourself back up again. Most people don't like to think about people like me, and it seems like the opportunities to get back on my feet just get fewer and fewer. It seems like all I can really hope for is just to make it until tomorrow.

(There's another silence between the two. Girl gives Man a pitiful look and, after a moment's contemplation, grabs the cup of lemonade. She holds it out towards the man, who gratefully accepts.)

Girl: Well, consider this an opportunity. I'll give your free lemondade if you keep bringing me good ideas like that hot chocolate thing. I may even throw in a free sandwich if you come up with something really good.

(Man quickly chugs down the lemonade then places the cup back on the stand.)

MAN: Thank you. That was delicious. I'll start racking my brain for a way to get you that bike by the end of next week.

GIRL: *(Excited.)* You think you could? If you do, I'll promote you to the head of research and you'll get fifteen percent of the profits. Plus I'll let you ring the bell whenever you want.

MAN: *(Chuckles, then rises.)* Well, then. I guess I'd better get to it. Thanks for the drink, kid, and the job.

GIRL: It's Ms. Starr, and you're welcome.

(Man crosses stage left then turns back to Girl, giving her a soft smile.)

MAN: See you on Monday, boss.
(He exits. Blackout.)

END OF PLAY

Biography

Marla DuMont earned her MFA in Writing for the Stage and Screen at Florida State University. She was a writer on *Mike & Molly* and currently lives in Los Angeles where she continues to write television. Marla is a member of WGA West, Alliance of Los Angeles Playwrights, and The Dramatists Guild.

Bedtime Stories

Marla DuMont

Bedtime Stories was written while Marla DuMont was at Florida State University. It received a production there, as well as at the Attic Theatre in Los Angeles in 2008 in which Laura Manchester and Allie Gerstein played Beth and Julie respectively. That production was directed by Marla DuMont with artwork by Outi Harma. In 2009, the play came in second in the "Script Tease of Short Plays" contest behind Ms. DuMont's one-act play, *An Drochshaol*. Both pieces received a reading by the San Diego Playwrights' Organization.

CHARACTERS
>BETH: 20 years old; a gentle rebel with no shortage of individuality.
>
>JULIE: Beth's pretty-in-pink, 8-year-old sister.

SETTING
>Beth's old bedroom.

TIME
>The present.

· · · · · · · · · · · ·

>*Paintings inspired by Greek mythology line Beth's old room. A few boxes have stacked up full of family memorabilia and junk. Beth sits at a bare desk wearing a black dress and smoking. Her sockless Doc Martens are propped up, revealing a self-designed crescent moon tattoo on her ankle. She is trying to write. Julie knocks lightly on the outside of the door.*

JULIE: Beth? Are you there?
>*(Beth doesn't respond.)*
JULIE: Your light's on.
>*(Conceding, Beth puts out her cigarette and waves a hand to clear the air. She crosses to the door, opens it. Julie is in her pajamas, rubbing her eyes.)*
BETH: What?
JULIE: I can't sleep.
BETH: Try harder.
>*(Beth moves to shut the door. Julie enters the room, sniffing.)*
JULIE: You're not supposed to smoke in the house. Mom said.
BETH: Mind your own business.
JULIE: It's gross.
BETH: What do you want?
JULIE: Nothing.
BETH: Then good night.
>*(Julie doesn't move. Annoyed, Beth crosses towards the desk to write.)*
BETH: I have to finish this.
JULIE: What's an orphan?
BETH: The service starts in nine hours, Julie.
JULIE: Billy said I was a dumb orphan.

BETH: You are not an orphan. An orphan has never had a mom or dad. You've had both.

JULIE: He told me that all the orphans no one wants go to this dirty place where they aren't allowed to eat and have to do chores all day long.

BETH: You tell Billy that he's an ass-hole.

(Julie's eyes grow wide.)

BETH: A jerk. Tell him he's a jerk. Now be quiet, I have to think.

(Beat. Beth tries to write.)

JULIE: What if no one wants me?

BETH: Julie...

JULIE: Aunt Kathy doesn't want me. I heard her telling Uncle Larry.

BETH: You're imagining things.

JULIE: Am not.

BETH: Of course people want you.

JULIE: Then how come Grandma said no.

BETH: Grandma's getting old, Jules. She can't take care of a little girl.

JULIE: And Uncle Joe?

BETH: He travels too much.

JULIE: But you? *(Silence.)* You want me, don't you?

BETH: I really need to figure out what I'm gonna say tomorrow.

JULIE: About Mom?

BETH: Yes, about Mom.

JULIE: Can I read it?

BETH: No. It's not finished yet.

JULIE: I can help.

BETH: I don't want your help.

(Julie moves around the room touching the paintings.)

JULIE: Your pictures are pretty.

BETH: They're not pretty. They're making a statement. And stop touching them. They're for my honors exhibition next week.

JULIE: At school?

BETH: Yeah.

JULIE: You're going back.

BETH: Knock it off.

JULIE: Everyone's leaving tomorrow.

BETH: They have to get back to their lives, Julie.

JULIE: What about me?

BETH: What about you?

(Julie backs away. Beth tames herself.)

JULIE: Why'd Mom call you Wonder Wild last week at the hospital?

BETH: It's just an old nickname. She used to say I was strong like Wonder Woman, but wilder.

JULIE: Why?

BETH: 'Cause I always did things my own way, I guess, whether or not she approved.

JULIE: Like when you stole her makeup to go to school?

BETH: Yeah.

JULIE: Or when you said the ants wanted me to pet them?

BETH: Yeah, I guess so.

JULIE: Or when you tricked Mom and made her twenty-dollar bill disappear and never gave it back?

BETH: Yeah yeah yeah. All of the above.

JULIE: I played a trick on Mason once. He made fun of my pink shorts, so I got to class early and dumped pink paint in his chair.

BETH: You showed him.

JULIE: Mom said I shouldn't have done it.

BETH: She said that to me all the time.

JULIE: 'Cause you were bad.

BETH: Because I was different.

JULIE: You loved her though, right?

BETH: Of course.

JULIE: And Dad?

BETH: Of course.

JULIE: And me?

BETH: You're my little sister.

(Beat. Julie notices a painting propped on the nightstand.)

JULIE: What's this a picture of?

BETH: Artemis in a cage.

JULIE: Artie-who?

BETH: Artemis. It's complicated.

JULIE: Why?

BETH: She lived a long time ago. Far away.

JULIE: What'd she do?

BETH: She was a huntress. She lived among the animals.

JULIE: What about her mom and dad?

BETH: Julie, I can't do this right now.

JULIE: Was she an orphan too? *(Silence.)* Beth?

BETH: She lived by herself because she wanted to, okay. She wanted to be left alone!

JULIE: Like you.

    (Beat. Then…)

BETH: Sometimes, yeah.

JULIE: And Aunt Kathy.

BETH: I guess.

JULIE: But not me. I don't wanna live with the animals.

BETH: I have to get back to work.

JULIE: *(Referring to the eulogy that Beth is writing.)* I wanna read it.

BETH: No.

JULIE: Why not?

BETH: Because I said so, that's why.

JULIE: You're not my mom.

BETH: I'm the closest thing you've got. Now go to bed.

    (Julie climbs onto Beth's bed defiantly.)

JULIE: Tuck me in.

BETH: Grow up.

JULIE: Mom always tucked me in.

BETH: Go to sleep.

JULIE: I can't sleep.

BETH: So count sheep.

JULIE: It's boring.

BETH: Then lie awake.

JULIE: Mom always sang to me.

BETH: Shut up, Julie! Just shut up! You think you can come to me and keep me up and ask me what's going to happen tomorrow, or the next day, or the day after that, and that somehow I'll have all the answers? That's not how it works, that's not how this is supposed to go. I have friends, and homework, and obligations that are completely separate from anything you've ever known. And then you, you just crash land in my lap overnight, and everyone expects me to put it all on hold, to sacrifice everything I've worked for, everything I've finally figured out about who I want to be, and spend the rest of my life raising my poor, parent-less, eight-year-old sister! So no, Julie. I won't tuck you in, and I won't sing to you. Because I'm not Mom. I'm not supposed to be a mom!

    (Julie leaps out of the bed and into action. She knocks the Artemis painting off the nightstand and begins to jump on it. Beth charges to stop her.)

BETH: What are you doing? What the hell do you think you're doing?

JULIE: I hate you! I hate your stupid pictures and your dumb stories.

BETH: Julie, stop it! You're ruining everything!

JULIE: It's not fair! IT'S NOT FAIR!!

> *(Beth seizes Julie fiercely and yanks her, still kicking, away from the painting. Julie tries to escape, but Beth's grip is too strong.)*

BETH: Julie! Calm down, Jules! Calm down!

> *(She pulls Julie to her roughly, and into a hug. Slowly, Julie's squirming stops as she gives into the hug, sobbing.)*

JULIE: I don't want you to leave me.

> *(Beth crosses with Julie to the desk and sits, holding Julie's hand.)*

BETH: There's a lot of stuff I've got to figure out, Jules. It's gonna take some time.

> *(Silence, then...)*

JULIE: I'm sorry I broke your painting.

> *(Beat. Beth looks at Julie.)*

BETH: I'm not so sure it matters anymore.

> *(Tenderly, Beth pulls Julie onto her lap. Together, their eyes fall on the eulogy. Lights fade to black.)*

END OF PLAY

Biography

Julie Lawrence earned her Bachelor of Arts degree in Theater in 1986, moved to New York in 1988, and created a theater company with Director, Kenneth Mitchell. In 1992, she moved to Orlando, Florida, where she worked as a Production Coordinator for Nickelodeon Studios, working on such shows as "All That" and "Allegra's Window." In 1996, Julie moved to Los Angeles and worked for Walt Disney Studios, creating original programming for their Educational Publishing division. In 1998, she moved over to Disney's Club Disney division and worked as a Production Supervisor, creating play areas based on Disney animated films. In 2001, Julie joined Tom Hanks and Gary Goetzman's production company, Playtone, where she continues to work as a Creative Executive in Development.

Bye Gones

Julie Lawrence

Bye Gones was written during Lisa Soland's All Original Playwright Workshop in 2002. The play was first produced in November of 2002 at the Tamarind Theater in Los Angeles, and then again in June of 2006 at the Lex Theater, also in Los Angeles. It was then turned into a short film and was shot in Florida in May of 2005.

CHARACTERS

> SUZANNA WEBBER: 37-years old, warm and sweet, but can't seem to get her life together. She drifts from job to job and appears to be searching for contentment of some kind. Nina's older sister.
>
> NINA WEBBER-SACHS: 34-years old, housewife, married, mother of two. She has that, "I'm-married-to-a-rich-man" edge to her. A perfectionist who is intense and tightly wound.
>
> DADDY: Only heard offstage, Daddy's voice is ominous and deep, as only memories can be.

SETTING

> The porch of a house in the woods of Martha's Vineyard. The childhood home of Nina and Suzanna.

TIME

> It is mid-July, late afternoon, present day.

• • • • • • • • • • • •

Suzanna is sitting on the steps of the porch, nervously waiting. There is a backpack and a beer next to her on the step. She holds some rocks in her hand and skims them out into the water in front of her. She looks in the bushes for better rocks and notices something. She digs at it with her foot.

SUZANNA: Oh wow. *(She digs around and holds up an extremely dirty, little, ceramic angel. She tries to wipe it clean.)* How long have you been under there? *(She chuckles.)* Wow.
(A car is heard approaching. The car stops, a car door is heard opening and closing and Nina enters struggling with a suitcase.)
NINA: Hey.
SUZANNA: Hey!
NINA: What are you doing on the porch? Did you lose your key?
SUZANNA: No. I knew you weren't here yet. I just thought I'd enjoy the fresh air. What timing. I just got here. *(She puts the angel on the step and stands up and hugs Nina.)* It's so good to see you. How are you?
NINA: Good.
SUZANNA: Here, let me... *(She grabs Nina's suitcase and places it on the porch.)*

Lisa Soland

NINA: Thanks. Ugh, that's a long trip. All the Islanders on the ferry staring at me like I was an alien. *(Sarcastically.)* Gee, I forgot how friendly the people are around here.

SUZANNA: You're an Islander too, you know.

NINA: I don't think anyone would consider me an Islander any more. Where's your car? I didn't see it.

SUZANNA: Oh, I walked.

NINA: You walked? Isn't it a couple of miles?

SUZANNA: I guess.

NINA: It's unbelievable. This place looks exactly the same. It's filthy though.

SUZANNA: Well, it's been pretty much empty since she died.

NINA: I thought you would've moved right in.

SUZANNA: No, I haven't been here since the funeral.

(Pause.)

NINA: Sorry I didn't make it.

SUZANNA: It's all right. You're busy.

NINA: So, she just dropped dead on the floor, huh?

SUZANNA: *(Winces.)* Yup. I saw her foot when I walked in. She was lying next to the table.

NINA: God.

SUZANNA: For a second I thought she was cleaning the floor or something.

NINA: I'm sorry you were the one to find her. Too bad Daddy's dead. He would've been here.

SUZANNA: Yeah.

(An uneasy silence falls. Suzanna holds out her beer.)

SUZANNA: Want a beer?

NINA: No thanks.

(She takes a designer water bottle out of her purse and takes a sip.)

SUZANNA: How's Chuckie?

(Nina glares at her.)

SUZANNA: Sorry, how's Charles?

NINA: He's good. How's...? Sorry, I can't keep track. What's his name?

SUZANNA: Bill.

NINA: Oh yeah. How is Bill?

SUZANNA: I have no idea.

NINA: Oh. Well, you should be happy you live the simple life.

SUZANNA: Yeah, that's me. The simple life.

(There's an awkward pause.)

NINA: Well, should we get started? Honestly, I want to get back as soon as I can. Charles gets a little freaked when he's left alone with the kids.

SUZANNA: Where's your nanny?

NINA: Visiting her sister in El Salvador.

SUZANNA: Bummer. How're the boys?

NINA: Good. Michael wants a tattoo.

SUZANNA: Isn't he like, four?

NINA: He's nine.

SUZANNA: Oh.

NINA: I'll probably come home to a biker child with a flaming skull on his face. Things like that tend to happen when I leave town.

SUZANNA: I know you've got a lot going on. I really appreciate you coming. I wasn't sure you would.

NINA: It looks so small.

SUZANNA: What?

NINA: The lake, the yard, everything. When we were kids it all seemed so huge.

SUZANNA: *(Crosses to the step and shows her the angel.)* Look what I found.

NINA: What is that?

SUZANNA: I found her in the bushes. Do you remember?

NINA: No.

SUZANNA: Remember? Mom bought her in town and we put her outside to protect us, like a talisman. The angel of the cabin.

NINA: Hmmm.

SUZANNA: She would put her on the windowsill, but we kept sneaking her outside.

NINA: Oh, yeah! Oh my God! *(She takes the angel gingerly.)* We had to put her by the steps. I can't remember why, though.

SUZANNA: When Grandma died, Mom told us she had turned into an angel who would always protect us. We thought if she was by the steps she would stop anything bad from getting in the house.

NINA: Gee, that worked didn't it?

(Nina hands the angel back and wipes the dirt off her hands. She goes to her purse and gets some hand sanitizer. Suzanna puts the angel down and goes back to her backpack.)

SUZANNA: Oh, I've got something for you. Well, for the boys. *(She pulls out two baseball gloves.)*

NINA: Suzanna —

SUZANNA: It's not much.

NINA: You shouldn't spend your money.

SUZANNA: I'm not that poor.

NINA: I know. I just meant you didn't have to get them anything.

SUZANNA: I know.

NINA: They'll love them, thanks.

(Nina takes the gloves and puts one glove on the porch next to her suitcase. She puts the other glove on her hand and stares at it for a moment.)

SUZANNA: I'm really glad you came.

NINA: Oh, well, yeah. I kept picturing in my mind what it would be like to be here. I wanted to see the place again, I was just...afraid it would be too hard. But, it's not so bad.

SUZANNA: Good.

NINA: Sometimes though, I'm just going along, you know, and suddenly... wham! All these feelings come rushing back and I realize, damn, I'm a teenager again and I... I'm still so mad!

SUZANNA: I know.

NINA: I mean, where does all that anger go?

SUZANNA: Into other things, I guess.

NINA: I guess. But, God, it makes you wonder. Is it ever gonna go away or will it always be lurking there, under the surface?

SUZANNA: I don't know.

NINA: What if the kids do something one day and I just release the holy wrath on them?

SUZANNA: You won't.

NINA: I hope not. *(She looks at the glove.)*

SUZANNA: *(Sitting on the porch.)* I remember you and Daddy used to play catch.

NINA: Uh huh.

DADDY: *(A gruff voice is heard from offstage.)* Nina!

(The lights change. Nina looks out expectantly. She is now 10 years old.)

DADDY: *(From offstage.)* Get your glove out!

(Nina awkwardly sticks her glove up in the air.)

NINA: Like this, Daddy?

DADDY: *(Offstage.)* No. Out in front of you.

(Nina does what her daddy says.)

Open your glove and turn your hand over! Get your other hand up.

(She puts her other hand up in the air.)

DADDY: *(Offstage.)* No, beside your glove.

(Nina does.)

DADDY: *(Offstage.)* Are you ready?

NINA: *(Terrified.)* Uh huh.

DADDY: *(Offstage.)* Here it comes.

(Nina flinches and closes her eyes.)

DADDY: *(Offstage.)* What are you doing? You can't close your eyes!

NINA: Sorry, sorry. I'll keep them open.

DADDY: *(Offstage.)* How do you expect to catch the ball with your eyes closed?

NINA: I won't close 'em, I promise. Throw it, Dad.

DADDY: *(Offstage.)* You can't be afraid of the ball.

NINA: I'm not, I'm not.

DADDY: *(Offstage.)* You gotta keep your eye on it. Maybe Suzanna can —

NINA: *(Cutting him off in a panic.)* No, no, no! I can do it. I can do it by myself. Throw it.

DADDY: *(Offstage.)* Okay, here it comes.

NINA: Okay.

DADDY: *(Offstage.)* I'm gonna fire it in there.

NINA: Okay.

(She waits a second, but flinches again.)

DADDY: *(Offstage.)* Nina, goddammit!

NINA: Daddy, I'll catch it!

DADDY: *(Offstage.)* You can't even keep your eyes open.

NINA: I will!

DADDY: *(Offstage.)* We're gonna keep trying until you get it right.

NINA: I'll catch it, I will. Throw it, Daddy!

DADDY: *(Offstage.)* Here, maybe you can catch this.

(Nina reacts like he's throwing random things at her, like sticks. She still keeps her glove out but flinches and ducks.)

NINA: Ow!! Daddy, stop!!

DADDY: *(Offstage.)* And this…

NINA: Stop!

DADDY: *(Offstage.)* How about this?

NINA: Daddy, stop!!

DADDY: *(Offstage.)* Forget it. I guess baseball isn't the game for you.

NINA: No, it's great! *(She punches the glove awkwardly.)* I love it! Throw the ball!

DADDY: *(Offstage.)* I'll be back later.

NINA: Throw it! *(Pause. Louder.)* Daddy, throw it! *(Pause.)* Daddy!

(The lights change back to present time. Nina takes the glove off.)

NINA: So, can we actually go in now?

SUZANNA: Um…yeah. I just like looking at the water this time of day.

(Pause.)

NINA: What's going on with you?

(Nina puts the glove on the porch with the other one, wipes the step off, then sits down next to Suzanna.)

NINA: You seem weird. *(Swats away gnats or flies throughout the next few lines.)*

SUZANNA: I'm good, I'm good. No, things are…good. I just wanna look at the water.

NINA: God, these bugs. You act like you haven't been here in years.

SUZANNA: *(Laughs.)* I know.

NINA: You really should have someone mow the yard.

SUZANNA: The grass grows fast. We had the yard all decorated for Mom's Birthday party.

NINA: Sounds nice.

SUZANNA: Sorry she wouldn't get on the phone. She —

NINA: *(Cutting her off.)* It's okay. At least you tried. I didn't really expect her to.

SUZANNA: Well, I was hoping she would.

NINA: It's okay.

SUZANNA: I just felt bad.

NINA: It's okay, really.

SUZANNA: I mean, now it's too late to —

NINA: Can we talk about something else? Please?

SUZANNA: Yeah, sure. Sorry.

NINA: So, how's the job?

    (Suzanna looks down.)

NINA: Oh God, what happened this time?

SUZANNA: Nothing, I just… It just didn't fit.

NINA: *(Annoyed.)* Didn't fit? What does that mean?

SUZANNA: I don't know.

    (She picks up a few rocks, stands up and starts to skim them across the water.)

NINA: God, you lost your car too didn't you?

SUZANNA: I didn't lose my car.

NINA: Where is it then?

SUZANNA: It's at my place. *(Pause.)* It doesn't work but —

NINA: God, Suzanna!

SUZANNA: What?

NINA: You're 37 years old and you have no job and no car?

SUZANNA: It's only temporary, Nurse Ratchett. Calm down.

NINA: Whatever. I just…whatever. *(Pause.)* I hate it when you call me that.

SUZANNA: Sorry.

NINA: *(Trying to change the subject and calm down.)* So, any new prospects?

SUZANNA: What, job-wise?

NINA: You know what I mean.

SUZANNA: Oh, you mean guys.

NINA: Yes, guys. Anybody new on the horizon?

SUZANNA: Well… Nope. No new prospects. As bad as they say it is out there, its worse. I'm not the greatest when it comes to relationships, either. I never seem to make the best choices.

(Suzanna crosses to her and hands her a few rocks, inviting her to try. Nina stands, accepting the challenge. Nina tries to skim one, but is obviously not successful. Suzanna laughs.)

SUZANNA: You suck.

NINA: Shut up.

(She tries again, but again is not successful. Suzanna skims one.)

NINA: Good one.

SUZANNA: God, it's been a long time since we've done this.

NINA: Yeah.

(Nina gives up and hands the dirty rocks back to Suzanna with disdain. She grimaces and tries to wipe the dirt off.)

SUZANNA: *(Laughing at her.)* You are so funny.

NINA: What? It's gross.

(Suzanna really starts to laugh.)

SUZANNA: Oh my God, do you remember what we used to do?

(Lights change again. Suzanna's laughter becomes shrieking giggles from both of them. Suzanna is 11 and Nina is eight. They are huddled together on the ground.)

NINA: That's gross!!

SUZANNA: Shhh! It's not gross. It's fun.

NINA: How do you do it?

SUZANNA: You just kinda close your eyes and mush your mouth together. *(She does it.)* Like this.

NINA: *(Does it too.)* Like this?

SUZANNA: Uh huh. *(She smushes Nina's lips more together with her hand.)*

NINA: *(Still with her eyes closed and lips together.)* Then what happens?

SUZANNA: Then he puts his mouth on yours and you count to five and then you're done.

(Nina squeals with excitement and rolls on the ground.)

NINA: Gross!!!

SUZANNA: Shhhh!!!

NINA: *(In a hushed voice.)* What does it feel like?

SUZANNA: It feels…I don't know. Smushy.

NINA: *(In a hushed voice.)* Gross!

SUZANNA: It's not gross!

NINA: It sounds gross!

SUZANNA: It's not. It feels like… *(She puts the back of her hand up to her mouth.)* Here, mush up your lips and put your hand up to your mouth, like this.

(Nina does but stops when she notices her hand.)

NINA: Gross, I'm all dirty. I'm not kissing me.

SUZANNA: *(Exasperated.)* Oh, brother! You're so weird. Here. *(She picks up a big rock and holds it out to Nina.)* Use this.

NINA: Suz!

SUZANNA: Just do it. I wiped it off.

(Suzanna wipes it off on her pants. Nina hesitates.)

Just do it!

(Nina closes her eyes, smushes up her lips, and Suzanna presses the rock to her mouth. Nina keeps her lips on the rock and Suzanna starts to count.)

SUZANNA: One, two, three, foooooooooooour, five.

(Nina immediately throws the rock away and wipes off her lips.)

SUZANNA: You did it!

NINA: It's slimy.

SUZANNA: Well, a person is…drier.

NINA: Smells like dirt.

SUZANNA: It's a rock, Dumbo. Boys smell better. Well, some of them.

NINA: How many times have you kissed?

SUZANNA: A lot.

NINA: Really?

SUZANNA: Uh huh. Everybody has. We played spin the bottle at Mary Devito's party.

NINA: Gross!

SUZANNA: You'll understand when you're older.

NINA: I hope not.

SUZANNA: I kissed Michael Poynten twice.

NINA: Ewwww!!

SUZANNA: *(Annoyed.)* Shut up! He's so cute! He's…perfect.

NINA: He has braces!

SUZANNA: So?

NINA: So, metal mouth.

SUZANNA: Shut up!

NINA: He's got weird hair.

SUZANNA: He does not!

NINA: He's a dork!

SUZANNA: Shut up!

NINA: You shut up!

SUZANNA: You shut up or I'll tell everyone you kissed a rock.

NINA: *(Jumping up and yelling.)* Daddy!!

SUZANNA: Shhhh!

> *(Suzanna tries to clamp her hand on Nina's mouth. Nina fights her off.)*

NINA: *(Yelling.)* Daddy!!! Suzanna is being mean to me!

SUZANNA: I am not!

NINA: She is too!!!

DADDY: *(Offstage, yelling.)* Suzanna!

SUZANNA: *(Yelling.)* I am not!!

DADDY: *(Offstage, really angry.)* Suzanna! Come inside, now!

SUZANNA: *(Quietly.)* Thanks a lot.

> *(The girls get up and head up the stairs, wiping their hands on their clothes. The lights change back to present time. Nina and Suzanna are back standing in front of the steps.)*

NINA: *(Laughing.)* God, the things we did.

SUZANNA: Yeah.

NINA: I never did look at a rock quite the same way again.

> *(Nina goes to her bag, sits down on the rocking chair, and pulls out hand sanitizer. She rubs some on her hands.)*

SUZANNA: *(Laughing.)* Well, at least you don't have to resort to that anymore! A rock is about the only thing I could get hard right now. Really, you have no idea. I think you married the last perfect guy.

NINA: Ha! Perfect? I think not.

SUZANNA: Well, he seems pretty close.

NINA: *(Smiling.)* He's a good guy. I got lucky.

SUZANNA: Yeah. How's his job going?

NINA: Good. We're holding our breath. I mean, the layoffs aren't definite, but God, it's so scary.

SUZANNA: I'll bet.

NINA: When you have kids and a big house and all, it's just a terrifying thought.

SUZANNA: I can imagine.

NINA: You're lucky in a way. Not to have those kinds of problems.

SUZANNA: *(Laughing.)* Gee, thanks.

NINA: No, you know what I mean. I know I could work, but it's been so long... I haven't worked since I got married. When I left here I was in such a hurry to just...make my own family, I didn't even think about what kind of job I wanted or what skills I was acquiring. I guess I didn't plan too well.

SUZANNA: It'll work out.

NINA: Yeah. *(Noticing something and gasping.)* Is that our tree?

SUZANNA: Yeah, can you believe it?

NINA: *(She gets up and walks closer to it.)* My God, it's huge.

SUZANNA: I know. Isn't it beautiful?

NINA: Didn't we name it?

SUZANNA: Yeah, Sam. Sam the tree. It was so tiny and fragile when we planted it, like "A Charlie Brown Christmas."

NINA: Not any more! Yeah, it was gonna grow and watch over us. We sure did have a lot of talismen around this place.

SUZANNA: Yeah.

NINA: They didn't help me, though. Did they?

(The lights change. Nina runs across the stage, crying. Suzanna comes after her. They are now teenagers.)

SUZANNA: Nina!

NINA: *(Crying and holding her arm.)* Where have you been?

SUZANNA: I was at Patty's. God, I could hear Daddy yelling. What happened?

NINA: He hurt my arm! I think he dislocated my shoulder.

SUZANNA: Oh God!

NINA: He kicked me out of the house.

SUZANNA: Why?

NINA: I don't know!

SUZANNA: What did you do?

NINA: Nothing!

SUZANNA: What did he say?

NINA: He thinks I had something to do with the IRS investigation, called someone and turned him in or something.

SUZANNA: What? That's crazy!

NINA: I know, I don't know anything about that stuff.

SUZANNA: God, he's so paranoid.

NINA: He said he never wanted to see me again.

SUZANNA: I'm sure he didn't mean it, Nee —

NINA: Well, he sounded pretty convincing!

SUZANNA: It's gonna be okay.

NINA: What am I going to do?!

SUZANNA: Just come back in a little while, he'll calm down.

NINA: You don't get it. He kicked me out of the house. He told me to leave now and never come back.

SUZANNA: He said that?

NINA: You should've seen his face. He grabbed me and threw me down. He kept shaking me.

SUZANNA: God...

NINA: I'm not kidding. He's never gonna speak to me again.

SUZANNA: Don't say that.

NINA: It's true. You know how he is.

SUZANNA: What did Mom do?

NINA: She just stood there.

SUZANNA: Okay, this is crazy. I'll talk to them.

NINA: Don't make it worse!

SUZANNA: I won't.

NINA: What am I going to do? If he sees I'm still here he's gonna kill me.

SUZANNA: All right, let's just think about this for a sec. Why don't you go to Patty's and see if you can stay there for a few days?

NINA: What if her mom calls here?

SUZANNA: No way, she hates Daddy. So, stay there and after a few days I'm sure everything will be okay.

NINA: What if it's not?

SUZANNA: It will be.

NINA: What if it's not?

SUZANNA: It will be!

NINA: *(Hugging her.)* I'm never gonna see you again.

SUZANNA: Nina, shut up. I'm gonna go in and get you some money and stuff —

NINA: Forget it! I don't want anything that's in that house.

SUZANNA: You can't just leave with nothing.

NINA: Will you call me at Patty's?

SUZANNA: Of course I will.

(Nina starts to leave)

SUZANNA: Nina, wait. It's gonna be okay.

NINA: Okay. Call me right away, okay?

(Suzanna nods, Nina turns away. Lights change back to present day. A moment passes.)

NINA: You know, I lied.

SUZANNA: When?

NINA: Before, when I said this wasn't so bad. Being here. Seeing this place again. It is. It's actually pretty awful.

Lisa Soland

SUZANNA: I'm sorry.

NINA: I can't believe I let you talk me into coming back here. How long will all this take?

SUZANNA: It's not too bad.

NINA: Then what do I have to be here for? Just throw it all out.

SUZANNA: This was your house, too, Nee. I'm sure there are things they wanted you to have.

NINA: Are you kidding me?

SUZANNA: No.

NINA: They kicked me out of here.

SUZANNA: I know.

NINA: And never spoke to me again.

SUZANNA: I know.

NINA: I was excommunicated like a bad, Amish "Movie of the Week."

SUZANNA: Nina —

NINA: "Shunned: The Nina Webber Story."

SUZANNA: That's not funny.

NINA: You think I give a crap about getting some of Mom's old plates?

SUZANNA: You never know. There might be something you want.

NINA: I seriously doubt it. For chrissake, can we go in now? I have to pee.

SUZANNA: It's all locked.

NINA: Well, unlock it!

> *(Suzanna throws her some keys. Nina awkwardly tries to catch them, but can't.)*

NINA: Ah! God. *(She picks up the keys and, at the same time inspects her nails for any damage.)* Which one is it?

SUZANNA: The one with the blue thing on it.

> *(Nina picks out the blue key and heads up the stairs to the front door. She stops just in front of it and hesitates for a moment.)*

NINA: Huh. *(Pause.)* Weird.

SUZANNA: What?

> *(Pause.)*

NINA: *(Softly.)* Come in with me.

SUZANNA: What?

NINA: Come in with me.

SUZANNA: Oh, you know what? I'm actually not gonna stay.

NINA: *(Turning around.)* Excuse me?

SUZANNA: I'm gonna take off.

NINA: What?

SUZANNA: I'm leaving.

NINA: Where are you going?

SUZANNA: Not sure.

NINA: When are you coming back?

SUZANNA: I'm not.

NINA: What in the hell are you talking about?

SUZANNA: It's not that complicated.

NINA: Was this some sort of trick to get me here and stick me with all this?

SUZANNA: No, no...

NINA: You're gonna leave me here?

SUZANNA: I want you to have the house.

NINA: You are on crack.

SUZANNA: Not any more.

NINA: What?!

SUZANNA: I'm kidding, God! I've been thinking about it and I want you
to have the house. What's the big deal? You can renovate it and
bring the boys out for the summer; you can sell it, whatever you want
to do. I don't care.

NINA: You are unbelievable.

SUZANNA: It's not bad, really. It just needs to be cleaned. And, hey, it's
waterfront property. Chuckie will love that.

NINA: This is great. I fly all the way out here so you can make some grand
gesture or do some stupid guilt thing?

SUZANNA: It's not a grand gesture. I just want you to have it.

NINA: What about you?

SUZANNA: I don't want it.

NINA: You think I do?

SUZANNA: I don't know. I thought maybe if you saw it you'd... I don't know...

NINA: Get all nostalgic and want to move in?

SUZANNA: No. That you'd come to terms with...stuff.

NINA: What are you, Dr. Phil?

SUZANNA: No.

NINA: Hey, if you want to run away from your crap, that's fine, but don't —

SUZANNA: Run away? I've been here all my life.

NINA: Well, that's not my fault. You could've left any time you wanted. I wasn't
given a choice!

SUZANNA: Well, now you have one.

NINA: You're right. I'm outta here.

(Nina puts the keys on the porch railing and starts to get her things together.)

SUZANNA: Nina, please take the key.

NINA: I must've been out of my mind to think that this was going to work out!

SUZANNA: Please, just take it. *(She goes to the keys and takes the blue one off.)* I really want you to have it.

NINA: Forget it.

SUZANNA: Just take it.

(Nina goes to leave but Suzanna tries to physically make Nina take the key.)

NINA: What in the hell are you doing? Get off of me!

SUZANNA: Take it.

NINA: Suzanna, stop it!

SUZANNA: Take it!

NINA: What are you doing, stop it!

SUZANNA: *(Screaming.)* Take it!!!

(Nina jumps back, shocked. Suzanna freezes. Pause.)

NINA: What is wrong with you?

SUZANNA: It was me.

NINA: What was you?

SUZANNA: I called them. I called the IRS on Daddy. And I said I was you.

NINA: You what?

SUZANNA: I said I was you.

(Pause.)

NINA: Jesus Christ.

SUZANNA: Let me explain...

NINA: You called the IRS?

SUZANNA: Yes.

NINA: Oh My God.

SUZANNA: It wasn't right, what he was doing. I just wanted to —

NINA: You told them you were me?

SUZANNA: Yes.

NINA: Oh God.

SUZANNA: I panicked! I was so scared. They wanted to know things. I —

NINA: How did Daddy find out?

SUZANNA: I don't know —

NINA: You did it on purpose, didn't you? You made sure he found out somehow.

SUZANNA: No, I didn't —

NINA: And you knew what Daddy was going to do when he found out.

SUZANNA: No, I didn't —

NINA: You knew he would kick me out, you knew he would never forgive me.

SUZANNA: Just, let me explain —

NINA: God, he might've killed me!

SUZANNA: No, he wouldn't have.

NINA: He went to jail, Suzanna!

SUZANNA: I know.

NINA: And you never told them the truth?

(Suzanna shakes her head no.)

NINA: You just let them die thinking…

SUZANNA: Just let me explain —

NINA: Why would you do that? Why would you do something like that?! You're such a liar! You told me everything was going to be okay. You stood right there and told me it was going to be okay and you just watched me walk away. Oh God! And you buy my kids gifts?! You never buy my kids anything ever again, you hear me?! Ever again!! *(She grabs a glove and throws it at Suzanna. Of course, it misses her. Suzanna ducks anyway.)*

SUZANNA: Please, let me say this and try and explain. I heard Daddy talking about his taxes one day, about how he hadn't paid them in years and how stupid they were and so I called the IRS and talked to them a few times on the phone. I told them I was scared of him. At least that wasn't a lie. I guess that's all it took. They started to poke around and investigate him. I mostly wanted to punish him and was… But, I swear, I never thought it would go so far. I didn't mean for it to go so far. I never thought Daddy would go to jail. I just thought he'd have to pay a fine or something and they'd be really mad at you for a while and they would pay attention to me for once. I wasn't even sure they'd believe it, but they did. And then everything happened so fast and time just kept going by and I couldn't tell them. I couldn't tell anyone. I was just…young and so stupid. And, God, I was so jealous of you I couldn't think straight. You were the baby and you always got all the attention and they loved you so much and Daddy never played catch with me —

NINA: What?

SUZANNA: You two would just walk right by me.

NINA: Oh, God.

SUZANNA: I wanted them to look at me the way they looked at you. Just once. But, they never did. *(Pause.)* I'm sorry, Nina. I'm so sorry. I'm… so sorry. *(She puts the house key on the step and grabs her backpack.)* I don't know what else to say to you. I don't belong here anymore. This house should be yours now. I really hope it makes you happy someday. *(She starts to leave.)*

NINA: Suz…

SUZANNA: I think you should go in.

NINA: You're wrong about them, you know. They didn't love me more. They didn't love anyone.

SUZANNA: Maybe.

(Pause.)

NINA: We're never gonna be friends are we?

SUZANNA: *(Stops.)* I don't know. Probably not.

(The look at each other. Suzanna slowly starts to exit. Nina stares after her. She turns around and looks at the house. She sits on the step and looks at the key. She reaches for it but picks up the angel instead and, crying, hugs it close. Lights fade to blackout.)

END OF PLAY

Biography

Greg Screws works as a television news anchor in Huntsville, Alabama. He recently completed a one-man show on the life of George Wallace entitled, *Guvnah*, but he also wrote and performed *Local Media Icon*, *Local Media Icon: The Sequel*, and *Don't Get Me Started Today*. Along with a career in news writing, Greg enjoys writing for local awards and comedy shows. His love for the stage began when smitten with an actress in "that Scottish play."

The Funeral Home

Greg Screws

The Funeral Home was written in the Lincoln Memorial University's Arts in the Gap summer program, June of 2013. The instruction was to write a play by placing two people in a room and they discover a secret.

CHARACTERS
SANDY: 40s.
AMY: Five years younger than her sister Sandy.

SETTING
Waiting room at a funeral home.

• • • • • • • • • • • •

Two adult women sitting in chairs.

SANDY: I'm glad she's dead.
AMY: Stop it. Someone will hear us.
SANDY: I don't care. What that woman put us through… This is like Christmas.
AMY: She did the best she could.
SANDY: She did the best she could…finding a drunk.
AMY: *(Deep sigh.)* She did find some winners. My favorite was Earl.
SANDY: *(Disgusted.)* Jesus God he was the worst.
AMY: Ya think?
SANDY: God yes. He's the one that, when you were five years old, I would cover your ears so you couldn't hear them fight.
AMY: We hid in the closest. I used to think we were playing a game.
SANDY: That closet was the only place they never found us.
AMY: *(Pulls out a box of white Tic-Tacs.)* I'm glad I was so young. I still see a box of white Tic-Tacs and think about teeth.
SANDY: I was hoping you would forget that.
AMY: Forget that? There are still nights I lay awake scared of wondering what I'm going to dream.
SANDY: I remember the night she had us looking for her tooth.
(She rises and crosses to the back of the chair.)
AMY: That was a bad night. I just remember that Momma would scream at us every time we tried to cut a light on. We were trying to find a tooth on the kitchen floor in the dark. *(Deep breath.)* At least when he hit her, she hit that son-of-a-bitch back.
SANDY: I kept slipping on the kitchen floor. Thought it was water. Until Momma left with the gun to chase his worthless ass down, I thought it was water I was stepping in. Or a spilt drink…
AMY: We had to throw those pajamas away. Washed them a dozen times and

Lisa Soland

the blood still wouldn't come out.

(Silence, maybe 10 seconds.)

ANNA: When is that report coming back from the doctor?

SANDY: I don't know.

AMY: You act like you don't care.

SANDY: You know what…? I don't care what killed her.

AMY: What do you know?

SANDY: Know what?

AMY: You started to say, "You know what?"

SANDY: I did not.

AMY: *(Rises and crosses to the back of Sandy's chair.)* You know what killed her, don't you?

SANDY: Yes.

AMY: *(Grabs Sandy's arm, whispers loudly.)* Sandy, what happened? Why hadn't you told me?

SANDY: *(Squares up to Amy and puts her hands on Amy's shoulders.)* Do you believe in us?

AMY: What?

SANDY: Do. You. Believe. In. US?

AMY: Well. Yes. Of course. We're survivors. *(Beat.)* You killed Momma. *(Stunned silence. Starts to giggle.)* That is so funny. Did you tell her I said bye? *(Starts to laugh out loud.)*

SANDY: *(Tries to put a hand over Amy's mouth.)* Be quiet! We are in a funeral home.

AMY: Did she, like, know you were doing it? How did you do it?

SANDY: Well. *(Motions for the chairs.)* Let's sit back down.

(They sit down and Amy leans in.)

SANDY: I know one of the nursing home activities people. She told me that one of the nurses screwed up old Mr. Hatfield's meds. She OD'd him on sleeping pills. That gave me an idea. So, when they brought the breakfast in that morning, before Momma had put her teeth in, I told Momma they had a kitchen foul up, and they couldn't get the big breakfast out…and everyone was eating oatmeal. Told her she may as well eat it before she put her teeth in. You know how she just scarfs that stuff up, especially if you put brown sugar on it. Well, I got a punch of brown sugar; ground up 30 Hydrocodone from Luther's gout attack and 15 Percocet from Darby's draw. Ground it all up and mixed it in her oatmeal.

AMY: Why does your boy have Percocet?

SANDY: He's an addict, but that is not what we're talking about.

Focus here, dammit.

AMY: When did Darby become an addict?

SANDY: *(Whispering as loud as she can, in almost strained voice.)* Dammit Amy, look at me.

AMY: Jeff lost some Cialis. You think Dylan stole it when he came over last week?

SANDY: *(Exasperated and bewildered.)* Dylan is 18 years old. He gets a hard-on when the wind blows. No, he DID NOT TAKE JEFF'S CIALIS.

AMY: You really killed Momma.

SANDY: How long has Jeff been taking Cialis? Does it really work? *(Starts giggling.)* Y'all getting those twin bathtubs.

AMY: Mother of God does it work. The other day, I had to tell him if he didn't hurry up I was going to pass out. You could hammer a ten-penny nail…wait. Stop. Back to Momma. Did she know what was happening?

SANDY: Yes, she did.

AMY: How?

SANDY: When she started to go sleep, she looked at me and she said, "Something is wrong, I'm about to pass out."

AMY: What did you do?

SANDY: I told her to lay down on the bed, and went to shut the door. She gummed, "I thought you were getting the doctor." I told her, "No… I'm not getting the doctor." I put my hand over her mouth, and put my back to the door, and told her she would never wake up. And I told her that from you and me… "Screw you and tell the devil hello." And I held my hand over her mouth till she shut her eyes.

AMY: *(Waits 10 seconds.)* Darby…?

SANDY: Momma gave him pain pills when he broke his jaw playing football. That's how he became hooked. And he can't beat it. Can't get clean.

AMY: You don't reckon anyone will want to do an autopsy do you?

SANDY: Not worried about it. I've been screwing the coroner for years.

AMY: Oh my…

SANDY: What…?

AMY: So, have I…

(Both look at each other – wait three seconds – crack up laughing. Lights out.)

END OF PLAY

Lisa Soland

Biography

Sharon Roddy Waters is an ordained Disciples of Christ pastor, teacher, writer, and musician. Her education includes: a Master of Divinity degree from Erskine Theological Seminary, a Master of Education degree in Counseling and Student Services from The University of North Texas, and a Bachelor of Music degree from Converse College. Sharon's writing mentors include Bar Scott and Lisa Soland. She and her husband currently live in Virginia. Together, they serve one demanding dog and two sly cats. *Garbage In, Garbage Out* is her first short play.

Garbage In, Garbage Out

Sharon Roddy Waters

Garbage In, Garbage Out was written in the Playwright Intensive Workshop in June of 2016, offered through Arts in the Gap, a summer arts program of Lincoln Memorial University.

CHARACTERS

MOTHER: 30 year-old mother of three children.

JAZZY: Age 14 female and the oldest child. Loves to write. Aspires to be a writer someday.

SETTING

Jazzy's bedroom, with desk and computer.

• • • • • • • • • • • •

Mother is sitting at the desk in Jazzy's bedroom looking closely at the computer screen.

MOTHER: Oh my, God! *(Continues to read, clicking as she scrolls through what is on the screen.)* Oh my God! This *will not* do! *(Calling out.)* Jazzy!

JAZZY: *(From offstage.)* What, Mom?

MOTHER: Get in here, now!

(Jazzy appears in the doorway.)

JAZZY: What? What are you doing on my computer?

MOTHER: Come in here and sit down this minute!

(Jazzy reluctantly crosses and plops in the chair beside her mother.)

JAZZY: What are you doing on my computer, Mom?

MOTHER: *(Points at computer screen.)* What is this?

JAZZY: What do you mean?

MOTHER: Where did you find this horrible story?

JAZZY: I wrote it.

MOTHER: What? You wrote it?? *(Looking upward.)* Lord, help me now.

JAZZY: Yes, Mom. You know I like to write stuff.

MOTHER: Yeah, but I had no idea you were writing trash like this. *(Points at computer screen.)* This story is about some kids agreeing to commit suicide together. You know we believe people that commit suicide are going to hell.

JAZZY: Mom, I don't happen to believe God punishes people for things they do when they're hurting really bad.

MOTHER: Hrmph. Where did you get that? The Ten Commandments say, "Thou shall not murder!" Suicide is murder and that's all there is to it. I wondered what that new fangled youth pastor was teaching you in Sunday School. Now I know. There's too much good stuff in the world to think about than to spend your time thinking about sad and

Lisa Soland

horrible stuff like this.

JAZZY: *(Rolls her eyes.)* Whatever.

MOTHER: *(Scrolling on the computer screen.)* And look at this…a poem about smoking pot of all things…and this ditty about whether there's a God or not. Some of the things in this folder are full of the foulest language I've ever heard. It's sheer heresy! Are you learning this stuff in school? I know you aren't learning this stuff at home because we live clean, respectable lives. *(Self-righteously.)* We're God-fearing people. *(Beat.)* So why, Jazzy, why?

JAZZY: Mom, just because I'm writing about certain stuff doesn't mean I'm doing it. It's just pretend. It helps me understand things sometimes. *(Mother takes hold of Jazzy's left arm, turns it over, and peels back the bandage on her forearm.)*

MOTHER: Well, it looks to me like some of the things you're writing happen to also be things you're doing – or at least thinking about doing. What is this?

JAZZY: No big deal, Mom. The razor slipped when I was shaving my underarms yesterday and cut my arm.

MOTHER: This looks too perfect to be a mistake. Lord in heaven, Jazzy girl, are you trying to kill yourself?

JAZZY: No, Momma. I told you it was accident.

MOTHER: I don't think so. This looks exactly like the places that were showing up on Ann Marie Sholwalter's arms before her Mom found out what she was doing. You're doing what she was doing! You're cutting, aren't you?

(Jazzy is silent.)

MOTHER Answer me. *(Beat.)* Right now. I mean it.

JAZZY: *(Reluctantly and with a small voice.)* Yes. *(Beat.)* Sometimes it makes me feel better.

MOTHER: Makes you feel better? It makes you feel better to try and kill yourself? A pretty girl like you with the world by the tail?

JAZZY: I am *not* trying to kill myself. *(Beat.)* I'm not. I swear.

MOTHER : For what other reason would you try to slice yourself up with a razor blade? Do you want to go to hell?

JAZZY: This may sound crazy, but I cut because I don't want to go to hell.

MOTHER: Golly Moses! I hope your daddy never hears you say that. How can you have been to church twice a week since you were a baby, listening to the sacred Word of God, and not know any better than that?

JAZZY: *(Defiantly.)* I know plenty, Mom. About a lot of things. Even about *The Bible.*

MOTHER: The stuff on your computer tells me you know plenty alright – plenty about lots of things you shouldn't!

JAZZY: Like I said, the stuff I write helps me understand things better some times.

MOTHER: All you need to understand, girl, is found in the pages of *The Holy Bible. (Beat.)* By the way, Pastor Karla wanted to put one of your poems in the church newsletter. Everybody in the church would be horrified if they read any of *this* crap.

JAZZY: Momma, those things are not all I write about.

MOTHER: Well, I've looked through a bunch of this stuff and found only one thing Godly enough to go in the newsletter. Maybe this poem called, "Daffodils," would work. It's pretty nice. I'll save it, but the rest of this stuff? It's going to go right now!

JAZZY: What do you mean, Mom?

MOTHER: Exactly what I said, girl.
(Mother puts her hands on the keyboard and starts deleting.)

JAZZY: *(Horrified.)* No...no, Momma!
(Jazzy fights her mother's hands, trying to get them away from the computer keyboard. Finally, she gets hold of them momentarily and looks into Mother's eyes.)

JAZZY: No, Momma! Don't erase me! *Please*, please, no!
(Mother pulls her hands away from Jazzy and places them in her own lap. Jazzy, still watching her mother closely, returns to her chair.)

MOTHER: Jazz, do you realize how much your daddy and I are spending trying to help you feel better? Between the counselor and medicines, we're dropping a chunk of change every month. Reading this stuff makes me feel like we're just wasting our money. No one who is feeling better would be cutting themselves and writing scary stuff like this.

JAZZY: But, Momma, I *do* feel better – especially when I write. I even feel better when I cut. The pain in my heart goes away – at least for a little while.

MOTHER: You couldn't tell it by me. And pain? You have no idea what real pain is. No idea! My momma used to say, "Garbage in, garbage out." Whatever we fill our minds with is what is going to play out in our lives. So, you write and think about things like suicide and drugs and doubting God and the next thing we know you're slicing up your arms. God help us all!

(Mother quickly reaches up and clicks twice on the computer. Jazzy leaps up to look at the computer screen. She sees her writing folder has been deleted. She falls into her chair sobbing.)

JAZZY: No. Momma, how could you do it? All the stuff I wrote in Ms. Green's English class, my journal, my stories, my dreams...gone. *(Looking upward.)* God, why? *(Sobbing again.)* Noooooooo... Nooooo.

(Mother tries to puts her arm around Jazzy, but Jazzy tosses it off.)

MOTHER: Jazzy, come on. See, now you have a clean slate. You can start writing about nice things like friendship, God's creation, going to college. It'll make you feel better all the way around. You'll see. It might even help you get off that gosh awful medication.

JAZZY: *(Looks at her mom in horror.)* I've always suspected it, but now I know for sure. You...don't love me.

MOTHER: What?

JAZZY: You don't love me. You've never loved me.

MOTHER: Well, I never! How could you say something like that? Look how hard your dad and I work to give you girls the kind of opportunities we didn't have. Heck, I was the first person to encourage you to write. I knew you had talent when I read your first little story about finding a kitten in the neighbor's mailbox.

JAZZY: Yep, it's all good — I'm all good — as long as it's all smiles and cotton candy. But, sometimes things are licorice, Momma. Licorice. Some times things go wrong and sometimes I cry.

MOTHER: There's no need to dwell on the bad, honey, when you have our Lord and Savior, Jesus, in your heart.

JAZZY: Would you love me if I didn't?

(Pause.)

MOTHER: Listen here, when your daddy got me pregnant at sixteen, we got married. We could have made other choices, but we didn't. You wouldn't be here, if I didn't love you!

JAZZY: See, Momma, that's the thing. If you can't love *all* of me, I would have been better off if you *had* made a different choice.

MOTHER: Well, I never! You shut that talk off right now, Jazzy! *(Shaking her head, to self.)* Kids today... I was told it could be bad, but I never thought hormones could be this bad! Lord, have mercy on my soul!

(Beat. Mother turns off the computer. Straightens up the desk a bit. Sighs a deep sigh and wipes sweat from her forehead. Jazzy continues to deflate, little by little, until she is slumped in her chair staring at nothing — almost catatonic.)

MOTHER: *(Not noticing what is happening to Jazzy.)* Now, get yourself together, Jazzy girl, and let's go to the Dairy Queen and get the girls some ice cream like we planned. That will make us all feel better! *(Mother rises and exits, calling to other daughters.)* Kara Lee! Emmy! Are you ready to go for ice cream? *(Pause, light-heartedly.)* Jazzy! *(Having been erased, Jazzy remains in the chair staring blankly. Lights fade out.)*

END OF PLAY

Lisa Soland

Biography

Melanie Ewbank is an award-winning actress, playwright, director, and voiceover artist. Her 10-minute plays have been produced in California, Arizona, and Idaho. Her one-acts toured Los Angeles area prisons, juvenile halls and assisted living facilities. Her full-length play, *Baby Jesus in the Cat Box?* received a staged reading at Pasadena Playhouse.

Old School

Melanie Ewbank

Old School was written during The All Original Playwright Workshop's April 2015 Writer's Retreat. It was a finalist in the 2016 Female Playwrights Onstage Project national festival of short plays, "Curves Ahead," and in May 2016 received a staged reading in Sedona, Arizona, as part of an eight city reading series.

CHARACTERS

> MABEL: 60s - 90s. Wilma's roommate. The alpha-dog (or at least wants to be).
>
> WILMA: 60s - 90s. Mabel's roommate. Politely passive until pushed too far.

SETTING

> Living room of an apartment in a retirement facility.

• • • • • • • • • • • •

Mabel and Wilma are in the midst of a scuffle at the front door of the senior living apartment they share. Wilma is blocking Mabel's exit.

WILMA: No! NO! You can't take it! I won't let you take it!

MABEL: Get out of my way! You can't keep me here! I'm LEAVING and this whole ROOM is GOING WITH ME!

WILMA: I'm paying for half of it! You have to leave my half!

MABEL: I had it first! It was mine and Ethel's! We shared it like mature grown-ups! When she died she said I could have it, so it's mine! MINE! MINE! MINE!

WILMA: Is not! IS NOT! I paid for it!

MABEL: Did not! DID NOT!

WILMA: Half of it I did! I paid for half!

MABEL: *(Physically indicating half of the apartment.)* Fine then! You can have THAT half!

WILMA: Ha HA! I get the bathroom and you can't use it!

MABEL: *(Indicating the front door.)* Well, I get this door and YOU can't use THAT!

WILMA: I paid for half of that door!

MABEL: Then you can have the top half! Good luck jumping those brittle bones up over my half!

WILMA: It's a vertical half, you nincompoop!

MABEL: Says who?!

WILMA: Says my cancelled check number 8227.

MABEL: Liar! Show me!

WILMA: So you can leave and take that with you too?! No way sister! I'm not moving from this threshold! You think I was born yesterday?

MABEL: You weren't born at all! You were hatched!

Lisa Soland

WILMA: You take that back! Take it back!

MABEL: Or what?!

WILMA: Two words! Laxa-Tives!

MABEL: Number one, laxatives is one word. ONE! Number two, what does laxatives have to do with anything?!

WILMA: Number one, laxatives is a "two" word. Number TWO, you do not have permission to use MY bathroom, which you gave me not TWO minutes ago, in which to do your TWO business!

MABEL: Who died and made you queen?

WILMA: Ethel did!

MABEL: Liar! Prove it!

WILMA: That's TWO, sister!

MABEL: What is it with you and deuces?!

WILMA: How's your stomach?

MABEL: My stomach is fine! I'm the picture of health!

WILMA: No cramping?

MABEL: No, why? Should there be?

WILMA: There shouldn't be! Not if you've kept your dirty paws off of the food in my side of the refrigerator!

MABEL: If you accuse me one more time, I swear I will —

WILMA: What?! What will you do?!

MABEL: I will leave, and I will take this whole apartment with me! The whole apartment —

(Mabel stands up very straight, then looks stricken, then bends slightly, holding her stomach.)

WILMA: How's your stomach?

MABEL: I did not eat your brownies —!! *(She bends over a little further, then looks more stricken, then stands up very straight. She realizes Wilma's meaning of...)* Laxa-Tives.

WILMA: Finally putting two and two together.

MABEL: You! You... You... *(Mabel doubles over.)*

WILMA: Well, that doesn't sound anything close to an apology!

MABEL: For what?!

WILMA: Number one, for eating my food. And number two, for calling me a liar when I confronted you about it!

MABEL: You ARE a liar!

WILMA: At this rate, even if — and that's a big if! Even if I let you use my bathroom, without a serious change of attitude on your part, each square of toilet paper will cost you five bucks!

MABEL: I will wipe my ass with a five-dollar bill before I'll pay you for a square of your toilet paper. *(Half bent over, Mabel walks to her purse, picks it up and moves toward the bathroom.)*

WILMA: Suit yourself. Word of advice, though. Five singles would better maximize your investment.

MABEL: Step aside, sister.

WILMA: Nope.

(Silence. A standoff. Neither woman so much as blinks.)

MABEL: Pass or impasse.

WILMA: Impasse.

MABEL: You sure? Last time I wiped the floor with your sorry impasse.

WILMA: I've been studying.

MABEL: Rock, paper, scissors on three. *(Beat.)* ONETWOTHREE!

(Mabel throws scissors. Wilma throws rock.)

WILMA: HA! I win! I'll receive.

MABEL: You're letting me go first?

WILMA: Scrabble rules.

MABEL: Let's do this.

(Wilma gets a pad of paper and a pen. Mabel prepares herself. Like a Zen master, she straightens her posture, wincing at first, then overcoming her cramping intestines, she takes a deep, cleansing breath, releases it slowly, and then busts out a little beat box rhythm and begins to rap.)

MABEL: **Don't even mess, bitch I'm the best.**
Your good ol' days are in the past.
Homecoming Queen's corsage is brown
And girl! That crown? Bitch put it down!
It's old, like you. Your days are few.
Dry is your dew. Soft food you chew,
with plastic teeth held in with glue.
You poor dumb broad; you have no clue,
that I done wiped the floor with you.
Yes, full of class, full up with sass,
attractive, smart, I kicked your ass!
Peace!

(Wilma has made a hash mark for every rhymed word and begins tallying Mabel's points.)

MABEL: Read 'em and weep! "Q" for homecoming queen equals ten points plus all the rhyming words. Yeah boyyyyyz! How many, how many, how many?!!!

WILMA: Hold on, I'm counting!

MABEL: Need a calculator?

WILMA: Ten points for "Q" plus sixteen phrase endings is twenty-six, but I'm deducting one point for trying to rhyme "best" with "past." First round, Mabel, twenty-five points. Not bad.

MABEL: Not bad? Wait till round two. I wasn't even warmed up.

WILMA: You wanna go ask Ida if you can use her bathroom before I start? Cuz after I'm done, that bathroom's getting a lock that can be opened only with a retina scan.

MABEL: *(Taking the pad and the pen.)* You better save the smack talk for the homeless shelter.

WILMA: *(She begins her rap.)*
There ain't nothin' like the feelin'
Of your wrinkled homie stealin'
All your Metamucil, denture cream and toilet paper rolls.
That beyotch and her Bunco playin' hoes have gone too far,
Eating all my brownies and then pawning my guitar.
But karma is like Santa Claus, ubiquitous, just sitting
And waiting while that hoe-bag pretends that she is knitting,
Cuz soon the special food she stole will cause her to be
shitting. I'm all a twitter, filled with hope, and if it's true
I'll squeal From pure delight as vindication I pursued with
zeal. Forgive me if I'm wrong but stealing's wrong and
although crass, Yo, the answer my friend should be blowing
out her ass.
(Mabel has made a hash mark for every rhymed word and begins tallying Wilma's points, when the urgency of her bowel issues collides with the realization of the meaning in the message in Wilma's rap lyrics causing Mabel to double over.)

WILMA: You lose, gangsta.

MABEL: The points aren't counted yet.

WILMA: Ubiquitous. Ten points. Squeal. Ten points. Zeal. Ten points. It won't matter what else you count, I've already won.

MABEL: *(Standing, trying to hold her explosive bowel movement in.)* House rules. The points have to be counted — Ghaaaaaaa! I have to go now.
(Wilma blocks her way.)

WILMA: There's no bathroom for you in here.

MABEL: I'm not fooling around, Wilma. I will do a Jackson Pollock on this carpet!

WILMA: I don't care. It's your carpet.

MABEL: Wilma, I'm in dire straights here! I've got food poisoning or something!

WILMA: Or something, all right! Admit it!

MABEL: Never!

WILMA: Suit yourself!

MABEL: I'm going to Ida's. *(She moves toward the door. She is barely hanging on.)*

WILMA: Good idea. Uh, no, no, Mabel. Not that side of the door. That's my side of the door.

MABEL: That's the side with the doorknob!

WILMA: You made the rule, you determined the boundaries. I'd say that is your tough shit.

MABEL: Wilma, I'm begging you. BEGGING YOU!

WILMA: *(Counting her points.)* You spelled "ubiquitous" wrong, and it is *to* the correct usage, and you have thirteen tally marks here, so thirteen plus thirty equals —

MABEL: I'm counting those points! I was the point counter and I will do the arithmetic!

WILMA: You were trying to cheat me. I got forty-three points.

MABEL: I have to go, Wilma. This is not at all funny. I am sick with E-coli or something!

WILMA: Or something! Like laxative-laced brownies, maybe?

MABEL: There's no way you got forty-three points!

WILMA: Say what you want, but I still win!

MABEL: How do you figure that?

WILMA: You ate that entire pan of brownies out of spite. SPITE, MABEL!

MABEL: Never! I will not admit guilt for something I am not guilty about!

(The phone rings. Wilma grabs it. The two women speak simultaneously, Wilma into the phone and Mabel shouting toward the phone.)

WILMA: Hello? Ida? What? Kaopectate? Really. You don't say. An entire pan of brownies while playing Bunco, huh? Isn't that strange. Sure, she's right here.

MABEL: Hello! Ida, Ida is that you? Ida you gotta help me. Wilma took over the door. DON'T ASK QUESTIONS! Wilma took over the door so I need you to walk down the hall and open it from the outside – THIS IS CRITICAL! Give me the phone, Wilma! GIVE ME THE —

WILMA: It's for you.

(Wilma makes a beeline for the bathroom and immediately reenters holding a grocery bag or a pillowcase containing the toilet paper, all of the reading material, and the towels. Basically anything that could be used as a substitute for a specific hygiene function.)

MABEL: Ida. Did you hear any of that? Wait! WAIT! Listen, Ida. You gotta come over – no, Ida, no! I'm not having any digestive issues! No, it's just that Wilma took the door – wait, what? Whadda ya mean, stuck? Cover to cover, huh? The entire issue in one sitting? Holy shi— *(Mabel drops the phone and doubles over with cramps. She urgently waddles toward the bathroom. Wilma starts to block her.)*

MABEL: Get outta my way, Wilma! Get outta my way or suffer the consequences!

WILMA: Oh, all right. Go ahead. I've made my point and I think you've learned your lesson, even if you are too hardheaded to admit it! *(Wilma steps aside and Mabel waddles to the bathroom as quickly as she can without soiling herself. Smiling, Wilma takes the toilet paper out of the bag.)*

MABEL: *(Calling out from off stage as she relieves herself.)* Oooooooohhhhhhhh. OK, Wilma. OK. Truce. I will try to be more aware of which side of the refrigerator my food is on, and you can be more...uh...Wilma?

WILMA: Yes, Mabel.

MABEL: I thought we had some toilet paper.

WILMA: We? No. I have some toilet paper. *(Wilma tears off one square of toilet paper.)*

MABEL: Ah, c'mon, Wilma! Let's let bygones be bygones. Clean the slate.

WILMA: Happy to. For five bucks a square.

(Lights quickly fade to black.)

END OF PLAY

Biography

Hunter Hawkins began his work in the theatre as a child, performing lead roles in multiple school and church plays. He was recruited to play football for Maryville College. While in college he worked in marketing for the theatre department. He then transferred to East Tennessee State University to study in their Radio/TV and Film department. Mr. Hawkins earned a Marketing/Management degree, and has hopes of building a career in the industry as a director, writer, and actor.

The Broken Line

Hunter Hawkins

The Broken Line was written during J-Term in a playwriting class at Maryville College, Maryville, Tennessee. It was then given a public reading in "Writes of Passage" on January 23, 2015 in Lawson Auditorium at Maryville College. The play starred James Francis in the role of Rob and Joe McBrien playing Vince.

CHARACTERS

    ROB: A college student.

    VINCE: His best friend.

SETTING

    In the locker room of a division one football team.

TIME

    Summer before the 2015 season.

• • • • • • • • • • • •

Two lockers side by side with a laundry basket stage right. Most of the teammates have already left. Rob is sitting in his locker, still in his pads with a towel over his head. Vince enters around the corner shocked to still see Rob in full gear.

VINCE: *(Upset.)* Dude what the hell are you still doing dressed?! I want to beat the lines at dinner!

    (Rob still sits there, like he never heard Vince. Vince walks over and sits beside the locker next to Rob, in a calm voice.)

VINCE: Is everything all right? You look like we just lost the national championship.

ROB: *(Looking down with a towel over his head.)* It's nothing man. Go on to dinner, I don't want to hold you back.

VINCE: I'm not going to dinner without my boy, you know that. *(Chuckle.)* Who would I sit with? The O-line? *(Laugh.)* Never in a million years.

ROB: *(Takes towel off, laughs.)* Yeah that's true...but man it's nothing.

VINCE: Well, it sure as hell doesn't look like nothing. You're still in full uniform and you look like your girlfriend broke up with you. So what's up? I'm your best friend, if you can't tell me who can you tell?

ROB: Dude...the tests came back.

    (Pause.)

VINCE: *(Concerned.)* Well...what did they say?

ROB: The trainers came up to me after practice and they told me that this will be my last one until they can run some more tests.

VINCE: Well, why?! What did the tests say?! Come on, man. Stop beating around the bush and say it!

ROB: They're not 100% sure what it is, but so far it's looking like avascular necrosis. *(Struggles to say avascular necrosis.)* Something like that. It's

Lisa Soland

AVN for me! I won't be able to practice for a few weeks. I'm going to miss camp, and I don't know what I'm going to do, man. I can't advance up the depth chart now. The season is over for me...and possible my career.

VINCE: Honest man, I don't think it's worth it anymore. Neither of us are here on scholarship. We're just two hitting dummies out there, and when we make those stand out plays the coaches are nowhere to say, "Good job." I'm tired of getting knocked on my ass all the time.

ROB: *(Nodding.)* You're right, but so many people are counting on me to go pro, to have some sort of career in football. Hell, I have to support my family. Coach said that if I didn't have so many injuries I could get a scholarship, and he said if I can stay healthy then I could get one.

VINCE: You have a great shot at making it pro. Hell, the only thing holding you back are the injuries. But man, I'm done with it. I was going to tell you at dinner that I wanted to quit, and honestly I suggest you do the same.

ROB: Dude, what the hell?! How dare you say that to me! You know how important this is to me, and everything that's riding on me making it.

VINCE: I know man, but your injuries are...

ROB: What?! What about my injuries? I have came back from every injury stronger than I was before. My sophomore year I came back from an ACL tear in less than four months. I can recover from anything!

VINCE: Dude, you're not Superman! AVN is serious. The lack of blood supply leads to breaking bones and eventually no bones at all. Bo Jackson, man. Bo lost his hip. It literally died and he had to quit. AVN ends careers, and I'm afraid if you play you could really hurt yourself. Please don't get mad at me, I'm just trying to help. You're my best friend. We've played football together for 15 years.

ROB: You don't know what you're talking about! I don't have AVN. Nothing has proven it yet, and if I did have it I would recover from it like I do every other thing. My career ends when I say it does!

VINCE: *(Chuckles.)* Do you even hear yourself?! Who are you?! In all our years together you have never been this hot-headed! *(Softly.)* What's gotten into you, man?

ROB: *(Almost in tears.)* I'm scared okay! There. Now you know what's wrong with me! I don't get scared! All through high school everyone told me that nothing could break me; nothing could bring me down. They said I was unstoppable, unbreakable. How can someone with that kind of reputation admit to being scared?

VINCE: Rob, you're still a human. It's okay to be scared. What you're going through is tough. No one will judge you for showing human emotions. We all get scared. You know I'm always here for you.

ROB: I know I should hang up the cleats, but my dad is depending me. Hell, my whole family is depending on me. I'm the only reason my brother plays football.

VINCE: How's your dad doing?

ROB: The cancer has spread from his lungs to his brain. The doctors don't know how much longer he has, and the only thing he wanted was to see me succeed in football and make a name for myself. My mom doesn't know how we are going to pay the bills, and if I was fortunate enough to make it somewhere, I could help with the bills.

VINCE: Listen, I don't want you to think I'm trying to convince you to quit with me, but I just want you to think about your future. Not only are you a great athlete, but you're also a great student. I know you can succeed outside of football. You will make great money in the future. Your business plan is already amazing. Just go that route. It will be easier on you, trust me.

ROB: Football is all I've ever known. If I don't go to the NFL, I can go somewhere else. I know I can!

VINCE: Yeah, but is it worth giving up your body? You don't want to end up crippled, do you? Crippled for life? What will make your dad happier – living a short life with football, or a long, meaningful life doing something without the physical risks? I'm just giving you the hard truth, just because you are my boy and I don't want you to have any regrets.

ROB: *(Suddenly angry.)* You can't tell the future! You don't know what will happen! I thought you were my friend.

VINCE: If your health is in serious danger you need to call it quits. No matter what you decide I'll still be by your side, but I'm quitting first thing in the morning. I'm going to be a veterinarian, and honestly football is just getting in the way of that dream. If I were you, I would quit with me tomorrow, and start working toward that awesome business plan of yours.

ROB: You know, I never thought I would be hearing all of this shit from my best friend, and honestly I'm tired of it. I will not quit with you tomorrow.

VINCE: You're making a big mistake, I'm telling you.

ROB: *(Rises, ready to leave.)* Whatever dude. I'm not sitting here listening to this any more.

(Crosses to leave.)

VINCE: *(Desperate to get Rob to stay.)* Remember when I wanted to quit in middle school?!

ROB: *(Stops and turns around.)* Yeah I do, and I told you, you would regret that decision?

VINCE: Well, what you don't know is I already quit.

ROB: So you told me you wanted to quit and you already did it?

VINCE: Yeah. I wasn't playing like I wanted to, and you told me that quitting during playing time, so early in the season, would be the biggest mistake I would ever make. Do you know what you told me after that?

ROB: Can't say my memory is that good.

VINCE: You told me the only honorable way to quit is when you lose passion for the game, or if your health is in jeopardy. You made me realize that I still had the health and passion to continue playing, so the next morning before school I asked coach to let me come back.

ROB: I never knew that...

VINCE: I never wanted you to think I bailed on you and the team. That night, our conversation made me realize that you were right. I didn't have a good reason to quit, but Rob, you do. Bo Jackson, man. Please just think about it.

ROB: How do I know you're not just lying about that to get me to quit?

VINCE: *(Annoyed.)* Do you really think I would do that to you?

ROB: I just don't remember saying that.

VINCE: Well, I remember it, and you said it! *(Laugh.)*

ROB: Vince, you never told me why you want to quit.

VINCE: I told you, I'm tired of being the hitting dummy and never being noticed.

ROB: Dude, I know it's something more than that. You knew freshman year of college football you have to prove yourself. So what else is it, man? I was honest with you, so you better be honest with me.

VINCE: *(Hesitant.)* My mom lost her job last week, and you know my dad is too hurt to do anything, so that leaves no money to feed three kids. I told my parents that I'll transfer to the local community college, and I'll get a job and help out. Don't bother talking me out of it. I already have my transfer papers sent in.

ROB: When where you going to tell me?!

VINCE: At dinner. Dinner was going to be a very informative and eventful night.

(They smile.)

ROB: I know you're doing what you have to. I'm just upset we can't go to the same college together anymore. We had a lot of things to accomplish together during these four years.

VINCE: *(Laugh.)* Let's be honest. It would of taken five years to get out of here. *(They laugh.)*

VINCE: What happens from here?

ROB: Regardless of if I play football or not, I'll still be at this college. I love it here.

VINCE: I wanted to stay here, I really did.

ROB: It's all we've talked about for over a year.

VINCE: Everything seemed a lot simpler a year ago. Everything seemed to be lined up just right. My mom had a great job. Both of our dads were healthy. Our college plans seemed so real. The money was right. All of the stars were aligned.

ROB: Yeah, it's funny how fast life changes. I didn't have this disease, and I was healthy enough to make it in the NCAA.

VINCE: I don't want to drift apart.

ROB: We've been best friends for 15 years. That's way too long to worry about some stupid distance.

VINCE: I can come up here and you'll still be coming home, so it's all good!

ROB: No worries brother! *(Accepting the truth.)* Hey Vince, they're 99% sure it's AVL.

VINCE: Yeah? That's no good. No good. Bo Jackson, man.

ROB: Yeah. Yeah. You're right. I know you're right.

VINCE: *(Excited.)* So you're going to quit?

ROB: With football how am I going to see my best friend all the time?!

VINCE: You will look back and realize this is the right thing to do.

ROB: *(He nods.)* Are you hungry dude?

VINCE: Seriously, dude? I have been waiting on you for 30 minutes! I'm starving!

ROB: Well, let's go eat!

VINCE: Hey Rob, before we go anywhere, you should take that smelly ass uniform off!

ROB: I forgot I still had it on! *(Laugh.)*

VINCE: Oh, and please take a shower!

(Blackout.)

END OF PLAY

Lisa Soland

Biography

Randy Springer's most recent credits include the new media production of *Dreamcatchers*, the feature film *Nine Shades Of Pleasant*, and a staged reading in Los Angeles of his short farce, *Abe's Big Night*. He is presently developing and producing works for stage, screen, and television.

Company Benefits

Ⓐ

Randy Springer

Company Benefits was written by Randy Springer in conjunction with Maryville College's playwriting class in Maryville, Tennessee, where it was given a public reading in "12 X 10 X 2" in April of 2012 at the Haslam Family Flex Theatre at the Clayton Center for the Arts. It featured Randy Springer starring in the role of Davis, and David Stair in the role of Ross.

CHARACTERS

DAVIS: An employee in the Accounting Department of a
Financial Services Firm. He's about 40 years old.

ROSS: Davis' supervisor, about 45 years old.

SETTING

A financial services office in a large Metropolitan area in
the United States.

TIME

Mid-afternoon, spring of 2010.

• • • • • • • • • • • •

*Lights up on the accounting department supervisor's office. It has a fairly large
window behind the main desk, where there resides a large swivel chair, and another
chair placed askew, in front of the desk. The lull of the day has come. Ross peruses
a file. He holds his hand on his head as if he is suffering a headache. Davis enters
in a nervous, but determined manner.*

DAVIS: Ross, I need to speak to you —

ROSS: Can't it wait until — ?

DAVIS: *(Paces erratically.)* No, it can't. I've had enough of tomorrows.

ROSS: Well, no problem then, Davis, come on in and make yourself at home.

DAVIS: I have been trying to get a request done for weeks now, and I am not
getting anywhere. It's been weeks.

ROSS: What did you need? What's going on?

DAVIS: Well, you see it's not for the company. It's for me.

ROSS: Oh...

DAVIS: I've been to personnel, but I'm not hearing anything at all, and now
I call and call, and they just keep putting me off. Tomorrow-tomor-
row-tomorrow!

ROSS: Davis, there's not much I —

DAVIS: *(Emphatically.)* They don't care, Ross. They're not listening. Will you
at least hear me out!?

ROSS: Sure, what's going on?

DAVIS: *(Takes a breath. Calmly.)* Thanks. I need some kind of loan, advance,
whatever... I'm losing it.

ROSS: Oh, uh...okay, well, what happened?

DAVIS: *(Increasingly upset.)* It's all slipping away, Ross. Everything. Our house, our cars. I can barely afford to eat lunch. We're under water, and it's really bad. I've got banks all over me.

ROSS: Oh, no.

DAVIS: Yeah, Betsy was off for a while, and I can't keep it together. I'm really trying here, but nothing I've tried works.

ROSS: I'm real sorry to hear it.

DAVIS: Everyone is sorry to hear it. It's getting fucking ridiculous.

ROSS: Now Davis...just calm down, and take a seat for Christ's sake.

(Davis takes a seat and tries to relax.)

DAVIS: I...I'm sorry. I've been a good employee here, haven't I?

ROSS: Yes, we haven't had any problems. You're top notch.

DAVIS: I've put in twelve years here, and I'm wondering why can't I get any help?

ROSS: I...oh, man. I don't know. It's aggravating. This is something I've been hearing a lot lately...not just here, but everywhere.

DAVIS: Well, we're here now. I have been trying for six weeks. Six weeks. You're my supervisor. *(Shrugs.)* So, I figured...

ROSS: *(Muses.)* Yeah. I am. I'm the supervisor. You're the employee.

DAVIS: Can you do anything to help push things through for a loan, or an advance?

ROSS: Uhhh... Not much, I'm afraid.

DAVIS: Yeah, but can't we do something here. Anything?

ROSS: Such as what, Davis? This is accounting. We just count here.

DAVIS: Jesus, I should have known –

ROSS: Hey, I want to help you, Davis, but I'd have a lot of explaining to do. I could lose my job. You understand? *(He moves forward in his seat.)* Please know...it's not that I don't want to. I can't even give it to you myself, or I would. Kids in college. So much uncertainty. I know this is a tough time now, and it's a real tough time here too. The benefits package is shrinking before our eyes every day. I mean you've got to pick your battles. And this company is no exception. They don't like a rocky boat. And they're looking at everything right now. Everything. It could thwart advancement, and I'm sure you don't want that. You've worked too hard.

DAVIS: Yeah, but advancement in the future doesn't matter much when everything is coming apart now... And, I don't see why you can't, at least, take my advance request to Bill and Susan's team upstairs.

ROSS: I wish I could, but...

(Davis leans back in his chair, and touches his hand to head, slightly covering his eyes.)

DAVIS: *(Softly.)* We've got cash accounts. A lot of them.

ROSS: What are you suggesting?

DAVIS: It could be quick and easy…nobody has to know. Move a little out of each account. I could do installments, or something to pay it back, little by little.

ROSS: That's not going to happen, Davis. And, I'm going to forget you even asked it.

DAVIS: We've done it all the time for Bill and Susan. All the time.

ROSS: Yeah, well they're running the show here. They own it.

DAVIS: You know as well as I do they keep another set of books. I'm sure the SEC would be interested.

ROSS: I don't know that for certain, Davis. Do you? But I can tell you one thing for sure: they don't want the help dipping into the till. And, as far as the SEC is concerned, don't make me laugh…really…you think Bill and Susan don't have it wired there? They're not stupid, and they've got friends everywhere.

DAVIS: Can't you even ask them for a loan?

ROSS: I'm not going to ask because —

DAVIS: CAN'T YOU EVEN TRY —

ROSS: I know what the answer's going to be, Davis. You think you're the first one to come in here with this request? C'mon. You're not the only one with troubles, Davis. I've got some of my own here. And then, I get the thrill of hearing this over and over. 18 times now from good people. It feels too hopeless for words.

DAVIS: So, what now?

ROSS: Now?

DAVIS: Ah, the familiar refrain. I don't understand. You know, if I spent my career here saying, "There's nothing I can do," I wouldn't have been here this long.

ROSS: I know that.

DAVIS: Bit of a cheat, don't you think?

(Ross let's out a sigh. He pulls out a bottle of Scotch, two glasses, places them on his desk and pours.)

ROSS: A few years back, I remember I could have gone to Bill and Susan with your problem, and this could have happened. But, not now. We live in a pull yourself up by your own bootstraps kind of world now, Davis. Nobody gives a shit. I go up there all the time, and want to stop the bleeding. I've had to let a whole bunch of people go. It's not my favorite thing to do in the world. I wish it were different. I wish

Lisa Soland

we could go back before this whole thing hit the fan a few years ago. But it's not reality. And nobody wants to hear it, or hear about anybody's troubles. It's like we all want to bury ourselves in media graphs, sound bytes, or some goal planning bullshit, or go into hibernation until things get better. Only it's not getting much better. It's a helluva thing.

DAVIS: Yeah, I know it sucks. But it doesn't help me much, does it?

ROSS: My hands are tied on this, Davis.

(Davis rises sharply, and paces frantically around the office.)

DAVIS: You've got to do something, Ross. I have been a great employee here, and I am not taking no for an answer anymore. I can't.

ROSS: What would you have me do?

DAVIS: Your job, goddamnit.

(Ross rises angrily from his seat, and explodes on Davis, but manages to contain his boundary from behind his desk area.)

ROSS: You think I'm being negligent, do you? You think I like this? It's bullshit. I know it. I have to take a fucking handful of Adavans every single day just to get through it. I know you don't want to hear this, but I'm the company shit conduit 'cause I get from both ends, you hear me? So, don't come in here throwing your weight around and making demands. I'm numb to it. I can't fire another person without wanting to pull a fucking trigger on my own ass.

(Davis quietly takes a seat, tries to regroup, and takes a different approach.)

DAVIS: Look...I don't know where else to go anymore. I don't know what to do. Nobody seems to know anything. I'm in a real bind here...

ROSS: Yeah, aren't we all!? So, just calm down and have a drink. Want an Adavan?

(Davis refuses, waving his hands.)

ROSS: It may do you some good.

(Ross pulls out a bottle of Adavan from his desk, and starts taking some pills. He washes them down with his scotch.)

DAVIS: I realize I've stepped over the line today.

ROSS: Don't worry about it. You're not the first. I doubt you'll be the last.

(Ross pours more booze. Davis takes a glass from Ross' desk, and drinks.)

DAVIS: You know, I've been watching a lot of vampire shows and movies on TV lately, Ross. It's no accident there's this cultural thing with vampires, you know? I mean look at us. Look at our world here in good ol' America. A bunch of monsters on top of everybody...guys and gals like the people we work for...decide to just put it to everybody one day, and start sucking us all dry until there's nothing left. No benefits. No retirement. And then, no job.

ROSS: Seems to be a matter of time.

DAVIS: Why can't we just go up there, and straighten them out old school? *(Ross laughs.)*

My wife, Betsy, she left me.

ROSS: Oh, man, no.

DAVIS: Couldn't take it anymore. The bank is foreclosing on our house... could be any time. And there's this deluge of creditor calls morning, noon, and night.

ROSS: Change your number.

DAVIS: She called me a loser, and left.

ROSS: That's terrible.

DAVIS: Well, we've been up to our ears in debt for a while. Started with an expensive honeymoon, and it just kept ringing upwards from there. That big freaking house, we really didn't need for just the two of us in New Vernon, furnished with the finest things, expensive vacations to places like Monaco, new cars every year, really sweet jewelry, clothes. Betsy had exquisite taste. She really enjoyed the good life...and so did I. *(Pause.)* Boy, what I'd do to give it all back.

ROSS: Sounds familiar.

DAVIS: I guess that's what makes it so hard working in our business. We see people coming in here awash in wealth. They've got everything you want: dressed in the best, sporting the latest tech...bringing their entourages in here with their fat wallets. When you see that every fucking day, day-in and day-out, you want it. Soon, you start doing things that don't make sense, but you fool yourself into thinking that you can do it. You've got all these credit cards, or equity in your house that can be used as leverage for investing in stuff some expert says is a sure-fire, first-mover, and the next thing you know, everything starts closing in on you.

ROSS: Where are you living now?

DAVIS: Still hanging on to the castle. For the moment.

ROSS: The castle. What will you do?

DAVIS: Survive, I hope. It'll be hard. I know this is the end for me here.

ROSS: Probably.

DAVIS: *(Rises.)* Working here in financial services, you can't just go bankrupt la-ti-da, you know?

ROSS: So sorry, Davis.

DAVIS: But as a parting gift, I wanted to share something. *(Davis pulls what*

Lisa Soland

appears to bean automatic handgun from his trousers, and lays it on Ross' desk.)
I brought this in today.

ROSS: What the hell is that for?

DAVIS: I wanted to see if I could get it past security.

ROSS: Davis, are you kidding?

(Davis stalks about the office.)

DAVIS: It's fake, Ross. Plastic, or something. But then, if I was really nuts, and I am not saying I'm not. I would probably start bringing in pieces of this weapon here, and just start putting it together...if I was nuts, I'd do that. If I had lost everything, like I have, and I was nuts, I would probably want to put together a weapon like this, made of a composite material, slip it all past security, and quietly put it together at my desk at lunch times with my baloney and cheese sandwich. It would be my new project in our accounting department. Then, I would wait a few more days or so, or until I was really convinced I had no more hope, like right now, and then I would go upstairs, and give Bill and Susan a party they'd never forget.

ROSS: But you're not going to do that, are you Davis?

(Davis is visibly shaken.)

DAVIS: It's not that I don't want to... I just can't.

ROSS: Good. Davis, why don't you go back to your desk, and...or just go on home. Take the day and figure things out for yourself. We'll see what happens tomorrow, you know? It'll be a new day. It'll be like this never happened. Between us guys. Okay?

DAVIS: Yeah, okay. Sorry about stepping over the line, Ross.

ROSS: No need to apologize, Davis. It's hard to figure out where the lines are anymore. You just go home. And, try to be okay. It'll all work out. One way, or another.

DAVIS: Okay, Ross. Thanks for...at least, listening.

ROSS: Sure.

(Davis exits. After a few moments, Ross picks up Davis' weapon and studies it. He sits it down on the desk, and then pulls out his own weapon from the desk drawer. Ross picks up Davis' weapon with his free hand, and compares. He spins his chair around toward the window, holding the guns pointed upward in each hand, and then quickly a loud bang reverberates simultaneously with...)

(Blackout.)

END OF PLAY

Biographies

Darnell Arnoult is a novelist, poet and educator. Her most recent book is *Galaxie Wagon: Poems* (Louisiana State University Press, 2016). She is the recipient of the 2005 Weatherford Award for Appalachian Literature. She teaches writing at Lincoln Memorial University in Harrogate, Tennessee.

Marcus Burchfield is a writer and a journalist for the Independent Herald, Tennessee. A former student of Darnell Arnoult, Marcus graduated from Lincoln Memorial University in 2016. He's at work on a novel.

Karen Spears Zacharias is a novelist and journalist. Her debut novel, *Mother of Rain* (Mercer University Press), was the recipient of the 2014 Weatherford Award for Appalachian fiction, and is now a stage play.

Death Row

Darnell Arnoult, Marcus Burchfield, and
Karen Spears Zacharias

Death Row is the result of a playwriting class in June, 2014, offered through Arts in the Gap, a summer arts program of Lincoln Memorial University.

CHARACTERS
    INMATE #100689: female, mid 40s.
    INMATE #100293: male, early 20s.
    INMATE #100786: female, early 20s.

SETTING
    Prison meeting room.

TIME
    Present day.

• • • • • • • • • • • •

Three chairs in a prison meeting room. Inmates in orange jumpsuits, shackled, flip-flops.

INMATE 100786: It looks so easy on TV, you know? Sharp, glistening blade, a butcher knife, or maybe one of those scary chef knives like Emeril Lagasse uses. Some old guy, or innocent schmuck standing at the wrong place at the wrong time, some mean-ass boy high or scared or mean jabs something sharp through his bloated belly. I figured if you put the knife somewhere in the middle it would feel like forking a rump roast. And there in the middle, there's so much that's hard to fix: stomach, colon, liver if you get up under the ribs. In westerns, you never want the cowboys you like to get gut shot. That's the worst thing, where you see 'em jerk and fall with their hand on their stomach — over their wound, blood oozing between their fingers, blood spreading out into their shirts, that red spot getting bigger and bigger, and then they peel back their hand and see what they don't want to see, and there's this look they have then, they know they've been gut shot, that there's no way they'll live, but some friend leans over them and looks under the bloody hand and lies to them then and says, "Na. You'll be okay. It ain't that bad." And the gut-shot guy has to wait for it then. Wait for the lights to go out and the noise to stop and the sting of it.

INMATE 100689: I was always good with children. Everybody said so. Once, when I was playing in the front yard with the neighbor kids, I heard Mama say to Aunt Sue, "Sarah Ann is such a natural with kids, I worry sometimes that she won't be able to have any." I was only 12, hadn't yet started my period, but I memorized Mama's words that day. *(Beat.)* I always did like proving Mama wrong.

INMATE 100293: It's God's will, you know, that I'm here, locked up like some caged animal. Everything has been God's will. I was just 22 when I heard Him a-calling, beckoning me to bring the "Lambs" to slaughter. I hid myself at first, ashamed of my unfaithfulness, but like we learned from Jonah and his whale, ain't nobody able to escape the call of the Lord. I'd been a-running nigh on a week when He caught up with me at Park Inn just 20 miles south of Jackson. Yes, sir, I remember clear as day how she looked in them shorty shorts. Her hair was wet. She'd went for a swim and her skin was still cool under my hands and my lips well, lets say she was as sweet. Yes, sir, she was my first. They found her up next to where the river runs off into Stormy Creek. She was in a shalla' grave, no mo' than two or three feet deep and covered in lye. After all, I didn't want her to stank.

INMATE 100786: That's what I wanted. To see that look on his big old grubby face. The look that says, "Wait a minute. She couldn't do this to me," and then I wanted to see him peel back his hand and see that hole, that real hole in his gut — like the one I feel everyday. I wanted him to have that look that said, "Oh shit, I'm dying." I wanted him to look at me and think, "You did this to me? With the knife I gave you for Christmas?"

INMATE 100689: That first one? I got shed of her pretty quick. I must've been 16. That crop of red hair set me off. Reminded me too much of him, you know? Mama tried her best to steer me clear of him. She warned me that he wasn't nothing but trouble shod in shoe leather. As much as I hate to admit it, Mama was right. *(Beat.)* I didn't let that one live long. Dropped her right in the toilet at Taco Bell after Friday night's game against Bell County High. We won that game so everybody was shouting and carrying on. Nobody noticed when I dished her out of the toilet and carried her to the trunk of the car in that garbage bag.

INMATE 100293: I never thought serving the Lord would bring me so much pleasure, but I never thought serving the Lord meant buying Durex condoms at the corner market and picking a new girl every other Friday night. Don't wanna waste my seed, ya know. I had this thing for sixteen-year-olds, ones with red hair, had collection of it in a nice little Ziplock bag, till police took it from me. Some say I was sick, that I still am. It's hard to explain how squeezing the life out their eyes made me feel. I remember one girl, picked her up hitchhiking, trying to head west to Hollywood. She was sweet, talked a little whilst I drove us a ways. Full of dreams that girl, dreams that would never come true. I decided to ease her pain. She was a virgin. I could smell it. Weird to say, but I could smell a virgin across the room in a crowded place. They smell sweet, like apple blossoms on the spring breeze. I took her down on Cannon Creek, and made love to her. She fought back a little but after a while she stopped moving, and just laid there enjoying herself, crying it was so good.

INMATE 100786: I got everything I wanted — except that look didn't last as long as I thought. It faded pretty quick and then that look I'd seen so many other times came over his face, that, "You bitch!" look. The other thing that kinda surprised me was how it feels to stab a belly, a big belly that hangs over a belt you've felt slap and slide over your own skin more times than you can count. It feels like poking a rump roast and popping a balloon all at the same time. And then I found out you don't always hit a vital organ when you stab a man's belly. Sometimes you just make a mess. *(Beat.)* He took that knife and threw it in the sink, and he took off that belt faster than I could figure out he wasn't dying. And he whipped me like I was nothing even human. All that day I thought about him saying, "I brought you into this world and I can take you out of it."

INMATE 100689: I've had eight children. I didn't name them all. Only the ones I really felt connected to. Katy. She was my favorite. I think it was that dark hair of hers. Or maybe it was the way she held her baby dolls tight as she rocked back-and-forth, singing them lullabies that she made up. There was something so familiar about her.

INMATE 100293: I was caught one Thursday morning, mid-...September, I think it was, at a Gas-N-Go in Aberdeen. I was in there getting me a Snickers and some Pall Malls, when the police come in the door. They told me I was under arrest for the rape and murder of seven girls. I didn't cause no scene, but went real quiet like, praying the entire time. "It be Your will Lord, not mine." Makes me laugh, cause they was at least ten more they wasn't accounting for, you see.

INMATE 100786: One night when Daddy tied on a good one, I waited till he was passed out on his bed, and I took his own fishing line and sewed him up in a blanket with one of his own upholstering needles, the one shaped like the moon. And then I got that knife again and I counted every single time I popped that balloon. Two hundred and thirty-seven times. I've decided that's my lucky number. And when they ask me, Connie Francis Blakenship, for my last words, 'cause I hear they ask you that, I'm going to say, "Who took out who, you sorry excuse for a son-of-a-bitch?"

INMATE 100689: I won't deny it. I planned the killings. *(Beat.)* I had to be extra careful. How else could I have gotten away with murdering that many babies before anyone caught me? *(Beat.)* It's not as difficult as you might imagine. The killing. It's easier to do when they are itty-bitty. *(Beat.)* What did me in finally was my own fault. Can't blame nobody else. I let myself be a fool for Katy. I knew I should've gotten shed of her sooner. Killing the others didn't bother me like killing Katy did. *(Beat.)* That last blow caused her to puke something fierce. They said in court that there was blood splatters on the ceiling but I know they was lying 'cause I cleaned up that room myself. Scrubbed it down good and clean with bleach water before I called the police and told them Katy had fallen in the tub and hit her head. *(Beat.)* I can't recall now if she was my fifth child or my sixth one. Time isn't the only thing a person loses track of on death row. A person loses track of their memories too. I've always counted that a blessing. There is so much about my life and the choices I've made that I wish I could forget.

INMATE 100293: The trial was short. My lawyer said that the evidence against me was too much to deny, and that if I had killed any more girls, I'd tell the police where they was buried in exchange for my life. But that is not the Lord's work. Where they's buried is a holy place, a place of offering, where the Lambs go to slaughter. So here I am, Leonard Harper, the Mississippi Mud Killer. Waiting for my time.

INMATE 100689: Everybody in Middlesboro, Ky. expected such big things out of me. Shoot, I expected them of myself. I was Valedictorian of the 1989 graduating class, went to University of Kentucky on an academic scholarship. That's where I got my nursing degree. *(Beat.)* I was a good surgery nurse. All the doctors used to request me. That kind of work can be demanding for some, but I was skilled with a knife and blood didn't bother me none at all. *(Beat.)* I'm a disappointment to the entire state of Kentucky. Everybody back home talks about me — Sarah Ann Wiley — in hushed whispers, as if just saying my name might unleash the forces of hell. *(Beat.)* I heard tell that after I was arrested, Preacher Ray give a sermon about me. He said I wasn't mental. I was plumb evil. *(Beat.)* He's one to talk.

INMATE 100293: They say that when they plunge the needle into your vein, it's just like going to sleep. No pain. No suffering. Not that I am scared of that. Lord deliver me from the hands of my enemies, and forgive my iniquity, with covering of your blood and the blood of your slaughtered Lambs. Yes, dear Lord, please, don't let it be bad.

INMATE 100786: It can't get too quiet for me.

INMATE 100689: Truth be told, I'm looking forward to the day my time comes. *(Long pause.)* When I put my babies to sleep, I used to sing to them, "Heaven is a wonderful place, filled with Glory & Grace. I can't wait to see my Savior's face. Heaven is a wonderful place. I wanna go there."

(Blackout.)

END OF PLAY

Biography

D.W. Gregory writes in a variety of styles and genres, but a recurring theme is the exploration of political issues through a personal lens. The New York Times called her a "playwright with a talent to enlighten and provoke" for her most produced work, *Radium Girls*, which has received more than 500 productions worldwide since its premiere at Playwrights Theatre of New Jersey. Her drama, *The Good Daughter*, was nominated for a Pulitzer Prize by the drama critic for Variety when it premiered at New Jersey Rep, where Gregory is a resident playwright. Other plays include *Molumby's Million*, *Salvation Road*, *October 1962*, and a musical, *Yellow Stockings*.

Five-Cent Girl

D.W. Gregory

Five-Cent Girl was commissioned by Rorschach Theatre in Washington, D.C., and produced as part of its Klecksography Series: D.C. Underground, in March 2012.

CHARACTERS

ANGUS: A barman.

CUSTOMER: A mysterious gentleman with a secret agenda.

SILE: (pronounced 'Sheila') An Irish immigrant, anywhere between 19 and 30.

SETTING

A corner pub in an Irish slum. This one is in the Swampoodle section of Washington, D.C., once notorious for vice, crime, and ignorance...now long gone.

THE TIME

1896, spring.

Note: The accents are suggested in the dialogue but it's up to the actors to find what works for them in performance. The intention is that Sile's accent is more pronounced than Angus's, and that Customer is clearly not of this place.

• • • • • • • • • • • •

A run down bar in the Swampoodle section of Washington, D.C. 1896. Angus the barman is on his knees scrubbing the floor, as a well-dressed Customer at the bar observes him. He has a glass of whisky, his bowler hat beside him.

ANGUS: Not for me to ask about the private lives of my customers, sir. What they do when they leave here is their own business. But this mess...Lord help me. We was closed three days because of it. *(Beat.)* But in answer to your question – no. I don't think Bill danced with anyone that night. Though I can't be sure. But I know that captain did. Five-cent girls – we got a few in here. Though some will dance just for a pint.
(Offstage, Sile, pronounced Sheila, approaches, singing a melancholy drinking song...)
SILE: *(Offstage.)* "Now stick to the craythur, the best thing in nature..."
ANGUS: And speak of the devil —
SILE: "...for sinking your sorrows and raising your joys." *(She enters, then pauses. Sile has a bowl of apples in her arms, a canvas sack over her shoulder.)*

Lisa Soland

Angus. Are ye a sight fer sore eyes!

ANGUS: You got yer nerve comin' in here. After all this. *(He moves to the bar, where he busies himself.)*

SILE: I can pay. *(Beat.)* Buy an apple. Two fer a penny?

(Angus snorts.)

SILE: It's an honest livin', I'm here to make, Angus.

ANGUS: That's a first. *(He makes no move to pour her a dram.)*

SILE: *(Overdramatic.)* And how am I to put me achin' heart to rest then? With me poor lad about to swing?

(Customer eyes her intently.)

ANGUS: If you'd left him alone he might not be about to swing.

SILE: Ye think I don't know that? It's all I can think about this last week. I can hardly sleep for thinkin' of it. Oh, Angus, if you'd known what I suffered —

ANGUS: Seems to me, it's that police captain done most a the sufferin'.

SILE: He died so quick. Couldn't a hurt that bad.

ANGUS: Now what drives a man to do that, do you think? What would make a man so angry he'd pump three bullets into another man's skull?

SILE: Could be anything.

ANGUS: Could be. But usually it's one specific thing. Or have you not bothered even to ask?

SILE: How can I ask Bill anything? They won't let me in to see him. *(Bitterly.)* Family only.

(Customer taps a coin on the bar.)

ANGUS: Another?

(Customer indicates Sile.)

ANGUS: *(Sliding coin back.)* We ain't servin' her tonight. Or any other night.

CUSTOMER: *(Grabs hold of Angus. Firmly.)* She'll have a whisky.

ANGUS: *(After a beat.)* Fine, sure. It's your funeral. *(He frees himself and pours a whisky.)*

ANGUS: Piano player comes on at six, if you're int'rested. Five cents gets ya the Fox Trot. *(Confidentially.)* Don't ask me what a dime will get ya.

SILE: Go on with ye.

(Angus moves away. The customer pushes the glass towards Sile.)

SILE: You're a true gentleman. Unlike some I could name. *(Lifting the glass.)* Cheers.

(Customer lifts his glass but does not drink. A silence as Sile grows uncomfortable under his gaze.)

SILE: Now don't get the notion I'll do somethin' special for ye. Just because ya bought me a drink. *(Beat.)* Truth is, I've suffered a terrible loss. And I ain't in much mood for company.

(A beat. Customer is still looking at her.)

SILE: He loved me, ye see. Though I din't deserve it. He loved me too much and now he's goin' to pay. *(Beat.)* And I'll pay too. *(Turning to Customer.)* Oh why did ye buy me a drink? Was it a dance ye were wanting? Not sure I can dance no more.

(Customer moves his hat off the bar. Sile takes that as an invitation.)

SILE: But I don't even know yer name.

CUSTOMER: My friends call me J.D.

SILE: J.D.? All right, then J.D. I'll tell ye what, I haven't had a drop in me since the tragic events. You must know what I mean, it's been in all the papers. The police captain —

CUSTOMER: Shot by his own officer.

SILE: Ye know the story.

CUSTOMER: I know what happened. What I'd like to know is why.

SILE: Billy ain't sayin'. *(Beat.)* William, yes. They call him William some times. I suppose they called him William down to the precinct house. But he was always just Billy to me. And he was a sweet one, me Billy. Bought me things. Not just a drink now and then. It's only now and then I'd have one, mind ye. But he bought me this. *(She pulls a red photograph album from the sack.)* It's filled with dreams. And last night, when I put it under me pillow, an angel come to me.

(Angus snorts quietly.)

SILE: 'Twas a dark angel with a dark message. I've laughed me very last, ye see. No more smiles for me. No more joys. Me youth is done.

There's a man dead, and I did na pull the trigger, but it's me doin' all the same. 'Cause I killed him with a wish.

ANGUS: *(Unimpressed.)* He really said that did he? Yer youth is done?

SILE: 'Twas a lady angel. And yes that's what she said.

ANGUS: That's an odd one to deliver a message a doom, don't you think, Sile? Usually the message a doom comes from a big, burly angel with a sword, swingin' wide – or a blowin' a big loud horn. Repent, repent! Ye sinners!

SILE: She was quieter than that. Whispered to me. "Time fer yer penance, Sile. Take yer penance." *(A burst.)* Well, I can't very well do a penance without a pint in me, can I?

ANGUS: Now it's a pint yer wantin'? Ya just had yer drop.

SILE: Just because I ain't in widow's weeds, don't make it any less a grief. To lose the man ye love!

ANGUS: Which was it then?

SILE: What?

ANGUS: The man ye loved. Was it the patrolman or the captain? You never did say.

SILE: Must you torment me so?

ANGUS: You're not the one in the lock-up, Sile. When mornin' comes you'll still be here. While that poor fool is down to the courthouse for his sentencin', and that police captain is still rottin' in his grave —

SILE: All I did was dance with him!

ANGUS: Aw, ya lyin' tramp. No man in the world shoots another just because of a dance!

(Angus is in Sile's face by now, and Customer quietly pulls out a revolver and places it on the bar.)

ANGUS: Jaysus!

CUSTOMER: I wouldn't speak to her like that.

(Angus lets go of Sile and backs away.)

ANGUS: Better be careful, flashing that about. Some policeman might see ya.

(Customer produces a badge.)

CUSTOMER: Sorry I forgot to introduce myself. J.D. Springer. Metropolitan Police.

ANGUS: I already spoke to the police.

CUSTOMER: I'm not here on police business. I'm here because Bill Collier is my friend.

ANGUS: Regards to officer Collier then. But I've nothin' to do with these events. She's the one – lured 'em both…into an entanglement.

CUSTOMER: Then leave me to my business.

ANGUS: I will that. I want nothin' to do with any a this business.

(Angus backs away. He grabs a broom and busies himself cleaning. Customer puts his revolver away. A beat.)

SILE: Yer the one. *(She approaches Customer.)* Yer the one Billy said was in the army. Fought the Indians. Captured Geronimo.

(Beat.)

CUSTOMER: Show me the book.

SILE: 'Tis a private matter.

CUSTOMER: *(Intently.)* If you cared for him at all. You'll show it to me. *(Beat.)* I can help him.

(Another beat. Sile slides the album down the bar. He opens the cover, discovers it is a photograph album.)

SILE: Last summer. He'd bought me a little Brownie. But he took most of the pictures. Said I was to keep it all...for the time when we could be together permanent.

(Customer turns a page.)

SILE: This one's me favorite... We took a drive out into the country for a picnic. Way out into Maryland...where the fields were comin' in green and gold. There was a farmer. Sold us some milk. And took the picture of us together. *(Beat.)* Oh we live in dreams, don't we? As if Billy and me could ever have been together permanent.

CUSTOMER: You knew about his wife?

SILE: *(After a beat.)* I knew. Billy never spoke of her...but I knew.

CUSTOMER: *(After a beat.)* When did you see him last?

SILE: Saturday a week. But only fer a moment – one awful moment. And I've not seen him since, nor been able to ask his forgiveness.

CUSTOMER: And Captain Matthews? How long were you going about with him?

SILE: I wasn't goin' with him. I only danced with him. And only because he paid.

CUSTOMER: Did you know who he was?

SILE: He never told me his name. But he come in regular. I can't turn down a regular customer.

CUSTOMER: What happened Saturday?

SILE: He come in wantin' his dance. And he danced so rudely too, grabbin' at me in ways I don't dare say. And don't usually tolerate, except... *(Almost whisper.)* ...he promised me extra. Well, I look over and there's Billy, at the bar, starin' at us. Ye have to understand, Billy never come in on Saturday nights. *(Ashamed.)* He'd never seen me dance! *(Beat.)* I look back and there's that Captain grinnin' at him, like he'd been expectin' to see him. I told him, "That's yer last dance with me. And may the devil take ye to an early grave!" I never dreamed it would be Billy put him there. *(A burst.)* Oh, I'm the one should be goin' to the gallows, not Bill! *(Beat.)* Will ye see him at all? Before he swings?

CUSTOMER: I plan to.

SILE: Can ye tell him fer me? Because I swear, I loved no other but him. I swear it. On me very soul. I swear it.

CUSTOMER: He can have letters. Why don't you write to him?

SILE: Write to him! *(Beat.)* You think a girl like me had ever got to school?

(A beat as Customer regards her.)

CUSTOMER: Can you make a mark?

(Sile nods. Customer reaches into his pocket for a pen. He turns the photograph over, gives her the pen.)

CUSTOMER: Make it here. I'll write your name below it.

(She makes an X. He takes the pen back.)

SILE: Sile. *(As he writes.)* Can ye make it say, "All me love, Sile?"

(He writes exactly that, then closes the pen.)

SILE: That's so very kind.

CUSTOMER: I'm not doing this for you. This is for Bill.

(He puts the photograph in his pocket, picks up his hat and takes the album.)

SILE: No, ye can na take that. It's all I have left of him.

CUSTOMER: Listen to me, my girl: An act of passion can get a man 20 years to life. A cold-blooded murder means the gallows. And he's confessed to murder. *(Beat.)* Now, if you care for him as you say you do, then you will give this to me. And let me use it to make a case.

(Sile releases the album to him. Customer starts to go.)

SILE: Will ye tell him what I said?

(Customer stops. He extends the album to her.)

CUSTOMER: Take one. Take your favorite.

(Sile opens the album and selects a photograph. She closes it. He takes it, starts to leave again.)

CUSTOMER: If this works, it will mean a trial. And that will mean a scandal. You understand, don't you? That's why he isn't talking.

SILE: To save his poor wife from all that.

CUSTOMER: Or to save you.

(Customer crosses off, leaving Sile with that notion for comfort. A beat. Angus returns to the bar and pours a drink for Sile.)

ANGUS: You think he's really done the things they said? Captured Geronimo – conquered the West – all those wild stories?

SILE: We're all full a stories, Angus. *(Sile lifts the glass as she regards the picture in her hand.)* All we have are stories.

(Lights fade.)

END OF PLAY

Biography

Debbie Lamedman is a playwright and author/editor of eight acting books published by Smith & Kraus, Inc. Debbie's produced plays include *Phat Girls, Triangle Logic, Eating in the Dark, Snowflakes,* and *You Belong to Me.* Debbie is a proud member of the Dramatists Guild. www.debbielamedman.com

Mind Control

Debbie Lamedman

Mind Control was written in The All Original Playwright Workshop and first performed on November 3, 2005 in AOPW's production of "The Playwright's Vehicle," directed by Rob Mersola, starring Julia Sommer as Gwen, Joshua Biton as Rob, and Kim Cottom as Melissa in North Hollywood, California. The play was then selected to participate in the 35th Annual Samuel French Off Off Broadway Short Play Festival in New York City, and remained in the top 40 finalists. *Mind Control* was then produced for Second Fig Theatre Company in New York City, the New York City Collective Theatre Company also in New York City, and the University of Montana in Missoula, Montana.

CHARACTERS

GWEN: Mid to late 20's. Former smoker. Roommates with Rob and Melissa.

ROB: Mid to late 20's. Trying to cut out sweets from his diet Melissa's boyfriend.

MELISSA: Mid to late 20's. Caffeine-addict. Rob's girlfriend.

SETTING

The kitchen of Gwen, Rob, and Melissa's apartment.

TIME

Early morning.

• • • • • • • • • • • •

Gwen is sitting in the kitchen drinking a cup of coffee and smoking an imaginary cigarette. Rob comes in from his morning jog, helps himself to some coffee and watches her for a moment as she continues to smoke a cigarette that isn't there.

ROB: Can I ask you? Exactly what are you doing?

GWEN: I'm smoking. I'm pretending to smoke. I'm fantasizing about smoking. God, I wish cigarettes weren't bad for you.

ROB: Get in line.

GWEN: Do you miss it?

ROB: Not enough to hold air between my fingers.

GWEN: It calms me.

ROB: How depressing that we've reached an age where we have to be careful what we do to our bodies.

GWEN Sucks.

ROB: You know what I miss? Doughnuts.

GWEN: Doughnuts aren't as bad for you as cigarettes. No one ever got lung cancer from a doughnut.

ROB: No...but have you heard of cardiovascular disease? Doughnuts...major contributor to clogged arteries. Not to mention love handles.

GWEN: I guess you're right. *(She takes a hit off her imaginary cigarette – inhaling deeply.)*

ROB: You've got that down. It looks like you're really smoking.

GWEN: I am really smoking. In every fiber of my being, I feel like I am smoking. If my mind believes it, the body will follow.

ROB: But if your body believes that you're really smoking, you still might get
    lung cancer...so I think you should quit.

GWEN: Do not rain on my parade.

ROB: I'm just saying...

GWEN: Try it.

ROB: What?

GWEN: Try it.

ROB: Try what?

GWEN: You want a doughnut? *(She mimes picking up a doughnut. Licking her fingers,*
    she places it in front of Rob.) There you go...knock yourself out.

ROB: *(Looking down at the imaginary doughnut.)* What kind is it?

GWEN: *(Seductively.)* What kind do you want it to be?

ROB: Krispy Kreme. Chocolate glazed. Hot off the rack.

GWEN: You got it.

    (She licks her fingers again sensuously. Rob continues staring down at the "dough-
    nut.")

GWEN: What's the matter? Aren't you going to take a bite?

ROB: I can't see it.

GWEN: Sure you can.

ROB: *(He stares down at the table for awhile. Then looks up at Gwen.)* I can't do this.

GWEN: Concentrate. Close your eyes.

    (He does.)

GWEN: It's chocolate. It's dripping with glaze. Sweet...cake...bursting with
    flavor. Your salivary glands are alive with the amazing flavor of this
    indescribably delicious treat. Open your eyes.

    (Rob opens his eyes. He groans softly. Licks his lips. Gwen watches him careful-
    ly as she continues to smoke.)

GWEN: *(Whispering.)* Eat it.

    (Rob slowly picks up the imaginary doughnut. Gwen leans forward in anticipa-
    tion as he takes his first bite. He throws his head back in ecstasy as he chews
    slowly. Gwen sits back in her chair victorious.)

ROB: *(Chewing.)* That is amazing.

GWEN: I told you. The body believes anything the mind tells it. Now you can
    eat all the doughnuts you want – cholesterol and calorie-free!

ROB: What other stuff can we do?

GWEN: Anything you want. The sky's the limit.

ROB: OK, how about....um....heroin? Wanna try heroin?

GWEN: NO! I don't do drugs. Never wanted to.

ROB: But I want to try this again. I can't believe I achieved such satisfaction without actually eating a real doughnut.

GWEN: You want to achieve satisfaction?

ROB: Yeah!

GWEN: Then sleep with me.

ROB: Gwen... You know I can't do that.

GWEN: This way – not the real way.

ROB: It still would be cheating. I'm not cheating on Melissa. I love her too much.

GWEN: So I guess Melissa controls every thought in your head?

ROB: No!

GWEN: Haven't you ever thought about it?

ROB: Cheating on her?

GWEN: Sleeping with me.

ROB: No!

GWEN: Really? Last Halloween I seem to remember...

ROB: OK. OK. You looked hot that night. So, yeah...maybe from time to time I've entertained the idea. But I'd never go through with it. And you wouldn't either. You wouldn't do that to Melissa and you know it!

GWEN: OK...if Melissa walked in right now with a box of Krispy Kremes.... all chocolate glazed, by the way, would you eat one?

ROB: No. They're poison.

GWEN: But you did just eat one.

ROB: An imaginary one. That doesn't count.

GWEN: Exactly.

ROB: Ohhhh. I get your point.

GWEN: So what do you say?

ROB: Well, how do we do this?

GWEN: The same way we did the cigarette and the doughnut.

ROB: There can be no touching!

GWEN: Nope. No touching. It's all in your mind. The body will follow. OK?

ROB: All right. God what am I doing?

GWEN: Don't worry so much. OK. So...close your eyes.

(They both close their eyes. Gwen continues to issue instructions.)

GWEN: We have to look at each other, but we won't touch. We won't even move. Just look at me though, like you looked at that doughnut, OK?

ROB: But we can't move.

GWEN: Right. You stay where you are, and I'll stay where I am.

ROB: Deal.

GWEN: And keep your hands on the table.

Lisa Soland

ROB: Really?

GWEN: I don't think we should touch ourselves either, Rob. That's getting a little too...

ROB: Weird.

GWEN: Right.

ROB: OK.

GWEN: Ready?

ROB: I guess.

GWEN: Open.

(They both open their eyes and stare at each other for a while. Nothing seems to be happening. Rob looks away.)

GWEN: Stay with me, man.

ROB: This isn't working.

GWEN: Concentrate. I am the doughnut.

(Rob looks back to Gwen. A beat. Then Gwen starts to smile, her breathing becomes shallower. She lets a soft groan.)

ROB: Hey...no groaning!

GWEN: I said no touching...groaning is fine! Groaning is encouraged!

ROB: It is?

GWEN: You did it when you ate the Krispy Kreme, you didn't even know it. Pleasure makes you groan.

ROB: OK. Just don't be too loud, OK? What if Melissa walks in?

GWEN: What if she does? We're not doing anything. We're sitting across the table from each other. Perfectly innocent.

ROB: Sitting across from each other groaning.

GWEN: Do you want to do this or not?

ROB: OK. Let's get back to this. But I have to close my eyes for a second.

GWEN: Go ahead.

(Rob closes his eyes. Gwen continues to stare at him. Rob opens his eyes and they begin. Gwen's breathing becomes heavier. Rob adjusts his position in the chair and lets out a heavy sigh. During this section, their movements should be as minimal as possible, but their breathing and groaning, though it doesn't have to be loud, should become more and more climactic. Towards the end, they are both gripping the edge of the table tightly.)

GWEN: Ummmmm...

ROB: *(Releasing a loud sigh.)* Haaaaaaaa...

GWEN: Oh...ohhhh...

ROB: *(Breathing heavily.)* Aaahhhhh...

GWEN: Oh God...oh...

ROB: *(More heavy breathing.)* Haaaa...haaaaa...

GWEN: Oh baby...oh yes...yes...

ROB: Ohhhh...ohhhhh...

GWEN: *(Reaching climax.)* Oh my God! Oh God!

ROB: Whoa...oh God...

GWEN: *(Catching her breath.)* Unbelievable. That...really...worked...for me...
(Beat.) Are you OK?

ROB: *(Obviously aroused.)* Oh man... 'Scuse me... I gotta go use the bathroom.
(He carefully gets up and leaves the room. Gwen smiles and lets out a huge satisfactory sigh, leans back in the chair contentedly and resumes smoking her imaginary cigarette. Melissa enters.)

GWEN: Morning, sleepy head.

MELISSA: Hey! What are you doing?

GWEN: Smoking.

MELISSA: Thought you quit.

GWEN: I did. That's why I'm smoking this brand.

MELISSA: Clever girl. Is Rob up?

GWEN: Oh yeah. He's up all right.

MELISSA: Is there coffee?

GWEN: Yup. But I thought you were giving up caffeine.

MELISSA: I'm trying. But I need my fix. I'm so addicted.

GWEN: I could probably help you quit.

MELISSA: Really? You think so?

GWEN: Yeah. Sit down here.
(Melissa sits at the table.)

GWEN: Now...close your eyes...

END OF PLAY

Lisa Soland

Biography

Stephanie Hutchinson is an award-winning Playwright/Composer/Lyricist. Four of her 10-minute plays are published by Smith & Kraus in The Best 10-Minute Plays anthologies: *More Precious Than Diamonds* (2009), *Carwash; Or in This Town, You Are What You Drive* (2010), *Super 8 Versus Bacara Resort and Spa* (2009), and *Model Home* (2007). *Carved-Out Light* will be published by Applause Theatre & Cinema Books (Hal Leonard Publishing) in January 2017.

Stephanie's plays have been produced in festivals at Naugatuck Valley Community College (Connecticut), the University of Montana, Western, Redwood High School (Northern California), Kent-Meridian High School (Seattle), and The Colleges of the Fenway (Boston). Her first international production was in Germany, at the prestigious Schule Schloss Salem boarding school.

Super 8 Versus Bacara Resort and Spa was a winner (by audience vote) out of nearly 200 entries in Camino Real Playhouse's Showoff! International Playwriting Festival in San Juan Capistrano. *Speak Now or Forever Hold Your Peace* was one of 7 plays produced (out of 300 international entries) in the 2015 Showoff! festival, and the only play by a female playwright. The Secret Rose Theatre in North Hollywood produced "The Start of Something Real: Short Plays and Musicals by Stephanie Hutchinson," featuring six short plays and two short musicals. The show included 12 actors and 3 directors and ran for six performances. www.StephanieHutchinson.com.

More Precious Than Diamonds

Stephanie Hutchinson

More Precious Than Diamonds was published by Smith & Kraus in The Best 10-Minute Plays 2009. It received the AOPW Fellowship Award and was originally presented by The All Original Playwright Workshop as part of An Evening of Four 10-Minute Comedies on March 29, 2008 at The Actors Group in Universal City, California Cast: Michelle - Angela Rose Sarno; Julie - Michelle Mania; Salesman/Stewart - James McAndrew. Directed by Jonathan Levit. The play was then produced by Redwood High School in Larkspur, CA, in December of 2013, with Emily Newell as Michelle, Kyra Mowbray as Julie, and Jason Gorelick as Salesman/Stewart. The director was Pitarly D'Haiti. In addition, *More Precious Than Diamonds* was produced by International Baccalaureate students at Kent-Meridian High School in Kent, WA, for their Drama Fest 2014 in February. Cast: Michelle Martinez (Guatemala) as Michelle, Sabrina Madamba (Philippines) as Julie, and Darwin Robin (Philippines) as Salesman/Stewart. It was directed by Jimmy Aung (Myanmar). Another production was in May of 2011 at the University of Texas at El Paso: Michelle - Hieu Duong, Julie - Raquel Gomez, Salesman/Stewart - Brandon Graves. Directed by: Lluvia Almanza. Dr. Hutchinson adapted *More Precious Than Diamonds* into *More Precious Than Diamonds: The Musical,* doing triple duty as the Book Writer/Composer/Lyricist. CDs of the cast album are available on iTunes, Amazon and CD Baby on her website.

CHARACTERS

MICHELLE: Early forties, best friend of Julie, practical, married.

JULIE: Late thirties, imaginative, single.

SALESMAN: Thirties, upper-crust British accent, scientific mind, handsome but unconscious of it, single.

SETTING

Interior of Tiffany's Beverly Hills store. There is a jewelry display case and three chairs.

TIME

An afternoon. The present.

• • • • • • • • • • • •

Michelle and Julie enter.

MICHELLE: Don't do it, Julie, I beg you. You'll regret it.

JULIE: No, I won't.

MICHELLE: You know what I mean. Wait.

JULIE: I'm through waiting. I've dreamed all my life of getting a beautiful, big Tiffany diamond ring in a robin's egg blue box with a white bow. *(Beat.)* But here I am, facing forty, and my finger is still naked. *(She displays her left ring finger.)*

MICHELLE: They say that forty is the new thirty.

JULIE: Yeah, and thirty is the new fifteen, I mean, twelve.

MICHELLE: Don't do everything yourself. Leave space for someone to love you.

JULIE: I've given up on love. If it hasn't happened by now, it never will.

MICHELLE: What about Joe? The guy with the big house?

JULIE: Oh, I loved the house, but unfortunately, Joe came with it. It was a package deal.

MICHELLE: Wait for a *man* to give you a diamond.

JULIE: I can't wait anymore. My birthday is next week, you know.

MICHELLE: Turning forty isn't such a big deal, trust me.

JULIE: Michelle, who are *you* to talk? You've been married for twenty years.

MICHELLE: That's not the point.

JULIE: That's exactly the point! *(Dreamily.)* All these years you've watched your diamond glint in the sunlight, reflecting the colors of the sky.

MICHELLE: You've been reading *way* too many ads.

JULIE: It's now or never.

MICHELLE: But to buy yourself a diamond? That's pathe —

JULIE: — Go ahead, say it. Pathetic —

MICHELLE: — I didn't mean —

JULIE: — Sure you did. Whatever you call it, I want a diamond. There's nothing more precious than diamonds. *(She points to an engagement ring in the case.)* Would you look at that cushion cut! I bet it's four carats.

MICHELLE: You'd have to marry a rock star to get a ring like that.

JULIE: Leeza got a ring like that. Of course, she's a slut. *(Beat.)* I wonder if any decent women ever get rocks like that?

MICHELLE: Look, it's not too late – we can still walk out the door.
(Salesman approaches, the studious type. He wears a bow tie. He is handsome but unaware of it.)

SALESMAN: *(British accent.)* Good afternoon, ladies. How are you today?

MICHELLE: We were just leaving. *(She pulls Julie by the arm.)* Come on, Jules.
(Julie extricates herself and sits.)

JULIE: Hello. I'd like to see that ring, please. *(She points to the cushion cut.)*

SALESMAN: Certainly, Madame. *(He pulls the ring out.)* You have wonderful taste. This is one of our most expensive rings, due to its exquisite cut, color, clarity, and carats, the four Cs. *(Beat.)* Are you here today to pick out rings before your fiancé visits?

JULIE: *(Embarrassed.)* Uh...there is no fiancé. I was just...uh, I think I'd better leave. *(She rises to go.)*

SALESMAN: Oh, please stay and try it on. It's just your size!
(Julie sits.)

JULIE: *(Amazed.)* You can tell that just by looking at my finger?

SALESMAN: I was trained as a scientist. I've been researching rings for some time.

JULIE: Really?

MICHELLE: *(Impressed.)* How fascinating that a man is so interested in jewelry.

SALESMAN: The credit for that actually goes to my ex-girlfriend. I had hoped to marry her, but she ran off with a man who gave her a real diamond. I was only able to offer her a small cubic zirconia, being that I was just a poor graduate student at the time. *(Beat.)* I vowed then and there to research diamonds to find out why women are so attracted to them.

MICHELLE: Did she marry him? The other guy?

SALESMAN: Yes, I'm afraid she did.

JULIE: Oh, I'm sorry.

SALESMAN: She's the one who would be sorry now if she knew that I was working here and getting the employee discount.

MICHELLE: That's the spirit!

SALESMAN: *(To Julie.)* Go ahead. Please try it on.

(Julie squints as she puts the ring on. It is obviously too tight.)

JULIE: *(Self-deprecatingly.)* I feel like Cinderella's stepsister trying on the shoe.

SALESMAN: *(Gallantly.)* No, you're like Cinderella herself.

(They share a deep look. He smiles at her. Time stops. Michelle looks down at other rings in the case, oblivious to the unfolding drama.)

MICHELLE: We'd better get going before our parking meter expires.

(No response, as they gaze deeply into each other's eyes.)

MICHELLE: Julie?

(Michelle finally looks over and takes in what is transpiring.)

MICHELLE: Oh my...!

JULIE: *(Snapping out of it.)* Uh...yes... It's really beautiful, don't you think, Michelle?

(Michelle looks at Salesman.)

MICHELLE: Yes he is, I mean, yes it is.

JULIE: How much did you say it costs?

SALESMAN: *(Flustered.)* It's a mere $84,900, but with my employee discount —

JULIE: — Your discount?

MICHELLE: *(Disbelief.)* You'd give *her* your employee discount??

SALESMAN: Uh, that is to say —

(Julie tries to remove the ring; it is stuck.)

JULIE: Ouch – I can't —

(She pulls the ring but it doesn't budge; She begins to panic.)

JULIE: — I can't seem to get it off!

SALESMAN: Let me see.

(He takes her hand and again they gaze into each other's eyes, lost. He caresses her hand.)

MICHELLE: Well? Is it coming off?

JULIE: *(Dreamily.)* I really don't care.

MICHELLE: For $84,900 you'd better care!

SALESMAN: Don't forget my employee discount.

MICHELLE: *(Sarcastically.)* Your employee discount?!

SALESMAN: *(Coming to his senses.)* Ladies, please wait here while I get our

163

special liquid spray. *(He exits.)*

MICHELLE: Julie, what just happened?

JULIE: I don't know. I looked into his eyes and suddenly I forgot about everything, even the diamond!

MICHELLE: This is major! I've never seen you so excited. Your eyes are sparkling and... Why, you're blushing!

JULIE: *(Blushing.)* I don't know what's come over me.

MICHELLE: *(Getting practical.)* But we've got to get that ring off!

JULIE: *(Dreamily.)* Why?

MICHELLE: Snap out of it! I don't care how amazing this salesman is, you don't want to spend $84,900 on a ring, do you?

JULIE: Well, he said he'd give me his employee discount.

MICHELLE: Julie! Listen to yourself! Get a grip! You've got to get that ring off, now!

(Salesman reenters with the spray.)

SALESMAN: Here.

(He sprays Julie's finger; the ring gradually dislodges. All sigh with relief.)

SALESMAN: That certainly was a close call.

MICHELLE: Does that happen often, that rings get stuck?

SALESMAN: *(Hesitantly.)* I wouldn't know.

MICHELLE: Well, how many times has it happened while you've been working here?

SALESMAN: *(Guiltily.)* Today is actually my first day. *(Beat.)* The manager is upset that I miscalculated your finger size and that the ring got stuck.

JULIE: And you risked your job to let me try on a ring that didn't even fit? *(To Michelle.)* That's so sweet! *(She looks up at him, her face glowing with tenderness.)*

SALESMAN: So you're not angry?

JULIE: How could I be, when you risked so much for me?

MICHELLE: *(Cynically, to Julie.)* And *you* risked getting stuck with an $84,900 bill!

SALESMAN and JULIE: *(In unison.)* Less the employee discount.

(They laugh.)

SALESMAN: So why did you come shopping today, if I may be so bold as to inquire?

JULIE: The truth is, I'm facing a major birthday and I'm tired of waiting for a Tiffany diamond. *(Beat.)* I suppose that must sound silly to you.

SALESMAN: Not at all. I understand completely, now that I'm researching women and diamonds.

JULIE: Yes, diamonds are the jewelry equivalent of chocolate.

SALESMAN: Precisely. *(Beat; to Julie.)* I'm sorry, I never did introduce myself. I'm Stewart, and you are?

JULIE: Julie.

STEWART: A real pleasure to meet you, Julie.

(They shake hands, smiling, for a lengthy time; Michelle coughs to get their attention.)

MICHELLE: I'm Michelle. *(She extends her hand.)*

STEWART: Pleased to make your acquaintance, Michelle.

(They shake hands, then Michelle stands.)

MICHELLE: Julie, we really have to get going or we're going to get a parking ticket. It was nice meeting you, Stewart.

JULIE: *(To Michelle.)* Why don't you get the car and circle the block? I'll meet you outside in a couple of minutes.

MICHELLE: Okay, but don't take too long. You know how bad traffic gets around here.

JULIE: All right. Bye.

(Michelle waves and exits.)

STEWART: I hope you don't think that I'm too forward, but —

JULIE: — Yes?

STEWART: I should like to call on you someday, if I may?

JULIE: *(Unconsciously adopting his manner of speaking.)* That would be lovely, Stewart.

STEWART: I mean, I want to get to know you better, whether or not you ever buy diamonds here.

JULIE: I understand. After all, *some* things are more precious than diamonds.

(They smile and gaze at each other.)

(Lights fade out.)

END OF PLAY

Lisa Soland

Biography

Laura Grabowski-Cotton is an award-winning fiction writer. She has an MFA in Playwriting and Screenwriting from Florida State University's College of Motion Picture, Television, and Recording Arts, an MA in English Literature and a BA in Communication from George Mason University.

The Perfect Proposal

Laura Grabowski-Cotton

The Perfect Proposal was written in the fall of 2006, while Laura was attaining her MFA in playwriting at Florida State University. The play was originally produced on December 9, 2006, at Florida State University in an evening of ten-minute plays. The cast was as follows: David - Joele Davis, Shannon - Brenda Scott, Melissa - Donna Cross. The play was also published in The Best 10-Minute Plays for Three or More Actors, edited by Lawrence Harbison.

CHARACTERS

> DAVID: Mid to late 20's. A shy, nerdy guy, especially around females. He's been dating Melissa, for eight months now.
>
> SHANNON: Early 20's, David's best friend. Sharp, clever, easily excited. Has a huge crush on David, but has never told him. Always thought she'd wait for a better time.
>
> MELISSA: David's girlfriend. A queen-of-the-world type.

SETTING

> David's kitchen.

TIME

> Present day. Around six-o-clock.

• • • • • • • • • • • •

The table is beautifully set. A perfectly cooked lobster in the center. Champagne glasses and a wine bottle on the table. Chopin plays from a c.d. player. The lights are dimmed. David sits at the table, on the phone.

DAVID: *(Into phone.)* But we had plans. I made dinner, this was supposed to be our special... What...? No, no, I still can't hear you... That music, you know, it kinda sounds like...David Bowie! Are you at David Bowie's house...? Oh, a concert. But why didn't you tell me you were going to...? Yeah, sure, we can talk about this later.
(Hangs up the phone. Pours a glass of wine and drinks it. He sits there, listening to the Chopin, a glum look on his face. The doorbell rings. He opens the door. Shannon stands before him, drenched. Her hair is soaked, her clothes and jacket are wrinkled. A large canvas bag over her shoulder.)
SHANNON: David! David! Is it too late? It is, isn't it? Isn't it?
DAVID: Too late for what?
SHANNON: Oh, David, please, please don't play with me. Your mother called an hour ago and told me, told me that you were gonna ask Melissa to marry you. Tonight! I left work early, ran down eight blocks and nearly got hit by a Hershey's truck. And then, then it started raining. Why didn't you tell me you were gonna propose?
DAVID: I was afraid you'd...try to talk me out of it. I know you don't like

Lisa Soland

Melissa and...

SHANNON: We've been friends for five years, you and me. Five years. I love you like a...a... I don't know...like a someone. And you don't tell me! So what'd she say? After you asked her, I mean?

DAVID: Actually, I didn't. She canceled on me.

SHANNON: Then I'm not... I'm not too late?

DAVID: Too late for what?

SHANNON: For the...um...proposal planning. You have to plan your proposal. It's very important.

DAVID: Yeah, I know, I know. I worked it all out. I cooked her a lobster dinner, *(Motions towards the lobster.)* ...bought her a ring, *(Pats his shirt pocket.)* ...and put together a compilation of "romantic" music. *(Directs his gaze towards the c.d. player.)* I even got myself a knee pad, *(Rolls up his pants to reveal a knee pad on his one knee.)* ...so that I could easily get down on one knee and ask her.

SHANNON: A knee pad. A knee pad?

DAVID: I have bad knees.

SHANNON: Mmmm... So Melissa's definitely *not* coming over?

DAVID: Definitely not.

SHANNON: Good. *(She turns the lights onto their full power, turns off the music, grabs a lobster stick, breaks the shell off, and munches on it.)*

DAVID: What are you doing?!

SHANNON: I'm saving you...from...the biggest...mistake of your life.

DAVID: Huh?

SHANNON: How do I put this nicely...? Your proposal sucks, David. It's unoriginal, unexciting, and to be honest, a bit on the...smelly side.

DAVID: Oh... Really?

SHANNON: Yes.

DAVID: Uh...okay. How would you...? I mean, how do you think I should ask her?

SHANNON: Well, there are five types of proposals, David. But you probably already knew that.

DAVID: Actually, I didn't.

SHANNON: Well, there are. There's the adventurous proposal, the romantic proposal, the so casual-you-don't-know-it's-happening pro-posal, the sexy proposal, and of course, the ultimatum proposal. But that one is usually reserved for women and only to be used in the most dire of emergencies.

DAVID: Should I be taking notes?

SHANNON: Yes.

DAVID: I was joking.

SHANNON: I wasn't. *(Grabs a pen and paper out of her bag, hands it to David.)* Let's start with the adventurous proposal. Imagine this. You're taking Melissa hiking through the woods. Now, as we walk you're gonna pretend I'm Melissa. And at some point you should ask me to marry you. Okay?

DAVID: Uh, sure...

(Shannon opens her bag, takes out a c.d. Puts it in the c.d. player. The sounds of nature play. She also takes out two foldable walking sticks and two safari type hats. She puts one hat on, puts the other on David's head, and hands one of the walking sticks to him. David stares at her, curiously.)

DAVID: This is weird. Do you always carry around...?

SHANNON: No time for talking. Okay. I'm Melissa now. Ready, set, go!

(She walks through the kitchen, using the hiking stick. David watches, bewildered.)

SHANNON: Me o' my o, me o' my o'! It's a beautiful day today, isn't it, David?

DAVID: It's not day, it's night, and...

SHANNON: We're pretending, David. Remember?

DAVID: Oh, right. Right... *(He walks a little, uses the hiking stick.)* It is a beautiful day, Shannon.

SHANNON: Melissa.

DAVID: What about her?

SHANNON: I'm Melissa.

DAVID: No, you're not.

SHANNON: Pretending, David. Pretending.

DAVID: Oh, right. Right. Sorry. It is a beautiful day, Melissa.

SHANNON: Don't you think I look beautiful too?

DAVID: Yes, you are beautiful. Nature is beautiful. Everything, Melissa, is beautiful.

SHANNON: Oh my God! Oh my God!

DAVID: What? What's wrong?

SHANNON: There's a bug on me!

DAVID: What? Where?

SHANNON: You can't see it! It's a tick. I can just feel it. It's crawling, crawling all over me! Get it off! Get it off of me!

DAVID: How can I if I don't see it?

SHANNON: Just kill it! Kill it, you sissy man! Okay. Enough a' that. Now you see why the adventurous proposal is not always successful.

DAVID: Wait. Are you saying there really wasn't a bug on you?

171

SHANNON: Of course not. I said, several times, that we were just pretending.

DAVID: Oh. Right. I knew that.

SHANNON: Moving on. The romantic proposal. Imagine this. You ask Melissa to marry you after a full night of...tango dancing!

DAVID: I can't tango dance. I can barely...regular dance.

SHANNON: That's okay. Just follow my lead. And at some point, ask me to marry you.

(Shannon takes a c.d. out of her bag, puts it in David's c.d. player. Tango music comes on. Then she takes David's hands and begins to lead him through the Tango. He does the woman's part, she does the man's. At the end of the dance, Shannon dips David. It looks ridiculous.)

SHANNON: Now, David! Ask me now.

DAVID: Okay, okay... Will you...marry me, Melissa?

(Shannon drops David, causing him to fall out of the dip.)

SHANNON: Sure, I'll marry you.

DAVID: Really?

SHANNON: Right after you learn to dance.

(Shannon turns off the music.)

SHANNON: I'm just gonna say it. The romantic proposal isn't for you. Don't even think about it.

DAVID: I tried to tell you I couldn't d—

SHANNON: Let's move onto the so-casual-you-don't-realize-it's-happening proposal. You and Melissa are at the gym.

(She takes another c.d. out of her bag. Puts it in the player. Fast paced techno music plays.)

You're running... Well, run, already David!

(David jogs in place.)

SHANNON: Melissa's on the floor doing sit-ups. *(Sits down, does sit-ups on the floor.)* Now, we're gonna talk and at some time during our conversation, you're gonna ask me to marry you. Real casual, like it's no big deal.

DAVID: Okay... So Melissa...you're really...working that tummy a' yours.

SHANNON: You think I have a tummy?!

DAVID: Well, what I mean is...

SHANNON: You never mentioned a tummy before!

DAVID: Everybody has a tummy. Listen, Melissa, I've been thinking...and I think we should, you know, do what other people do.

SHANNON: Have wild sex?

DAVID: Well, yeah, I'd love that too, but...

SHANNON: 'Cause it's not happening. Never again. Not after what you just said about my tummy.

DAVID: What?

SHANNON: Okay. Enough. You're not exactly doing well here, David. You know that, don't you?

DAVID: I'm doing the best I can! Your sex comment, it distracted me.

SHANNON: Speaking of sex, let's move on to...the sexy engagement. *(Shannon dims the lights, then takes another c.d. out of her bag. Puts it in the c.d. player. Slow jazz music plays. She strips down to a sexy blue babydoll. Dances seductively.)*

DAVID: Uh... I feel kinda weird about this. I mean, I appreciate your efforts but...

SHANNON: David, if you want to have the perfect proposal you need to practice. Think of this. You're in the mood. But Melissa... She's... Melissa. A cold fish, as your mother calls her. So it's up to you. You have to seduce her. How about giving me...I mean...Melissa a massage?

DAVID: But Melissa doesn't...

SHANNON: Please, David. Just do it.

(David nods, walks over to Shannon, starts massaging her back.)

SHANNON: Wow. That feels really good... Do you...do this to Melissa a lot?

DAVID: Are you kidding? Melissa would kill me! She hates it when people touch her.

SHANNON: Hates it when people touch...? Why do you want to marry her?

DAVID: Why? Well... I've been with her for eight months. That's the longest relationship she's ever had. And all she talks about now is how all her friends are getting married. It's time, she says. It's time for me to ask her.

SHANNON: David, David, David, David. Are you in love with her?

DAVID: Well, she's not my dream girl. *(Beat.)* But I'd never get my dream girl.

SHANNON: David, I need to tell you something. *(Beat.)* I have always —
(Melissa enters.)

MELISSA: Well, lookie what we have here! *(Goes to the c.d. player, turns off the music.)*

DAVID: What are you doing here?

MELISSA: I left the concert right after you called. The guy beside me was like totally hitting on me. He kept trying to touch my knee. And you know how I am about people touching me! *(Glares at David.)* I didn't think you were the type to cheat, David.

SHANNON: We were just practicing. David was trying to figure out how he should...

Lisa Soland

DAVID: Propose to you.

MELISSA: Yeah, right.

SHANNON: He really was.

MELISSA: *(To David.)* Okay, so do it.

DAVID: What?

MELISSA: Propose to me. Now. Right now.

SHANNON: The ultimatum proposal.

DAVID: I don't think now is a good —

MELISSA: Ask me!

DAVID: No.

MELISSA: What?

DAVID: I'm not asking you. I don't even know why I was thinking of asking you.

MELISSA: Well, I wouldn't have said yes anyway.

DAVID: Good.

MELISSA: Good?! Are you crazy? Are you out of your mind?

DAVID: Melissa, you know we aren't right for each other, you know —

MELISSA: David. Please. Don't do this. You don't have to marry me right this minute. We could wait a few days.

DAVID: No. I'm not going to marry you. Not now, not tomorrow, not ever. It's over, Melissa. It's completely over.

MELISSA: But David it could be different, I could be different, we could be —

DAVID: No.

MELISSA: You'll never find anyone like me. Never! *(Storms out of the room.)*

DAVID: That's the point.

(Melissa leaves, slamming the door behind her.)

SHANNON: I'm sorry, David. This is all my fault.

DAVID: No.

SHANNON: Yes.

DAVID: No.

SHANNON: Yes.

DAVID: Yes.

SHANNON: No.

(David and Shannon look at each other and burst out laughing.)

SHANNON: Look, I was trying to tell you this earlier. The thing is I... I would never want to do anything that could in any way jeopardize our friendship but...

DAVID: What?

SHANNON: Do you want to go out sometime? On a date, I mean?

DAVID: What kind of date?

SHANNON: What kind of date?

DAVID: Yeah. You know, there are seven kinds of dates. There's the, "I like him, but I don't love him date," the "I just want to sleep with him date," the "we're just friends date," the "double date," the... *(Shannon laughs as lights fade.)*

END OF PLAY

Biography

Susan C. Hunter's credits include several published plays and numerous productions of her work across the country. With her partner, Thomas R. Shelton, she was the recipient of the national playwriting award given by the Landers Theatre in Springfield, Missouri, for their musical adaptation of the classic novel *Caddie Woodlawn* by Carol Ryrie Brink. They were also commissioned by the San Diego Opera to write a children's opera, *The Boy Who Ruled the Moon and Sun*, which toured schools as part of the company's educational outreach program. Her full-length play, *Flights*, has been produced both in New York City and Los Angeles. In addition, she has had several one-acts produced nationwide, including *Traffic Jam*, *High Hopes*, *Tired Feet and Dancing Shoes*, *Heart-to-Heart*, *The Camel's Back*, *Eternal Flame*, and *Springer Sprung*. Many of her works were developed in association with Lisa Soland's All Original Playwright Workshop in North Hollywood, California. Susan C. Hunter is currently a member of At Rise: Playwrights, and is part of the writers' pool with Playground-LA, both also based in Hollywood. As producer of Women Inventing Theatre at WriteAct Repertory, Ms. Hunter has helped other women playwrights bring their work to the stage.

Heart-To-Heart

Susan C. Hunter

Heart-To-Heart began as a writing exercise in Lisa Soland's All Original Play-wright Workshop. The members were told to just start writing. From that initial class-starter, it developed. *Heart-To-Heart* was then produced by the Laurelgrove Theatre in Hollywood. It has had many subsequent productions all across the country, most notably at The American Globe Theatre in New York City, The Found Theatre in Long Beach, California, and WriteAct Repertory in North Hollywood.

CHARACTERS

GRAMPS: about 70, very conservative-looking.

NANA: about 65, resembles a plump Betty Crocker, comes from Wisconsin.

JUNIOR: their fresh-faced grandson, about to go away to college.

SETTING

A middle-class living room in the Heartland of America.

TIME

About now.

•••••••••••

Nana and Gramps are having a serious "talk" with Junior.

GRAMPS: *(Quoting Rudyard Kipling's poem If.)* "If you can keep your head when all around you are losing theirs, then you will be a man, my son." *(As himself.)* You know what I mean?

JUNIOR: *(With thinly-veiled restlessness, hoping he can get back to his video games very soon.)* Yeah, Gramps. I do.

NANA: So, we just wanted to have this little talk with you.

GRAMPS: Now that you're going off to college. Meeting all those radicals.

NANA: Living in the dorm with a whole slew of wild fellas.

JUNIOR: And girls.

NANA: *(Fearfully.)* What?

JUNIOR: The dorms are co-ed, Nana.

NANA: Since when?

JUNIOR: Since 1983.

NANA: *(Ever more alarmed.)* Oh now, in that case…

GRAMPS: *(Interrupting wisely.)* All the more reason for this little heart-to-heart. My boy, there will be temptations out there of all kinds.

NANA: *(Trying to strangle her sense of rising hysteria.)* No one to guide you. Nothing to stop you.

GRAMPS: Except yourself. You will have to be responsible for your own actions. We won't be there. Your folks won't be there.

JUNIOR: I know.

NANA: But if you need us, we'll be here for you, sweetie. Just call.

Lisa Soland

GRAMPS: That's what you have a cell phone for.

JUNIOR: I will. I promise. And don't worry about me. I'll be okay. I was raised with strong moral values. I won't forget them, Gramps.

GRAMPS: I know you think you can handle this new environment, but take it from us, we know what's out there.

JUNIOR: How?

GRAMPS: How what?

JUNIOR: How do you know what's out there?

GRAMPS: *(With a wise little chuckle.)* Well, we were young once, you know.

NANA: *(Also chuckling.)* Oh my yes. We were, weren't we?

JUNIOR: *(Actually listening.)* Tell me about it.

GRAMPS: Eh?

JUNIOR: *(As if catching his grandfather in a lie.)* I want to hear about your wild and crazy youth.

GRAMPS: Oh, well, I don't remember any specifics.

JUNIOR: Aw, come on, Gramps.

GRAMPS: No.

JUNIOR: How come?

GRAMPS: It's none of your business, young man.

JUNIOR: Why not?

GRAMPS: Look here, we're not talking about my youthful indiscretions. We're talking about yours.

JUNIOR: How do you know I have any?

GRAMPS: Everyone has them.

JUNIOR: Do they?

GRAMPS: They do.

JUNIOR: Come on, Gramps. Just give me a hint. Did you ever drink alcohol?

GRAMPS: Well...

NANA: You might as well tell it to him straight, dear. He's nearly a man.

JUNIOR: So?

GRAMPS: So, I took a drink or two in my time.

> *(Nana snickers unintentionally.)*

NANA: Sorry.

GRAMPS: Now Nonie, we've already said enough on the subject of alcohol.

JUNIOR: Aw, come on, Gramps. Did you ever have a little too much?

GRAMPS: Oh, I...

NANA: *(In a sudden outburst.)* The first time I met your grandfather he was drunk as a skunk.

GRAMPS: I guess that's true.

JUNIOR: *(Scandalized.)* Gramps!

NANA: *(With a giggle.)* Head in a toilet drunk, as I recall.

GRAMPS: *(In retaliation.)* Well, you were dancing on the table, tossing your blouse to anyone who would catch it.

JUNIOR: Nana?

NANA: *(To Gramps.)* Oh, now, you didn't have to tell him that. What will he think?

JUNIOR: Nana!

NANA: See? Now, there ya go.

JUNIOR: Why were you doing that?

GRAMPS: Why do you think?

NANA: I just wanted to have a little fun, don't ya know? *(To Gramps.)* And as I recall, you were wearing your scanties on your head, mister. Smoked one too many of those happy cigarettes, I think.

JUNIOR: *(To Gramps, horrified.)* So, you were, what…into the whole sex, drugs, and rock and roll thing?

GRAMPS: Well, pretty much.

JUNIOR: You, too, Nana?

NANA: Oh, not like your grandfather was. Certainly not. He was mainlining at one point.

JUNIOR: Like, you mean heroin?

GRAMPS: Oh, I got off that right away. Just stuck to pot and acid after that.

NANA: *(In fond remembrance.)* He had some wild trips, I can tell you!

GRAMPS: Ended up in the emergency ward one time. Remember that, dear?

NANA: *(Lost in the memory, forgetting Junior is even there.)* Oh, sure. You'd had some bad peyote and I'm trying to drive you there, but I'm all toked up and kept veering off the road.

GRAMPS: *(With sentimental emotion.)* You saved my sorry ass that night.

NANA: For sure. But that's all water under the bridge now.

GRAMPS: Except for the occasional violent flashback.

NANA: Well, yes.

JUNIOR: This is…unbelievable.

GRAMPS: *(Getting nostalgic.)* Those were some bitchin' times.

NANA: Oh yeah, for sure. But we also had a bump in the road or two.

GRAMPS: That we did. *(Near whisper.)* Remember your miscarriage?

NANA: Whew! Saved me having another abortion.

JUNIOR: You had an abortion?

NANA: Well, I was too young to be having some brat to tie me down, don't you know?

JUNIOR: You and Gramps…?

NANA: Me and…? Oh, no! This was long before we ever met.

JUNIOR: You mean there were others?

GRAMPS: Dozens.

NANA: *(In a pleasant dream of reminiscence.)* Hundreds.

JUNIOR: No, no! This is a nightmare. You and Gramps and so many others… doing it…like dogs in heat.

NANA: *(Pointing to Gramps.)* Oh, we didn't "do it," dear.

JUNIOR: What do you mean?

NANA: *(With only slight reluctance.)* Well, if you must know, I never thought of him in a romantic way. How could I? We've always been the best of friends, but never lovers.

JUNIOR: What? Why not?

GRAMPS: Well, the truth is, I've never been interested in women, if you know what I mean. Women's clothing, certainly. But never women.

JUNIOR: You're gay?

NANA: Gay as the day you were born.

JUNIOR: So, you've been living a lie all these years?

GRAMPS: Oh, I think that's putting it rather harshly.

NANA: No one ever asked.

GRAMPS: Until now.

NANA: Oh, hon. It wasn't so bad, you know. Society looks down on unwed mothers…

GRAMPS: *(Using his fingers as quotation marks.)* And "queer" Republicans.

NANA: And children from single-parent households.

GRAMPS: It was a perfect arrangement.

NANA: So turn that frown upside down and get happy, Mister Gloomy Pants.

JUNIOR: This is horrible. It's disgusting enough thinking about your grandparents "doing it," but finding out that they don't do it is even worse! So what…you just ignored your…urges? You just… *(He cannot bring himself to continue his thought.)*

GRAMPS: Shut off the faucet, so to speak?

JUNIOR: Yes.

GRAMPS: *(With a scornful laugh.)* No.

NANA: Certainly not.

JUNIOR: *(Afraid to ask, yet compelled to find out.)* No? Then, who…?

NANA: You know all those poker nights at Uncle Jerry's?

JUNIOR: *(Confused.)* Yeah?

GRAMPS: Well, let's just say… *(With seedy innuendo and pelvic thrusts.)* Five-card stud is our favorite game.

NANA: Gives a brand new meaning to ace in the hole.

JUNIOR: *(Nearly nauseous.)* Ohhh! But then...if you're not Mom's biological dad, who is?

NANA: *(With a conspiratorial smirk to Gramps.)* Well... Uncle Jerry swings both ways.

JUNIOR: *(Screaming in horror.)* Ahhhh!

GRAMPS: So, you see, we know wherein we speak.

NANA: And we want you to behave yourself, you hear?

GRAMPS: 'Cause if you don't...

NANA: *(Scrubbing Junior's scalp with her fist.)* We'll just have to give you a good Dutch Rub!

> *(Junior runs screaming from the room. Gramps looks at Nana. They smile sweetly, oblivious to the havoc they have wreaked.)*

GRAMPS: I think that went well, don't you?

NANA: Yes indeedy.

END OF PLAY

Biography

Arthur M. Jolly wrote his first full-length play, the drama *Past Curfew* (Next Stage Press, 2010) in the 2008 All Original Playwright Workshop where it won the AOPW Fellowship Award; and began *The Ithaca Ladies Read Medea* in the 2014 All Original Playwright Workshop, which premiered in Los Angeles in 2016. In between, he has penned five full-length plays and numerous shorter plays, twice won the Joining Sword and Pen competition, was named a finalist for the Woodward/Newman Drama Award, and was a two-time semi-finalist for the O'Neill Conference. He is repped by Brant Rose Agency.

If You Could Go Back...

Ⓐ

Arthur M. Jolly

If You Could Go Back... premiered in June, 2011 at The Kraine Theatre in New York City, as part of End Times Productions' Vignettes of the Apocalypse V; featuring Michael Swartz, Rosie Sowa and Jamaal Stone, directed by Brad Raimundo. It had subsequent productions by Playwrights' Round Table at the Lowndes Shakespeare Center as part of the Orlando Fringe Festival; at A Shot of Theatre in Northampton, Massachusetts; and at Playzapalooza in Santa Paula, California.

CHARACTERS
    STANLEY
    JENNY
    MARK

SETTING
    An empty stage.

. . . .

Stanley tinkers with a square box with a blinking light on it, large enough to hold a person. Jenny enters, carrying a gun.

JENNY: Is it ready?

STANLEY: Just about.

JENNY: Stanley – you are a genius.

STANLEY: I am. And this is my masterpiece.

JENNY: Forget the frozen mice – this thing is gonna change the world.

STANLEY: I'd forgotten the mice.

JENNY: Like it never happened.

STANLEY: This will work. The first actual fully functional time machine – capable of sending a person back in time and bringing them home again.

JENNY: Not frozen.

STANLEY: Nope. Alive.

JENNY: Cool.

STANLEY: You ready?

JENNY: Yeah. I go back, shoot him – we're heroes.

STANLEY: Bear in mind, once you shoot him – history's gonna change.

JENNY: Whatcha mean?

STANLEY: Right now, Hitler's an evil despotic dictator who started a war and killed millions of innocent people. You go back to Berlin in '34; you're assassinating the chancellor of a minor political party. Which is the whole point.

JENNY: So when I get back, I won't have saved the world from an evil dictator, I'll have capped a minor political figure no one's heard of.

STANLEY: You will have saved the world. But the world won't know it. You'll just be a political assassin.

JENNY: Will I know?

Lisa Soland

STANLEY: Oh, you'll know. I won't. That's the whole thing with time travel – as soon as the world changes, that's the way it's always been. We could've done all this before – we wouldn't know. When you get back, explain to me why you did it – I'll trust you.

JENNY: Cool. Is it ready?

STANLEY: Done.

JENNY: Okay. Turn it on!

STANLEY: I'm switching it on! Stanley throws the switch.

(The lights go out. The light on the box flashes. Lights up.)

JENNY: I didn't even get a chance to get in.

(Mark walks out of the box and shoots Jenny dead.)

STANLEY: Whoa! Dude! What the —

MARK: Sorry – I had to.

STANLEY: You shot Jenny!

MARK: Yup. Didn't have a choice.

STANLEY: I think you did.

MARK: It was the only way.

STANLEY: Why did you shoot her?

MARK: She killed Hitler!

STANLEY: What are you, a Nazi?

MARK: No, but after Hitler dies, Göring takes over – and that guy – I mean, without Hitler to keep him in check – yeesh. Plus – he wins the war! He doesn't get bogged down in Russia, that whole thing with the giraffes —

STANLEY: What giraffes?

MARK: You know. The Berlin thing. With the giraffes. The Berlin zoo – in the middle of the – when Hitler diverted Rommel's Panzergruppe division during the Battle of El Alamein to get a pair of giraffes for the Berlin Zoo. Biggest blunder of the war.

STANLEY: That never happened!

MARK: Well maybe not now. Now, we're in a world where I stopped that idiot from killing Hitler. But before.

STANLEY: She was my best friend.

MARK: It was really important.

STANLEY: I can't let you do that.

MARK: Before you sent me back, you said if I explain —

STANLEY: No. I'm fixing this!

(Stanley throws the switch. Lights out. The light on the box flashes. Lights up. Jenny is fine. Mark has vanished.)

JENNY: So when I get back, I won't have saved the world from a dictator, I'll
have saved the world from a minor political figure.

STANLEY: There may be an issue.

JENNY: What issue?

(Mark walks out of the box and raises his gun. Stanley grabs it just in time.)

STANLEY: Thank you.

JENNY: Whoa!

MARK: Dammit – missed again!

STANLEY: Again?

MARK: This is like the fifth time we've gone through this.

STANLEY: We?

MARK: It was your idea.

JENNY: What's going on?

STANLEY: Don't kill Hitler yet.

JENNY: We've been planning this for months!

STANLEY: There may be a problem.

JENNY: Who the hell is this guy?

MARK: I'm his roommate.

JENNY: He lives with his mom.

MARK: He sent me back here 'cause I was short this month and owed him
a favor. Listen – if you go back in time and kill Hitler it makes things
worse. It's not the guy; it's the entire ideology. You can't shoot the idea.
I've explained this before.

STANLEY: I've never met you!

MARK: You will. Trust me – this doesn't work.

STANLEY: It's the entire ideology.

MARK: Yes.

STANLEY: What about the book?

MARK: Whaddaya mean?

STANLEY: The problem is his ideology. We get him before he writes Mein
Kampf – who's gonna know? 1924, he's in prison, formulating his
great plan, writing his book. Get him before that.

JENNY: He never writes Mein Kampf...

MARK: So he never inspires the party...

STANLEY: No Hitler, no Göring, no Nazis —

JENNY: Let's do it! I'm ready!

STANLEY: Right. *(He tinkers with the machine controls.)* 1923.

*(Jenny enters the machine. Lights out. Box flashes. Lights up. Jenny pops her
head out of the machine.)*

JENNY: Is Jenny here? Wait, did I just go to 1923?

STANLEY: Yeah.

JENNY: Send me five minutes earlier. Quickly!

(Jenny ducks back in. Lights out. Box flashes. Lights up. Jenny walks out of the machine, touching her chest tentatively.)

STANLEY: What was that?

JENNY: Freaky. I just shot myself.

STANLEY: What?

JENNY: Dude – you sent me back here to stop me going back there, but I missed me, so I had to go back five minutes before I got to 1923 and stop me. I shot me. Freakiest thing.

STANLEY: Why did you stop yourself?

JENNY: It was your idea! Go back and stop the idiot that made Hitler a martyr to the cause.

MARK: But —

JENNY: Hey Mark.

MARK: Have we met?

JENNY: Yeah. No. Later. Tough to say.

STANLEY: So Hitler's dead?

JENNY: No. But it could be worse. Much worse.

STANLEY: Worse than Hitler?

JENNY: You have no idea.

STANLEY: But we're cool now?

JENNY: We're back where we started.

MARK: Did the thing with the giraffes happen?

JENNY: What giraffes?

MARK: Okay – we gotta fix that.

JENNY: You're not gonna shoot me again.

MARK: When have I ever shot you?

JENNY: Like eight times!

MARK: Really?

JENNY: Not anymore! But in some of the alternate pasts, yeah. And it hurts! Listen – just 'cause you don't remember this – let me explain. We've tried this a whole bunch of times. You keep sending me back – I shot Hitler when he was a dictator, I shot him when he was a chancellor, when he was a student. In 1916, when he was a messenger in the First World War... It doesn't work. Every time, something just gets worse, and then you send your dumbass roommate back to stop me. Quit it! Now we've got it pretty much back to where it was – okay, awful and all. But just let it be. We can't shoot Hitler.

MARK: I got it.

JENNY: What?

MARK: Go back to Berlin, 1943, shoot the giraffe.

JENNY: What giraffe?

MARK: There's a giraffe in the Berlin zoo. Shoot it.

JENNY: What did a giraffe ever do to you?

MARK: It's important —

JENNY: I'm not gonna shoot an innocent —

MARK: It distracts the Nazi war effort at a critical time —

JENNY: It's a giraffe! You go shoot it.

MARK: Okay – I didn't want to do this in the first place! And I covered his half of the cable bill last month!

STANLEY: Okay, I'll do it!

JENNY: You? You've never done anything. You're like... You don't have the guts.

STANLEY: I can do it. You know why? 'Cause I understand historical causality. Sometimes you sacrifice one life to save millions. Hit this switch.

(Stanley grabs the gun and enters the machine. Jenny hits the switch. Lights out. Box flashes. Lights up. Stanley steps out.)

STANLEY: I couldn't do it.

JENNY: You wuss.

STANLEY: I stood there – looking into those big doe eyes, that sweet innocent face, peering down at me from that elongated neck —

JENNY: This is Adolf Hitler we're talking about?

STANLEY: What?

JENNY: You went back in time to kill Hitler.

STANLEY: No – we tried that. We might have tried it more than once. I went back to shoot a giraffe to distract Hitler. It's complicated.

JENNY: Not in this timeline you didn't – you went back to kill Hitler.

STANLEY: Did he start World War II in this timeline?

JENNY: Yeah.

MARK: Killed millions of innocent people. Real bad guy.

STANLEY: Then I couldn't have done that either. I can't do it. *(He drops the gun.)* I don't think that's the answer anyway. It's just more violence in a world that's already full of it.

JENNY: You just shoot him. One life to save millions.

STANLEY: I couldn't even shoot one giraffe to save millions!

Lisa Soland

JENNY: So what – we're just gonna give up?

STANLEY: No. I'm gonna go back earlier. Much earlier.

(Stanley heads for the box. He adjusts the controls.)

MARK: You forgot your gun.

STANLEY: No I didn't.

(Lights out. Box flashes. Lights up. Stanley walks out.)

STANLEY: You know, everyone says – would you go back and kill Hitler. If you could. It's like – a moral acid test. Against the death penalty? What if you could go back...? That's what they say. I found out – I can't. Even if that's the right thing to do – I can't do it.

JENNY: What are you talking about...? What did you just do?

STANLEY: I went back to 1895 – found this little Austrian kid crying 'cause his father beats the ever loving hell out of him on a daily basis and the other kids rag on him 'cause he's small and weak and has greasy hair. They call him Schickelgruber and taunt him about his Jewish mother, born out of wedlock. *(Beat.)* He was a six-year old kid with no friends. I talked to him, I told him it gets better. I dunno. *(Beat.)* So that's what I did. There's my answer – maybe you can go back and kill Hitler. I gave him a hug.

(Pause.)

JENNY: Who the hell is Hitler?

MARK: Never heard of him.

STANLEY: Huh.

MARK: If you're gonna go back and kill someone – kill Kubizek.

JENNY: There's a guy that deserves it.

MARK: Guy was a nutcase —

(The lights start to slowly fade.)

JENNY: Nazi dictator —

MARK: Total maniac – that thing with the giraffes – I mean – in the middle of a war!

(Lights out.)

END OF PLAY

Biography

Gary Garrison was the Executive Director of the Dramatist Guild of America from 2007-2016. Prior to his work at the Guild, Garrison filled the posts of Artistic Director, Producer and full-time faculty member in the Department of Dramatic Writing at NYU's Tisch School of the Arts, where he produced over forty-five festivals of new work, collaborating with hundreds of playwrights, directors and actors. He is on the Tony Administration Committee for the Tony Awards, and the program director for the Summer Playwriting Intensive for the Kennedy Center. In April of 2014, The Kennedy Center for the Performing Arts instituted the National Gary Garrison Ten-Minute Play Award given to the best ten-minute play written by a dramatist. In the spring of 2016, he was awarded the Milan Stitt Outstanding Teacher of Playwriting by the Kennedy Center.

A Whole Lotta Empty

Gary Garrison

A Whole Lotta Empty was written for the Boston Theatre Marathon in May of 2015. This short play is a complete revision of a short play, *Scream With Laugher,* and an extraction from the full-length play, *We Make A Wall.*

CHARACTERS
    ANGIE: 42, Danny's mother.
    DANNY: 17.
    BENNY: 45, Danny's father.

SETTING
    A completely bare room, but for a card table and a chair.

TIME
    Morning – three months after Angie's left her home.

• • • • • • • • • • • •

Lights up on a completely bare room – what looks to be someone's deserted living space. Center stage is a card table. One folding chair is placed around a side of the table. Angie sits quietly in the chair, mindlessly flipping through her copy of People Magazine. She checks her watch, stands, crosses to a window, looks out. She runs her finger across the windows sill, inspects her finger for dust, then rubs the dust off of her fingers. She checks the time, then quickly races to the door, opens it.

ANGIE: Daniel, tell your father he's got two minutes and I'm outta here! Two minutes. I got a life now, and I wanta live some of it. Ya' got that?
DANNY: *(From offstage.)* Got it, Ma!
ANGIE: *(Turning in.)* Jesus, why am I here? Like I got nothin' better to do than hear that guido make his excuses.
    (Danny bursts in the room, all smiles and a big hug for his mother.)
DANNY: Ma, look at you! Wow! Turn around… WOW! Ya' look great. Jesus, you got an ass on you, Ma. Did ya' know that? D'ya bring the sauce?
ANGIE: What do you think? Would I not make the sauce you asked me to make one hundred times on the phone yesterday? And don't look at your mother's ass, Danny. There is no support for that in the Catholic Church. Sauce is right there.
    (Angie points to a large paper bag sitting on the floor beside the chair.)
DANNY: And the meatballs?
ANGIE: Thirty-Five.
DANNY: Thirty-five?! Ma, that's nothin'. That'll be gone before lunch.
ANGIE: So you tell your father to keep his fat hands outta your bag, all right? Those are your meatballs, Danny. Not your father's. Your father gets

gotz. *(Nothing.)*

DANNY: Yeah. Right. Like I could keep him from your meatballs. Just the mention of your name and...

ANGIE: What is wrong with you, Danny? You're still lettin' your father push you around? I am twice your age and half your height, and I'm not afraid of him. Learn from the little people, Danny.

DANNY: Yeah, right.

(Angie crosses to the folding chair, sits. A little awkwardness between them, then...)

ANGIE So, big boy, how's Marla?

DANNY: Marla?! Forget her, Ma. She's, like, mad-whacked.

ANGIE: *(A beat, then...)* I'm supposed to know what that means?

DANNY: Whacked, Ma. She's...she's like tryin' to play me, but I'm not down with that.

ANGIE: Danny, what the hell are you talking about? Are you seeing her or not? And stop with the Justin Beaver talk.

DANNY: Bieber, Ma. His name is Justin Bieber.

ANGIE: Daniel, I do not care if his name is My Big Ass, talk to me so I can understand you. Now, are you seeing Marla or not?

DANNY: Not. Ever. Okay, maybe for the prom, 'cause she already got the dress and all. But after that, no. Because you know what I discovered, Ma? She snores. She's louder than dad. And I'm talkin' a lot louder. It don't feel right to hear that comin' outta such a pretty girl. So now what?

ANGIE: What do you mean, so now what? You love her, that's what. And like she was gold, Danny, 'cause she is, and 'cause she loves you. And 'cause she ain't never told you her laundry list of things you do that make her crazy.

DANNY You're wrong, Ma. She has.

ANGIE: Good, then she's smarter than I thought. But in spite of whatever, she loves you anyway. That's what women do...until they can't do it no longer.

DANNY: *(Looking around at the empty room.)* Is that when they empty out the house and leave?

ANGIE: Sooner, if they're smart. I wasn't so smart.

DANNY: No, but you were quick. I can't believe you emptied out this house from top to friggin' bottom in one day. How'd ya' do it, Ma? What did ya' have, like, thirty guys on it?

ANGIE: Daniel, I came here to see you. I did not come here to talk about that.

DANNY: Are you coming back, Ma? Is that why you're here? *(No response.)* You shoulda seen the look on dad's face when he walked in here and saw that you took everything but the floor. Jesus, Mary and Joseph, Ma. I thought he was going to stroke out or something. You know, he'd been fighting a fire for two days – that one on the lower east side in the City – so he was like exhausted and tired and he comes in here and swear to God, the veins were bulging in his forehead. It scared the hell out of me.

ANGIE: Don't' be afraid of your father, Danny. That's no good. Respect, yes. Honor, yes – I mean, he is a hero out there, like all the other firemen. But don't be afraid of him.

DANNY: I'm not afraid of him. I just can't leave him like you did. I got nowhere to go. I can't go with you 'cause I don't know why, 'cause you never explained it, but Dad says you say I can't. *(A beat, then…)* Is that right, Ma? I can't stay with you? *(A beat, then…)* Ma…? Goddamn it, answer me, Ma!

ANGIE: Where did you get that mouth?! And you want to kiss your mother with that mouth? No! I don't think so, Daniel!

DANNY: *(Quietly.)* Sorry, Ma', I just…you know, I don't know what to do with all these feelings I got. So they come outta me at a lotta the wrong times. It's hard here, Ma. You didn't just leave Dad, you left both of us. Alone. Together. I mean, Dad's hardly ever here and when he is, he and I don't really talk, 'except about you, and then all he does is scream and blame me.

ANGIE: You? Why blame you? What the hell did you do but be a good son to us both? See, that's your father's problem, Danny. He gets stupid when he gets angry.

DANNY: If he's not screaming, he just ignores me, Ma. No matter what I say, he don't listen. But that's not so unusual in this family. Nobody listens to nobody. They just talk and talk and talk and nobody hears a friggin' word you say.

(A long beat; a standoff.)

ANGIE: I hear every word you said, Danny.

DANNY: You do?! How, Ma?

ANGIE: Mothers can do things science can't explain. And this mother knows everything you're thinking and feeling without the words. I don't need your words, Danny. I see the face; I see the eyes.

DANNY: *(Self-conscious.)* Okay. So whatta ya' see?

ANGIE: I see you're lonely…and I see you're sad. And I see you're a little angry at me for leaving you here. Am I right?

DANNY: Wouldn't you be? Jesus, Ma, you walked out of here three months ago and you forgot one thing: me. I mean, if I were you I would have left him too. But I would have taken you with me. But you just left me here. Why did you do that, Ma?

ANGIE: I had to get out, Danny. And I had a day and I had a time and I had just enough courage to make that date and not an ounce more.

DANNY: So you just leave me here?

ANGIE: Daniel, I don't expect you to understand this, but I came today to...

DANNY: *(Tired of the fight.)* Look, let's just forget it, okay? Everything's all right. Everything's fine. You can look at me and see I'm okay. See? I'm smiling.

(Daniel offers up the weakest smile and starts to exit.)

ANGIE: Daniel, things are gonna get better. Every day that goes by. You'll see.

DANNY: An empty room is an empty room, Ma, until it ain't empty anymore. Right now, we still gotta a whole lotta empty here.

(Danny hesitates, then pecks his mother on the cheek and runs out of the room. Angie straightens her hair in the window's reflection. A moment later, Benny enters wearing a t-shirt. He takes a good long look at Angie, then takes a few steps towards her. She stops him.)

ANGIE: Don't cross the room, Benny.

BENNY: What "cross?" I was walkin' in the room.

ANGIE: Seventeen years I lived with you, and you don't think I know when you're gonna cross and when you're not? You were crossin', Benny. A wife knows these things. *(A beat, then...)* It's been three months since I left. You might think about moving away from the folding chair and getting yourself a little furniture. You know, make the apartment look – what – lived in? Start with a sofa, Benny.

BENNY: I got a sofa, Angie. 'Course I don't know where in this God-forsaken borough of Brooklyn it is, but I got one. It used to be right there, next to my glass-top coffee table. Maybe you remember it?

ANGIE: Remember it? I cleaned that son-of-a-bitch every night before you went to bed 'cause you couldn't keep your fat feet off of it. *(Quickly.)* You can have it back. All of it. I just took it to make a point.

BENNY: So make a point, next time. Send the Goodyear fuckin' blimp across the sky with my name in twenty-foot letters and a message, for all I care. But leave my goddamn stuff in my goddamn house! Look at this! What is this, Angie? This is space – things belong in a space. Three months I'm thinking about that. The worst thing you can do is take something that belongs to someone and leave them space. What are you going to do with space, Angie? You stare at it. You hate it for what's not there. *(Swinging fists through the air.)* Fuckin' space and nowhere to rest your head. And I need somewhere to rest my head, Angie, 'cause I keep a headache, see? Always pounding, day and night. Wake up with it, go to bed with it. Pain shootin' through my eyes.

ANGIE: SO TAKE IT BACK. TAKE IT ALL THE HELL BACK, BENNY!

BENNY: I don't want it back. I want you back. *(Pained.)* I want...my family all in the same place, at the same time.

ANGIE: That, you can't have.

BENNY: Why not? Why the hell not? Look, you don't even have to say I'm sorry.

ANGIE: Sorry? For what?

BENNY: I don't know. For walking outta here, leaving me all alone?

ANGIE: Aaaaaah, Father, here we go... Look, Benny. Let's get the record straight here: I knew you were going on that fishing trip. Forget that it was my birthday. Forget that you hadn't spent a birthday with me in ten years. So I was mad as hell and I planned the move. Ordered it up and it was a done deal. I had it planned for weeks.

BENNY: *(A step forward.)* Look at me, Angie. I'm calm. Calm. You ever know me to be this calm?

ANGIE: *(Uneasy.)* Good for you, Benny.

BENNY: So in my calm here, Angie, tell me: why did you leave? I want to know.

(She stands to leave, crosses to the door.)

BENNY: What'd I say, Angie? I'm just asking you why you left.

ANGIE: Because I had no reason then or now to stay. Not one more minute, of one hour, of one day.

BENNY: You got plenty of reasons to stay!

ANGIE: Name me one, Benny!

BENNY: *(Exploding.)* One: you got a son that needs you. Two: you got a husband that needs you more than anybody. I need you here to come home to. Three: you got no job and no education. What are you going to do? Four: you came – back – in this house today. Something brought you back here, Angie.

ANGIE: You scare me, Benny. You do.

BENNY: What'd I say, Angie?

ANGIE: The same thing you said seventeen years ago when you asked me to marry you. Same exact words. Danny was an unexpected bun in the oven, remember? And my old man was just seconds away from killing you. You asked my parents to leave the room. You dropped to your knees – I'll never forget it – on that brown and orange shag rug, took my hands and with all the emotion you could muster, and said, "You have to marry me, Angie." And I said, "What are you, an idiot? I don't want to marry you." You wanted to smack me, but I had three brothers and you knew you woulda been dead. So instead you said, "Angie, you got a kid that needs you. You got a man that needs you more than anybody. And you got no job and no education. What are you going to do?" Now here you are, all this time later, and you're asking me to stay for the same reasons you asked me to marry you. Something should have changed, Benny. Something should be different seventeen years later.

BENNY: Like what?

ANGIE: Like you. Like me. The whole world's changed, Benny. And it's changing even more with every second that goes by. But the sad truth is, you and I are the same people we were seventeen years ago, only a little older and a little meaner. But, there is one thing different in our lives, Benny. One thing I could not ignore anymore. And that's what pushed me out the door...Danny.

BENNY: Danny?! What the hell does he have to do with anything?

ANGIE: Listen to what you just said! Jesus God, he's your son. You and I? Yeah, I guess that's sad. I woulda liked to have a better marriage. Who wouldn't? So nothing changed in seventeen years between us. So who cares? Danny. Danny does. He cares, Benny. 'Cause he became one more thing we got used to. He was one more thing we talked over and looked around. It got to the point that his own mother and father didn't even see him in his own house. He'd be right there at the dinner table, get up and leave and there'd be that "space" you were talking about earlier. That space, Benny. Daniel took himself away from us and there was space. And you never even saw he was gone, did you? *(Quietly.)* Neither did I... I got used to seeing no one there. *(With more pain.)* I took everything out of this miserable apartment, Benny, so all you had left was him to see.

(Angie crosses to the door, turns from the door and looks back directly at Benny.)

ANGIE: And I came back today, to this empty, sad house, to really see our son for the first time in all his years. It's the only way to save him, Benny, from everything you and I became.

BENNY: But why not here? Why can't you do all that from here?

30 Short Plays for Passionate Actors

ANGIE: Because you're here, Benny. And you and I together make a wall that will one day fall and crush him. It's sad, but it's true.
(Angie exits. Benny looks around the empty room for a long moment.)
(Lights out.)

END OF PLAY

Biography

Joyce W. Leo's varied works include a poetry collection entitled, *Catching the Dream*. Her one-act historical choral play, *Voices of the Valley: Black Voices of a Company Town Called Alcoa, Tennessee,* was performed at the Martin Luther King Community House, the Shannondale Health Care Center, and the Blount County Library, all in Maryville, Tennessee. She has completed a screenplay, *Crossing the River,* and is currently working on a novel entitled, *Bones of Almalita.* Ms. Leo is a retired teacher and psychotherapist.

A Higher Calling

Joyce W. Leo

A Higher Calling was written in Maryville College's playwriting class in Maryville, Tennessee, where it was then given a public reading in "12 X 10 X 2" in April of 2012 at the Haslam Family Flex Theatre at the Clayton Center for the Arts. The play was then given a reading by the Tennessee Stage Company, produced by Tom Parkhill.

CHARACTERS

CLARA WATSON: An elderly Nursing Home resident.

NURSE: Dressed in daily clothes with blue uniform shirt.

MIRIAM LORDE: Young mother at home with a sleeping infant in a crib.

SETTING

A nursing home room stage right; stage left is a living room in a young mother's home.

TIME

Evening.

• • • • • • • • • • • •

The stage is divided into two playing areas. It is evening in a nursing home room, stage right. A living room in a young mother's home is stage left. The lights come up on the nursing home room of Clara, an elderly resident. The song "Amazing Grace" drifts in from the nursing station offstage.

CLARA: *(Looking toward the window.)* That sun. That beautiful sun is going down. My parents need to know where I am. They'll be out looking for me. My daddy never lets me stay out this late. *(She fumbles around for a call button.)* Where is that call button? *(Pause.)* Oh, here it is! *(She pushes the call button.)* The sun is setting. I have to hurry! They'll be very upset with me.

(Nurse enters.)

NURSE: Yes, Mrs. Watson?

CLARA: Can you tell my parents where I am? I need to go home before it gets too dark.

NURSE: Clara, dear, I'm sure your parents know where you are. Don't you worry.

CLARA: But they always want me home before the sun goes down.

NURSE: You're safe and sound right here. Just relax and let your dinner settle.

CLARA: It's been nice visiting with you…but I need to get home.

NURSE: Oh, I believe I heard that your parents were on vacation. I'm sure they're enjoying themselves and know you're just fine. They'll be back. Don't you worry. *(Exits.)*

CLARA: No, don't go! *(Waves the call button toward the door.)* Why do people always leave? *(She presses the call button again, hard.)* Where is everybody? My parents didn't tell me they were on vacation!

NURSE: *(Re-enters.)* Clara, you can't keep pressing that button. We'll have to take it away from you if you don't stop.

CLARA: Stop me? Ha! I can't even get started, much less stopped!

NURSE: Did you hear what I said? We'll have to take that away from you if you don't stop.

CLARA: Ha! You can't take anything more away from me. Look at me! What is there left to take? *(Waves the call button in the air.)* Go ahead. Take it!

NURSE: You can't keep playing with that call button, Clara! That's for emergencies! You must stop or we'll have to put you in a closer room with no call buttons so we can watch you.

CLARA: *(A bit touchy.)* Watch me? What are you going to watch – me dancing on the bed? Cartwheels in the air?

NURSE: Clara, dear, you have to realize you're perfectly fine here. We take good care of you. This is your home.

CLARA: Don't you hear me? This is not my home. I have to get home now! My parents...

NURSE: Really now? Do you think your parents are worried about you – you, a grown woman?

CLARA: Yes, of course! They never want me to stay out late. Do you think I'm a loose girl running around after dark? How dare you think that!

NURSE: *(Laughing.)* Does it ever occur to you that your parents might be having a good time and not be worried about you?

CLARA: They always worry about me. You don't know my parents, do you? My mother is a worrywart.

NURSE: Clara, dear, every evening when that old sun goes down, we go through the same old thing. You're already home. You know that! You don't need to go anywhere. We go through this day after day, week after week. Ooooh! Sundown Syndrome.

CLARA: What'dya say? The Sundown what?

NURSE: *(To self.)* This too shall pass.

CLARA: Don't you listen at all? Where is the phone book? I'll call my mother myself.

NURSE: *(Clearly relieved to leave.)* I'll go see if I can find one. *(Exits.)*

CLARA: *(Touching her forehead with the palm of her hand.)* Oh, I have a headache! Why can't they just let me go home! *(Looking toward the window.)* The sun is down. Now Daddy will have to come get me. *(She presses the call button again and again.)*

NURSE: *(Re-enters, exasperated.)* Clara, you're going to have to stop this.

CLARA: Who are you, anyway? Are you one of those kidnappers? My parents always warned me about kidnappers. I want to go home!

NURSE: Clara, for God's sake, don't you know the truth? Here you are – almost 90 and your parents have long been dead —

(A sudden shock comes over Nurse as she realizes she never should have blurted out that truth to Clara.)

CLARA: *(Clearly stunned.)* What do you mean? Dead? My parents aren't dead! They want to know where I am after dark. Where am I, anyway? *(Bewildered.)* Who told me my parents were dead? *(On the verge of tears.)*

NURSE: Who told you?

CLARA: Yes, somebody told me my parents were dead. Is that true? Did I dream it?

NURSE: Oh, no, no. I'm sorry, Clara. I'll let them know you're here.

CLARA: I don't want to be here. I want to be home. Why are you keeping me here? *(Clara looks at Nurse as if she were a person she is trying to remember.)* You're...you're that one that kept me up all night with your partying and loud laughing, aren't you? *(Looks around at the walls.)* And look! You've changed my pictures all around!

NURSE: Clara, you know these pictures have been on your walls all this time.

CLARA: This is not your house to change anyway you want. Why are you even here? *(Beat.)* Who are you? I ought to call the police!

(Nurse takes out her blood pressure monitor and places it on Clara's left arm.)

NURSE: Are you feeling all right, Clara?

CLARA: Why don't you go on into the kitchen and get yourself something to eat? It's in the refrigerator. Go help yourself. *(Waves toward the "kitchen.")* Everybody else does.

(Nurse notes the readings on the blood pressure monitor.)

NURSE: I'll have to call your doctor. *(Gently touches Clara's shoulder.)* I'll be right back. *(Hustles toward the door.)*

CLARA: Why do you run off all the time?

NURSE: *(On the way out the door.)* I'll be right back! Hold on! I'll get your doctor! *(Exits.)*

CLARA: My doctor? How am I going to pay for a doctor bill? *(Gets an idea.)* Bill? Oh...yes, Bill! *(Reaches for the phone and dials.)* 856..no. 865-99..oh no. 78..99.

(Suddenly the phone rings stage left before Clara thinks she has finished dialing. It is a quiet ring.)

CLARA: Oh, dear me...it went through! *(Sitting up expectantly.)* Good!

Lisa Soland

(Lights come up stage left on a young mother's living room where Miriam is watching her baby sleeping in a crib. The phone continues to ring, quietly. Miriam tries to ignore the phone, so as not to wake the baby, but it continues to ring as if it will never stop. She finally picks up the receiver.)

MIRIAM: Hel-loh.

CLARA: *(Feebly and mumbled.)* Is that you, Bill?

MIRIAM: Hello, who's calling?

CLARA: *(Finding her voice stronger.)* Bill, I need you to come and get me!

MIRIAM: I'm sorry, but Bill's not available right now.

CLARA: Tell Bill to come now. I need him here.

MIRIAM: Who's calling, please?

CLARA: I'm Bill's wife. He knows I'm here. Tell him to hurry up and get here.

MIRIAM: I'm sorry, you must have the wrong number. There is a Bill who lives here. I'm his wife. What number did you want?

CLARA: No, I'm Bill's wife. I want Bill to come here. Who are you? What are you doing in my house?

MIRIAM: But your Bill isn't here. Where are you calling from?

CLARA: He knows I'm here. They're trying to kidnap me. He knows.

MIRIAM: Who's trying to kidnap you?

CLARA: The nursing home. They won't let me go home!

MIRIAM: Which nursing home?

CLARA: Bill knows.

MIRIAM: What is your name?

CLARA: I'm his wife. He knows me – Clara. Tell him to hurry up.
(Suddenly seeing something in the room, Clara takes the phone from her ear.) Is that you, Mama!

MIRIAM: Is there someone there you can put on the phone?
(Almost trance-like Clara rises halfway out of the bed with both hands resting on the bed as she looks toward the foot of her bed.)

MIRIAM: Hello! Are you still there? Who did you say is with you?

CLARA: *(Remembering to put the phone back to her ear.)* Oh, I have to go now. My mother's here.

MIRIAM: Your mother is with you? Can you put her on the phone?

CLARA: Yes, my mother's here! She's standing at my bed and smiling. I don't know if she wants to come to the phone. I'll see. Wait a minute. *(Holds the phone out toward the end of her bed.)* Mama? Can you talk on the phone?*(Into the phone, while staring at the end of her bed.)* She doesn't want to take the phone. *(Looking at her mother, Clara is suddenly is overwhelmed.)* Oh, My God! You're beautiful, Mama! Yes, yes, I'm coming, I'm coming!

MIRIAM: Can you call a nurse to help you?

CLARA: *(Into phone.)* No, I buzzed them. They never come. My mother says to hurry up. How beautiful she is!

MIRIAM: Are you all right? Can your mother help you?

CLARA: She wants me to go with her. Tell Bill to hurry, please! I want him to come too. Mama says it's time we go.

MIRIAM: Where are you going? Should I call 911 for you? Hold on! I have another phone.

CLARA: 911? Is Bill there?

(Miriam's baby begins to cry.)

MIRIAM: Wait, wait just a moment. I'm a mother, too. My baby's waking up. Hold on.

(As Miriam comforts the baby, Clara is spellbound with the vision of her mother.)

CLARA: Mama, what have you done with yourself? You are so bright and beautiful! *(She opens her arms as if she will embrace her mother.)* Now I see… You came for me before dark.

(Clara's arms reach out and she rises from the waist up as if she is going to float up to the visage at the foot of her bed.)

CLARA: And you're so bright! You light up the darkness! *(Suddenly shrieks with joy.)* Bill! You came too! *(She gently falls back onto her pillow, lifeless.)*

MIRIAM: *(Picks up the phone again.)* Hello, Clara, if you tell me your husband's last name, maybe I can help you. *(Silence.)* Where do you have to go? *(Silence.)* Hello, are you there? *(Silence.)* Hello? Hello?

NURSE: *(Entering.)* The doctor is on his way. *(Notes that Clara is unresponsive.)* Mrs. Watson? *(Nurse checks her pulse.)* She's gone! *(Looking tenderly at the still figure on the bed.)* Oh, Mrs. Watson. What an easy passing. You look so radiant!

(Nurse pushes the call button and begins the process of rechecking pulse, closing eyelids, and pulling up the sheet.)

MIRIAM: *(Still holding the phone and hearing the commotion, Miriam begins to shout into the phone.)* Hello! Hello!

NURSE: *(Hearing the shouting, Nurse picks up the phone.)* Hello, are you related to Mrs. Watson?

MIRIAM: Oh, no, I didn't know her name. She called my number, looking for her husband Bill, and I have a husband Bill, but I kept telling her she had the wrong number.

NURSE: We're sorry about that. Whatever you said must have made her very happy. She has the most beautiful smile on her face.

MIRIAM: Oh?

NURSE: Thank you for being with her in her last moments. Maybe she had the right number after all.

MIRIAM: Maybe...but her mother was there too, right?

NURSE: Excuse me? Her mother? No, she was here alone.

MIRIAM: But she said someone was with her —

NURSE: Mrs. Watson is in a lock-down unit. She's had no visitors at all.

MIRIAM: Oh...I see...but I didn't —

NURSE: Sometimes we just never know how our words can affect people. Now excuse me. *(Nurse hangs up the phone.)*

MIRIAM: But I didn't... She must have... Hello? *(Beat.)* She's gone.

(The baby cries again. Miriam puts down the phone and picks up the baby, holding the baby tight, as the lights fade.)

END OF PLAY

Biography

Sue Lange is a novelist, playwright, and screenwriter. She has four books of published speculative fiction satire and numerous published short stories in various venues, such as Nature's Futures. She is the resident playwright for the Reading Theater Project who has produced her full-length plays, *Speakeasy* and *Marriage Expo(sé)*. Her short film, *A Perfect You*, has been nominated for best comedy in the Southampton International Film Festival.

The Glass Ceiling

Sue Lange

The Glass Ceiling won 2nd place in the 2013 Frostburg University Short Play Competition in September of 2013. In March of 2014, the Reading Theater Project in Reading, Pennsylvania, performed a staged reading.

MARLENA: 35, junior executive of Dazzle Beverage.
SYLVIE: 33, junior executive of Dazzle Beverage.
GLENDA: 54, junior executive of Dazzle Beverage.

TIME

One afternoon after a managers' meeting.

SETTING

Ladies restroom on the 17th floor of the company
headquarters for Dazzle Beverage.

• • • • • • • • • • • •

Marlena sits on the throne in a stall stage right. We see her stockings and high heels. The door to the hallway outside the restroom is in the center of the upstage wall. A large, detachable magnetic strip with the words "Out of Order" has been placed sideways on the door. It is quite legible to the audience, despite it being at a 90° angle. On either side of the door are two full-length mirrors. Stage left are two or three basins, with mirrors on the wall. There's a trashcan somewhere visible. The door opens and Sylvie sticks her head in and looks around.

SYLVIE: You in here?
    (Sylvie steps in. She has short hair and is smartly dressed in pants and jacket. She sees the stall is occupied. Once she is inside, the door closes behind her.)
SYLVIE: Marlena, I saw you come in here.
MARLENA: I'm peeing.
SYLVIE: Why'd you kick me like that?
MARLENA: I'm peeing.
    (Sylvie removes the magnetic strip from the door and places it horizontally over the outside of the door. She reenters and lights up a cigarette.)
MARLENA: There's no smoking in here.
SYLVIE: *(Annoyed.)* I thought you were peeing.
    (The toilet flushes, Marlena enters from stall. She has shoulder length hair and is wearing a skirt. She's sharp and just a shade sexy.)
MARLENA: I'm done.
    (Marlena crosses to the sink and washes her hands. Throughout the following conversation she is fixing her makeup, adjusting her clothes, combing her hair. Sylvie smokes and paces.)

SYLVIE: Why'd you kick me in Codgins' meeting?

MARLENA: Can I just pee in private?

SYLVIE: I had something to say. You made me look ridiculous.

MARLENA: You don't need me for that.

SYLVIE: I really didn't need you cutting me off like that.

MARLENA: Believe me, Sylvie, I was doing you a favor.

SYLVIE: How's that? Forget it, forget it. I have something else I want to talk to you about. How long have we been doing this?

MARLENA: I don't know. Five minutes.

SYLVIE: You know what I mean. This thing. This...female cabal? This "out of order..." *(Taps the door.)* ...meetings coming to order, this —

MARLENA: Oh, no, why'd you put the sign out. Now Glenda's going to think we're having a meeting. She'll be in here any minute with some feel good crap. I don't want to talk to her today.

SYLVIE: Don't worry about Glenda, she's flitting around the office, happy as horse shit.

MARLENA: You think?

SYLVIE: Yeah, she's all excited: "the announcement, the announcement!" She's writing her acceptance speech, if you can believe that. She'll be occupied for hours.

MARLENA: I don't know why she's doing that.

SYLVIE: Because "the announcement?" Hello?

MARLENA: She shouldn't be counting her chickens.

SYLVIE: She has the most seniority.

MARLENA: They can pass over her. They've done it before.

SYLVIE: Yeah, but now there's only three eligibles and we're all women.

MARLENA: Doesn't mean she'll get it. They could give it to one of us.

SYLVIE: Answer the question.

MARLENA: What question?

SYLVIE: How long have we been doing this... *(Taps the door.)* ...thing?

MARLENA: This glass ceiling initiative?

SYLVIE: This —

MARLENA: Affirmative reaction?

SYLVIE: This —

MARLENA: Equal time, equal pay, equal opportunity dump?

SYLVIE: This.

MARLENA: Couple years.

SYLVIE: *(Stubs cigarette out on floor.)* It's not working.

(The bathroom door opens a crack and Glenda pokes her head in.)

GLENDA: Is there a meeting? I saw the sign.

(*Marlena grunts. Sylvie clears her throat. Glenda steps in. She's got shoulder length hair, plain skirt to her knees, neat but out of date and beige. Indistinguishable from wallpaper. She heads into a stall. Marlena and Sylvie exchange glances; Marlena glares, Sylvie shrugs.*)

MARLENA: Sylvie thinks we should stop having these meetings.

GLENDA: Oh, no! Sylvie! We can't! I live for these —

SYLVIE: I didn't say that.

GLENDA: Besides these meetings are working. I mean, today's the day. We rule!

SYLVIE: One of us is getting promoted by default, Glenda. These meetings don't have anything to do with it.

GLENDA: It has everything to do with it. Before they would have passed us over. If anybody knows that, I know it. But they'll come through this time. You know they will. They know if they don't we'll —

SYLVIE: What? Come in here and have an encounter session?

GLENDA: Take action. I was going to say we'll take action. They know we'll stick together on this. Keep in mind they already announced they weren't going outside to hire. They can't change their minds.

SYLVIE: They can do anything they want, Glenda. Even change their minds and hire some schmuck just out of college, somebody they only have to pay a couple of bucks to —

(*Toilet flushes. Glenda steps out from the stall. Washes her hands.*)

GLENDA: Into middle management? They're not going to do that. They need people that know the company. Fulfillment's having problems and… Did you hear about that Appletini —

MARLENA: Well, then, congratulations, Glenda, you've waited a long time for this. And you deserve it. You've been loyal and god knows you've been an inspiration for us.

GLENDA: Thank you, Marlena. And I'm not going to forget our little girls' room meetings. We've still got battles and knowing we're all here for each other when they start pulling their chauvinistic bull is going to…help me. A lot.

SYLVIE: "Chauvinistic." Now there's a word right out of the 70s.

GLENDA: It may be old-fashioned, Sylvie, but it hasn't gone away. Just because sexual harassment is against company policy doesn't mean they don't still practice it insidiously.

MARLENA: Glenda, please don't preach. We all know about the unspoken discrimination. We've heard the war stories. Can we just move on? I

215

Lisa Soland

want to make my own stories but it feels like we're laboring under the ghosts of feminists past.

SYLVIE: That's not really fair, Marlena. Things have definitely gotten better, but right now over on the other side of the wall there's probably two VPs jerking off over pictures of Glenda downloaded from the Internet.

(Marlena has a hard time not laughing at the idea.)

SYLVIE: I don't necessarily mean to be funny. What I'm trying to say is —

MARLENA: Well, if you're so understanding of the problem and know Glenda's right, why do you want to dump these bathroom meetings?

SYLVIE: I never said that.

GLENDA: So what's the problem, dearie? *(Pause.)* Sylvie.

SYLVIE: I'm not saying there's a problem.

MARLENA: What are you saying then?

SYLVIE: I'm saying it's not working for me.

MARLENA and GLENDA: That sounds like a problem.

GLENDA: And why is it not working, sweetie? I mean…Sylvie. Are we not showing support for you? For your efforts?

SYLVIE: No, no it's not that. You've both been great. Just great. And I want to be supportive of you, as well. Always. I want you to know that. No matter what happens, I will always be supportive. But I just get the feeling that sometimes we're going about it all wrong.

MARLENA: A minute ago I wasn't being fair to Glenda. Then you wanted to talk about it. You're, like, not being consistent.

SYLVIE: I don't know what I'm saying, really. I just —

GLENDA: You do know the demographics of suicide, right? I told you that, right?

SYLVIE: The statistics, yes.

GLENDA: It's not because they're men, you know. It's because the power structure, the social constructs, the whole cultural mess, leads to such things. There's no nurturing going on in a corporate environment. Leads to self-loathing and what all, but it's not genetic.

MARLENA: *(Campy.)* It's cultural!

SYLVIE: *(Glares at Marlena.)* Of course. That's one of the reasons we started this. We didn't want to end up like that. Like them. We can't be like them. We need to celebrate the traditional feminine style, stick with each other. One of us… Glenda, for instance…is moving into position and we can't let her be there alone. She needs psychological support and —

MARLENA: *(Still a bit campy.)* We have to do things differently.

SYLVIE: That's what we said, but maybe not being like them is not actually being different. Maybe what we really need to be is more like th—

GLENDA: Don't say it. Don't ever say it. Do not deny your femininity.

SYLVIE: *(Looks from Glenda to Marlena to Glenda again.)* Did it ever occur to you that maybe the so-called "glass ceiling" is a mirror? It's reflecting back. You don't really see to the other side. What you're seeing is what's in your own head. *(Knocks on Marlena's head.)* Maybe we need to stop being so self-obsessed. We question everything we do and then we head in here to analyze it with our homegirls. We go over the motivations, the results, come to conclusions, and then go back out to conquer. But we never conquer. If you're getting promoted, Glenda, it's by default. That's not really conquering.

GLENDA: Don't shit on this, Sylvie. It's a step forward. There was a time when this wouldn't happen. Our support for each other has them on the run. Don't shit on this.

SYLVIE: All I'm saying is that maybe we should skip the post game analysis and just muddle forward, do the best job we can, and let the chips fall. Divide. And conquer. We need to get out of the bathroom. *(Glenda and Marlena gasp.)*

SYLVIE: Something's out of order here. *(Taps the door again.)* Maybe it's us!

GLENDA: *(Thoughtfully.)* Well, we could do that. We could get out of the bathroom. Sure. Meet for lunch or after work over at the Marriott. But remember we started this in here for a reason. We needed to support each other during the work day. In the moment. When things happen. Their comments, their back handed compliments, their… shenanigans. We need to be here for each other when shit happens, exactly when it happens. We'll lose all that if we move out of here. Out of our little hive.

SYLVIE: I know all that, but —

GLENDA: Let me finish. *(Pause to collect her thoughts.)* I've been here at Dazzle Beverage longer than you two. I've been here almost from the beginning. I was here when old man Codgins was fresh out of college heading up Development. I was here when he invented Snorkle 180. I gave him the tagline —

SYLVIE and MARLENA: "When under the table isn't enough."

SYLVIE: We know that, Glenda. We know you never got credit. It was wrong.

GLENDA: But you still don't get it. You still don't know what it was like. Before the sexual harassment laws, before there were any women at all above the fold. There was no such thing as maternity leave and no one would listen if you had a complaint about your pay. And behavior? Forget it. No recourse whatsoever. Not even a word for it. Same for psychological support from your co-workers. There was nothing. You don't know what we've got here. You take it for granted and forget we have to stay vigilant. We could lose it all easily. Take it from me, I know. We have to be supportive.

SYLVIE: I do know, Glenda. I totally know. I'm not trying to belittle your past experience. I wouldn't do that. I know it's important.

GLENDA: I know you do, sweetie. Sylvie. I just need to hear it sometimes. I just need... *(Opens her arms.)* C'mon. Let's love, ladies.

(Sylvie and Marlena grudgingly move in for a group hug.)

SYLVIE: *(Stepping back.)* I'm just frustrated at the moment, I guess. *(She rifles in her pocket for her cigarette pack.)* Things are all right. I just needed to —

GLENDA AND MARLENA: Vent!

SYLVIE: *(Smiles sheepishly.)* I guess.

GLENDA: Well, I've got to go. *(Kisses them.)* They're going to announce pretty soon. I need to be at my desk when that happens. *(Stops at door and turns to Sylvie.)* Stick with it, Sylvie. We need you. And by the way, there's no smoking in here.

SYLVIE: *(Puts the pack back, waits for the door to close, pulls it back out.)* Why did you bring her into it?

MARLENA: She came into it. I didn't invite her. It's your own fault. She saw the sign and came in.

SYLVIE: I'm trying to get my thoughts together on this and I wanted to know how you felt about...things.

MARLENA: So you weren't just venting.

SYLVIE: I love Glenda, but —

MARLENA: She's so —

SYLVIE: Nurturing and...she's living in the past. I can't take it sometimes. And she's never going to understand what I'm saying.

MARLENA: I don't understand what you're saying.

SYLVIE: Why did you kick me when I had something to say?

MARLENA: Kicked you?

SYLVIE: In Codgin's meeting. The monthly head-'em-off-at-the-pass, air-your- grievances, let's-fix-it-before-it-breaks, what-have-you, do. You kicked me just when I was getting ready to fix something before it broke. You were so...

MARLENA: Unsupportive?

SYLVIE: Well…

MARLENA: Oh, now you want support. Tell you what, Sylvie, you were getting ready to shoot yourself in the foot. That's what you were getting ready to do. How's that for support? I was only making sure you didn't make an ass of yourself.

SYLVIE: I was pointing out how Fulfillment lost another Appletini·Time shipment. Second in two months.

MARLENA: Everyone knows about that, you don't need to remind them. You were heading for harpy mode.

(Sylvie forces a laugh.)

MARLENA: No one in that meeting wants to hear how inept Fulfillment is. Elderman was practically rolling his eyes when you started. And you don't want to get on his wrong side, believe me. Elderman's got Codgins' ear. More than the rest. Anyway, what I'm trying to say is we all have problems. Facilities is slow with the software upgrades, Legal is forever setting up contracts. That's all lost revenue. The only group that seems on time is payroll.

SYLVIE: Yeah, well, that's because we get such shit from everybody when we screw up.

MARLENA: Well that's humble of you.

SYLVIE: All I was trying to do was point out how Fulfillment has been getting slower and slower. You know that from running the storeroom. You know how those people are, how Stoddard is. I'll be glad when he retires, but whoever gets that spot is going to have a mess to clean up. And they're going to need —

MARLENA: The point is you need to check your style. Take the meetings, since you brought it up. You always have something to say. Instead of just plowing through like everyone else and getting the damn thing over with, you've always got some point to make. It makes me squirm. I'm telling you, no one likes a complainer. I keep seeing images of Elderman rolling his eyes. They want you to figure out how to work with everyone, with Fulfillment, however bad they are.

SYLVIE: *(Laughs for real.)* So what you're saying is, if we're losing customers because some department is slacking, I can't bring it up in a meeting held to find out why we're losing money?

MARLENA: They don't want to hear it, believe me. You need to just cowboy-the-fuck-up and figure it out. Attacking anyone in this company is the same as attacking one of them personally.

SYLVIE: I'm just trying to fix something before it breaks.

MARLENA: Don't fix it before it's broken.

SYLVIE: Oh for Christ's sake.

MARLENA: You got ambition? You want to move up the ol' corporate ladder, you need to get behind your fellow employees, not kick them in the butt.

SYLVIE: So now you're spouting some of Glenda's crap?

MARLENA: It's not crap.

SYLVIE: And you're, what? An expert? Ms. Stockroom with a staff of two, lowest exec in your department. You've done so well, you're going to show me how it works.

MARLENA: Well, actually...

SYLVIA: Actually what?

MARLENA: Look, I'm older than you. I've —

SYLVIE: By two years, Marlena. Two years.

MARLENA: I've been here longer. By —

SYLVIE: By six months. In the big scheme, we've pretty much got the same amount of experience.

MARLENA: And, AND, I'm not naïve, like you. Don't give me that face. You are so effing earnest. Earnest gets you nowhere, Sylvie. That's your problem. That's our problem. The problem with women all over the world. In our saintly demeanor, we run about, trying to change the world with our shrill, little girly voices, when all they want is for us to play the game.

SYLVIE: How 'bout I just do a good job? Isn't that playing the game?

MARLENA: That's just how you get into the game. Once you're in, you need to play. For instance: what do men like more than anything in the world?

SYLVIE: Money, power, control...which they'll get if their organization runs smoothly which won't happen unless Fulfillment starts delivering Appletini·Time on time.

MARLENA: Would you shut up about the Appletini·Time? Stay focused. Yes, they want to be on top like that, I agree, but mostly they don't want change. They want the world to stay the way it is. They want the women, us,...to be sexy. There I said it.

SYLVIE: Oh god!

(Marlena looks her up and down again.)

SYLVIE: What?

MARLENA: Why don't you wear a skirt, for Christ's sake?

SYLVIE: *(Hits her forehead with her hand.)* If Glenda could only hear you now.

MARLENA: Oh, now Glenda's an authority. A minute ago she was so "living in the past." Anyhow, she'd agree with me. You're too mannish. They don't want to see that. Not in a woman. Glenda knows that. A mannish woman is a threat.

SYLVIE: Your breasts are more threatening than my pinstripes. They're scaring me, for cripe's sake.

MARLENA: They should. You don't seem to have any. What have you got on under there? A jog bra?

SYLVIE: Let me tell you something, Ms. I-demand-equality-but-I'm-not-a-feminist-oh-no-not me! We've had thousands of years of skirt-wearing, breast-thrusting, lip gloss-wearing. Where's it gotten us? What deep-seated progress have we made? Can you really say that we're not one president away from the burkah? Men are afraid of femininity, girly-girl, the so-called "woman's power."

MARLENA: Has lip gloss been around that long?

SYLVIE: If wearing a skirt makes such a big difference, what's up with ol' Glenda? She's been here what? Thirty years now? And wearing a skirt the whole time. Looks great, fit, neatly combed hair. Why hasn't she busted through before now? And that is one compliant-assed mama. I have never heard a discouraging word from her. Ever. And she's the office manager, thank you very much.

MARLENA: True, but a bad example.

SYLVIE: Yeah? Why?

MARLENA: You heard her speech. She's been here, like, forever. She got in before the E.R.A. went into effect. That's wicked bad timing. Way too early. She got passed over because of sexism and then became a fixture long before equal opportunity rolled around. They see her as a fossil. Something stiff and inflexible.

SYLVIE: You just said they don't like change. And by the way, the E.R.A. never passed.

MARLENA: Whatever. All I'm saying is —

SYLVIE: All I'm saying is we need to try something different. Divide – split up, every man for himself – to conquer. Maybe just a little? Stop being so… *(She looks in the mirror.)*

MARLENA: So what? Feminine?

SYLVIE: Well, yes. You know what's feminine? Tampons. You wear feminine, men see feminine products. You want to really put them – Elderman – off, use the word "Kotex" in a sentence. That'd be the equivalent of wearing a blinking neon sign on your back: "I am the 'other!' "

MARLENA: The "other?"

SYLVIE: C'mon, Marlena! You know what I'm talking about. You remind them that you're different. You said they don't want change. That's true in a way, but it's not the full truth. What they really don't want is something different. No matter how many clichés you cling to, how much you stick to the stereotype, you're always going to remind them that you are different. Bring them one stinking cup of coffee, girlfriend, and you are sunk.

MARLENA: *(Smugly.)* We'll see, Sylvie. We'll see if your theory is right.

SYLVIE: *(Snaps her head up.)* You know something?

(Marlena shrugs. Pause.)

SYLVIA: What?

MARLENA: *(Pause.)* I'm going to be getting Stoddard's position.

(Sylvie's jaw drops.)

MARLENA: I've been filling in for him for a while. He's on leave of absence. Wife's got cancer.

SYLVIE: Marlena…

MARLENA: Aren't you going to congratulate me?

SYLVIE: I'm just…

MARLENA: What? You're just what?

SYLVIE: I mean…what about Glenda?

MARLENA: She's not going to get it.

SYLVIE: I suspected it, but…well, she's so confident.

MARLENA: She's confident because they said they weren't going outside the company. Out of us three, she's been here the longest so she thinks she's going to get it. But she's not. Old man Codgins called me in to the office yesterday. Said I'd been doing great at it and he sees great things for me and they're very appreciative, and, what can I say?

SYLVIE: Great things…?

MARLENA: They don't want anyone, well, the board basically, to know because Stoddard's so close to retirement. You know how they are. And Codgins said I'd be remembered for stepping up so…well. All but said I got the promotion. They'll announce it today and —

SYLVIE: So that's why you kicked me. You've been running Fulfillment. Now it makes sense. You didn't want me —

MARLENA: Not true! Not true! Not true! I'm only thinking of you. You were shooting yourself in the foot.

SYLVIE: And why do you care about my foot?

MARLENA: Because you're my friend maybe?

SYLVIE: You're not going to start with that sister crap are you? I mean, maybe I should pull Glenda's head out of the clouds and tell her all this. She's going to need some sisterly love after she hears the news. She'll be in this room for a week, calling hourly encounter sessions.

MARLENA: You're my sworn sister, yes, but it's not just that, Sylvie. I swear to god, I'm bust —

SYLVIE: Goddess.

MARLENA: I swear to goddess, I'm busting through this glass ceiling. I'm going straight up and I'm going to need you on my team. I need you right behind me, sister. I'm moving up. This year Head, next year when the VP slot opens, I'll be there. When that happens, I want you to take over Fulfillment. But you can kiss that dream goodbye if you don't... I mean, they won't promote you if they don't like you, no matter what I say. And they're not going to like you, trust you, if you keep throwing your men's style and whiny complaints at them. You're a damn good worker, Sylvie. I can see that. Everyone can see that. So get on board! Just cowboy the fuck.

SYLVIE: *(Pacing in earnest.)* So Codgins is giving you Fulfillment. Codgins, not Elderman, talked to you. *(Stops and turns to Marlena.)* He said the words, right? "Head?" "Fulfillment?" Same breath?

MARLENA: *(Throat clearing.)* Not in those words exactly, but he said they'd remember me when the time came and the time's coming today.

SYLVIE: Let me ask you something, Marlena. How are you going to deal with Glenda?

MARLENA: Glenda?

SYLVIE: Yeah, I mean, she's going to think you're stabbing her in the back.

MARLENA: I should turn this down? Make them give it to her?

SYLVIE: That's the way she'll look at it.

MARLENA: She's incompetent.

SYLVIE: What?

MARLENA: I mean... Not incompetent, just not right for the job. She has been here too long. She's so second wave. You have to be more —

SYLVIE: So it's not going to bother you that it's going to bother her.

MARLENA: A little, maybe. But she'll get over it. She has to. I mean what's she going to do?

SYLVIE: She can't quit. She'll never find a comparable job somewhere else. Not in today's environment. Age discrimination is worse than gender, race, creed – what have you – discrimination. She'll be here every day, glaring at you from her cubicle. How are you going to stand it?

Are you going to go and apologize to her?

MARLENA: For what? I haven't done anything wrong. I'm just jumping at an opportunity. Anybody would do it. Glenda would do it. You'd do it.

SYLVIE: So you're not going to go and apologize to her?

MARLENA: Have I done something wrong?

SYLVIE: Of course not, but it might give you an opportunity to let her know that you care about her feelings and you want her on the team and she's important and...

MARLENA: So what you're saying is that maybe I need to have a good old-fashioned, feminist cabalistic, enlightenment, encounter session?

SYLVIE: I just think you need to let her know you care about her.

MARLENA: I get it. This is about you, isn't it?

SYLVIE: Maybe.

MARLENA: Sylvie, I'm not leaving you behind. That's why I kicked you. I agree, this whole secret meeting thing isn't important. It's not that it's not working, it just isn't necessary. Maybe before it was, but...you'll see after today. This is going to work out well for both of us. Well, it will if you... *(Looks her up and down.)* ...get a new strategy. You don't have to love these guys, but maybe you could, sort of, I don't know.

SYLVIE: Flirt with them?

(Marlena shrugs.)

SYLVIA: Which one? They're all so...attractive.

MARLENA: Well...look at Elderman, since we keep bringing him up. He's cute in a virile sort of way.

SYLVIE: Cute and virile are mutually exclusive. He's what? Like, sixty-two. That's so, totally...Oedipal.

MARLENA: *(Starts packing up.)* I have no idea what you're talking about. Anyway, there's time for you to embrace your femininity. I'm telling you, Glenda's right about that.

SYLVIE: Glenda. Funny you should bring her into it.

MARLENA: I hope you're not going to hold me... I mean, you're going to be supportive of me, even though Glenda is being passed over yet again.

SYLVIE: Of course. Anybody would accept the position. Anybody.

MARLENA: Okay then. You're on board, but you do need to loosen up and enjoy the ride. Watch what I do. While I'm inching up towards upper management, we'll get you into middle.

(Heads toward door and stops to check herself in the full-length mirror.)

MARLENA: Stick with me, honey. I'll have you wearing horse turds as big as diamonds. Well, ta!

(Marlena exits and then returns to replace the "out of order" sign sideways on the inside of the door. Sylvie paces madly. Starts to light the ciggy, changes her mind and heads into the stall. We hear the unmistakable sound of a cell phone ringing Wagner's Ride of the Valkyries.)

SYLVIE: Hello, Mr. Elderman. *(Steps out of the stall, pauses as she listens, inhales deeply.)* I'm, I'm well, yes, thank you. Oh yes, I'm very excited… Yes, I've spoken to them both, just now. I'm sure they'll be fine. Oh and this bathroom thing is definitely…gone. I'll see to that…certainly. I'll be up in Mr. Codgins' office right away. And thank you so much for this opportunity. *(Sylvie snaps phone shut, does a victory dance, checks herself in the full length mirror, and yanks the sign off the door before tossing it into the trash can.)*

END OF PLAY

Lisa Soland

Biography

Sara Ljungkull has written for Interior Design Magazine in New York and Charles Patteson Public Relations of New York. Her plays include *Polished Manicure*, which has been produced worldwide and published by Heuer Publishing, *Perception Deception* which won Honorable Mention at the Drury University One-Act Play Competition and Honorable Mention at Hollywood One Act Play Competition, and *The Toast*, a mini-musical produced at Theatre Building Chicago. She currently resides in Illinois and teaches in Iowa.

Polished Manicure

Ⓐ

Sara Ljungkull

Polished Manicure was developed in The All Original Playwright Workshop, published by Heuer Publishing, and has since had the following productions: Johnston High School in Johnston, Iowa, Madill Public School in Madill, Oklahoma, Bertrand High School in Bertrand, Nebraska, Alonzo and Tracy Mourning Senior High School in North Miami, Florida, CGGS - Can berra ACT, Australia, World-wide school supplies in Miami, Florida, I SS in Princeton, New Jersey, Moscow Senior High School in Moscow, Idaho, Somerset Academy Charter School (Chapel Trail) in Pembroke Pines, Florida, Red Lion Christian School in Red Lion, Pennsylvania, AGWSR High Shool in Ackley, Iowa, EquipMySchool.com in Lincolnshire, United Kingdom, McClintock High School in Tempe, Arizona, Powell County High School in Stanton, Kentucky, Horner Junior High School in Fremont, California, White Station High School in Memphis, Tennessee, Garvey Intermediate School in Rosemead, California, and Ainsworth High School in Ainsworth, Nebraska.

CHARACTERS
> MARY: A Vietnamese woman in her forties. She is the
> manicurist.
> ALEXIS: A woman in her thirties. She is very wealthy.
> TIFFANY: A woman in her early thirties, also very wealthy.

SETTING
> The interior of a nail salon.

TIME
> Present day.

• • • • • • • • • • • •

Inside a nail salon. One table and two chairs. On the table is a 3 x 4 photograph.
Mary, a manicurist, is sitting at her station. Alexis enters stage left carrying many
shopping bags: Bloomingdale's, Saks, etc. Mary looks up. She laughs to herself.
It is a knowing laugh, not condescending.

ALEXIS: Do you have time for a fill?
MARY: *(Gesturing to a rack of polish.)* Yes. *(Laughs.)* Pick color.
ALEXIS: *(Not understanding.)* What did you say?
MARY: *(Taps her nails.)* Pick color.
ALEXIS: *(Pulls polish from purse.)* Oh, I brought my own.
MARY: Okay.
> *(Alexis puts down her bags and sits.)*
ALEXIS: Would you mind hurrying a bit? I'm meeting someone for lunch.
MARY: What time you lunch?
ALEXIS: Twelve-thirty.
MARY: Don't worry, I be done.
ALEXIS: *(Takes off her watch and rings.)* Where are you from?
MARY: Vietnam.
ALEXIS: *(Nods.)* I see.
MARY: You have pretty jewelry.
ALEXIS: Thank you.
MARY: I used to have pretty jewelry. But I have to sell. I had pretty necklace,
> black pearls. You know black pearls?
ALEXIS: Yes, I do, but I don't have any. *(Beat.)* Don't file my nails too much.
> I like them just the way they are.
MARY: *(Nodding.)* Don't worry.

Lisa Soland

ALEXIS: And make sure the fill is even. One time, I came in and the girl made my nails too thick and I had to come back.

MARY: I do a good job. Trust me.

ALEXIS: *(Alexis rotates her head to loosen up her neck.)* It feels good to take a break.

MARY: You married?

ALEXIS: Yes, I am. He's an investment banker at Golden Slacks. *(Beat.)* That's a joke. It's really called Goldman Sachs. He does very well for himself. Of course, he'd have to, being married to me. *(Waits for a nod of recognition from Mary, but doesn't get one.)*

MARY: I married, once. My husband American soldier. He officer.

ALEXIS: Oh, I don't know anyone in the military.

MARY: Why not?

ALEXIS: Well, I'm not in that circle. I hope he was… Not all Americans are like that.

MARY: Like what?

ALEXIS: What?

MARY: Like what?

ALEXIS: Well, it's just that I've heard that soldiers in Vietnam would get girls like yourself pregnant, marry them, and then leave. Not all American men are like that.

MARY: You think he get me pregnant and leave?

(Alexis doesn't reply.)

MARY: He no left me. He died in Vietnam, fighting war. He a war hero. We love each other.

ALEXIS: I'm sorry, I just assumed…

MARY: What you know about war?

ALEXIS: Which one?

MARY: *(Annoyed.)* Vietnam!

ALEXIS: Well, I know that…it was very ugly.

MARY: *(Calmer.)* Yes, ugly… I married when I was sixteen. Then I have two children. They were beautiful. They look like their father. You want to see picture?

ALEXIS: Sure, why not.

(Mary shows the old photograph in the frame on the table.)

ALEXIS: They look very young here. How old are they now?

MARY: The boy, he was fourteen month and the girl two years old.

ALEXIS: How old are they now?

(Mary puts the picture back, slowly, gingerly. It is a treasure to her.)

MARY: You have children?

ALEXIS: Yes, two.

(Mary massages Alexis' hand.)

ALEXIS: Oh, I *love* the massage. It's the best part of a manicure.

MARY: *(Nods.)* You children in school?

ALEXIS: No, they are with their nanny.

MARY: How old?

ALEXIS: One is four months and the other is, no, one is six months and the other is three. One boy and one girl.

MARY: Like me.

ALEXIS: Uh huh.

MARY: You lucky.

ALEXIS: Thank you.

MARY: You husband successful, you have two children, you very lucky. You have nanny to raise children, so you don't have to.

ALEXIS: Nooo, I have a nanny so I get some things done.

MARY: *(Looks at packages.)* You like to shop, you have nanny for children. Where you children now?

ALEXIS: My children?

MARY: Yes, where are children? You know?

ALEXIS: Yes, of course I know. They are with their nanny. Are you almost done?

MARY: You not know where your children are?

ALEXIS: *(Astonished.)* They're with their nanny.

MARY: I was like you. I was very rich. In my country, we had people to care for us. I had woman care for my children. We had money. Before Saigon fall, my family have picnics. My clothes were handmade, very fine silk. We go to Hong Kong and get kimonos. My father, he have suits made of silk. We go to arts. My father was very influential. Did I say right? Influential?

ALEXIS: Yes.

MARY: But that not help in war. That not help my children. The Americans, they all start to leave Saigon. Everyone get scared. We not know what to do. My husband killed by Viet Cong, my father too... No one help us. Everyone just trying to get away. They close embassy. They only take Americans. I try to give them my children, they look like their papa, but they lock gates. We suppose to go because I married, but no one let us in. We saw the helicopter leaving. Pretty soon, there no one left to protect us. We know we in danger because we help Americans. My children and I, we try to escape, but nowhere

Lisa Soland

to go. Then the soldiers came. They take Saigon. I try to hide my children. I try to keep them safe. Everybody gone. No one help us. *(Beat.)* One night, they come to my house. Say they know we help Americans. Say people told them about us, that we traitors. They shot my father. He was old man. Then they take my children from me. They took my babies. I tried to stop them. I was screaming, but one of the soldiers hold me. I tried to get away, but the soldier, he only laughed. They say my children look like American so they shoot them. My baby was crying for me, and I couldn't do anything. Then they shoot me, but they not kill me. They thought I dead too. They left me. I saw them kill my children. I saw them, and I couldn't do anything. Then someone find me and hide me. I no want to live. Now I the only one left, so I come here.

ALEXIS: I'm sorry, I didn't know.

MARY: People say we were traitors. I not traitor, just in love. You understand? You lucky. What you do all day without children?

ALEXIS: Lots of things. I go to the gym, and meet friends, and I do some charity work.

MARY: You children be your charity.

ALEXIS: We don't need charity.

MARY: You no need charity? We all need charity. What you do with children when you away? They need Mama and Papa to teach them things like charity.

ALEXIS: My children are well cared for, and it's really none of your business. I'm sorry you lost your children, but don't take it out on me.

MARY: Yes?

ALEXIS: Yes. Are you finished?

MARY: Yes, I almost finished. *(Beat.)* You children, one day they grow up, or maybe one day they not there. I thought I protected, too. But I not. You Americans too busy for your children. There is nothing more important than them. I know. I know! If you no have money you have time with children. No choice. I wish I have more time with my children. Now they gone. I miss them. If you children gone forever, you miss them, too.

ALEXIS: *(Finally getting it.)* Yes, I would. I'm sorry. You must miss them very much.

MARY: Yes, I miss them very much. All I want is my family back. You lucky, you have your family.

ALEXIS: I guess I am.

MARY: *(Nods.)* You children are very precious.

ALEXIS: I know. The oldest one, Garrett, he is so smart. He already knows his ABC's. And the baby, Veronica, is already the apple of her dad's eye. He adores her…when he's home. He has to work late a lot, so he doesn't get to see them very much. They're usually asleep when he gets home, and he's always in a hurry in the morning. So it's just me.

MARY: Maybe you children need to have you not so busy like their father. Maybe they need you.

ALEXIS: *(Pondering.)* Maybe they do.

MARY: Good. All finished.

(Alexis gives her some money. Mary looks at the money.)

MARY: Thank you.

ALEXIS: *(Gets up to leave.)* You're welcome. And…thank you.

MARY: You're welcome.

(Alexis picks up bags and dials her cell phone while exiting stage.)

ALEXIS: Cissy? Hi, it's Alexis. How are you? Good, thanks. Hey, I am sooo sorry, but I can't make it for lunch today. Yes, I'm fine. I don't mean to beg out, but my children need me today. I hope I'm not ruining your day. Oh, good. Thanks for understanding. Maybe you can come over for lunch or we can meet in the park or something. Okay, thanks. I'll call you and we'll figure something out. Bye. *(She dials another number.)* Lupe? Where are you? Well, stay there. I want to take the children for lunch. I'll be there in about twenty minutes. Okay, bye. *(Before she hangs up.)* Wait! LUPE? Can I talk to Garrett? Hi, honey! It's Mommy. I'm going to meet you for lunch today. Would you like that?

(Alexis exits stage left. Mary laughs. Tiffany enters stage left.)

TIFFANY: Do you have time for a fill?

MARY: Yes, you have color?

TIFFANY: My nail broke and I need it fixed. I'm in a hurry. I'm meeting some friends.

MARY: Okay, don't worry.

TIFFANY: I brought my own polish.

MARY: Okay.

(Tiffany sets her bags down and sits across from Mary, who arranges a clean white towel in front of Tiffany.)

MARY: You married?

TIFFANY: Yes, I am.

MARY: You have children?

TIFFANY: Just one.

MARY: Your child in school?

TIFFANY: No, home with a babysitter.

MARY: You can bring child with you.

TIFFANY: *(She takes off her rings and bracelets.)* Thanks, but it's easier for me to leave her at home.

MARY: I see... Pretty jewelry.

TIFFANY: Thank you.

MARY: I have pretty jewelry once...

(Blackout.)

END OF PLAY

Biography

Cameron Hite received his BA from Maryville College in Theatre Studies and English. He wrote and starred in his one-person show on Tourettes called, *Impulse*, and the play premiered in the Haslam Family Flex Theatre, October 3, 2014. With three other friends, Cameron started the State Theater Project, an endeavor focused on the revitalization, renovation, and reopening of an abandoned theater in downtown Kingsport, Tennessee. Cameron presides as the Executive Artistic Director of the State Theatre Company, Inc.

Move-In Day

Ⓐ

Cameron J. Hite

Move-In Day was written in a playwriting class at Maryville College, taught by Lisa Soland. The play received a staged reading in "12 x 10 x 2" and was produced at the Clayton Center for the Arts on April 28, 2012.

CHARACTERS

    CHARLIE PETERSON: A freshman in college, 18.
    GREG STEVENS: Charlie's roommate, 18.
    JEFF: Charlie and Greg's neighbor, 18.

SETTING

    A college dorm room at a University.

TIME

    Fall, mid-afternoon.

• • • • • • • • • • • •

We are in a dorm room with two beds, two desks, and two chairs. Charlie is stage left, unpacking various boxes. Greg enters carrying two boxes and doesn't say a word. Charlie fails to notice Greg at first. Greg crosses stage right and begins to unload his desk accessories. It is apparent that he is afraid to approach his new roommate. Unsure of what to do, Greg continues to unpack his belongings. Charlie finally notices that his new roommate has arrived, and turns to Greg, hoping to say something to greet him. But neither says anything, so they both continue to unpack their belongings. After a long, awkward silence, they both look at each other, then instantly turn away. Finally, Charlie sighs and speaks.

CHARLIE: Greg, right?

GREG: *(Looking to Charlie with ease, yet still nervous.)* Um, yeah. Greg Stevens. Charlie...Peterson?

CHARLIE: Yep, that's me! How long have you been in here?

GREG: I'm sorry I didn't say anything when I walked in. I'm not really the conversationalist type.

CHARLIE: No, no, it's fine. *(Tries to appeal to Greg's humor, if there is any.)* I'm really in the zone right now with all of this unpacking business.

GREG: Right.

    (Greg continues unpacking. They say nothing else. Another awkward silence is created as Charlie turns again toward Greg to say something, but instead turns back to his box. A few moments later, Charlie finally breaks the silence again.)

CHARLIE: Okay, this isn't going to work. What's wrong?

GREG: *(Confused.)* What do you mean what's wrong?

CHARLIE: I mean what's your deal, man? You sneak in on move-in day, you don't even say one word to your new roommate, and you just go on putting your stuff away like no one else is in the room! Would a "Hey,

237

roomie, how's it going?" kill you? I think not.

GREG: No, it's not like that at all. I'm just a shy person at first. I told you I wasn't a conversation-type. *(Exits with one of his boxes.)*

CHARLIE: Hey, wait a second! Greg! Come on, man, I was just messin' around with you! You don't have to leave! *(Pause.)* Great. Just great. *(Pause.)* I've been here for 10 minutes and I already scared my roommate away. Way to go, Charlie, you sure can spark conversation.

GREG: *(He enters with sarcastic enthusiasm.)* Well, hello there roomie! Boy, what a lovely day it is outside! Have you seen the sun today? It is absolutely GORGEOUS! Even though this is our first time talking, I'm sure we'll get along great from the get-go!

CHARLIE: *(Crossing arms, sternly.)* Okay, now you're just being a jackass. I wasn't saying you had to walk in here like you're Pee Wee Herman. I was just trying to tell you that you didn't have to be shy around me.

GREG: *(Crosses to imaginary 'halfway' line dividing the room.)* I was just trying to give you the roommate you wanted!

CHARLIE: *(Crosses toward Greg until their noses are touching.)* Yeah, but I didn't ask for some Disney channel television host to waltz in and tell me the forecast!

(There is a pause, then Greg bursts with laughter. Charlie is slow to start laughing, but eventually they are both cracking up.)

GREG: Look, I'm sorry. I'm really not much of a talker. I probably shouldn't have been that much of a jerk. Honestly, I'm surprised I even had the guts to do that whole re-entrance thing.

CHARLIE: No, no! It's fine! I was the jerk. Actually, I should have been the one to talk first, but I just didn't.

GREG: Well, it's all right. I mean, we've never even talked to each other before today, so what can we expect?

CHARLIE: *(Chuckling.)* Yeah, I guess you're right... So, I've actually got a couple boxes left in my car, so I'm just gonna run down to the parking lot and get those real quick. *(Crosses to door.)*

GREG: Okay! Do you need help with anything? I could help you carry one of the boxes...

CHARLIE: *(Stops and turns to Greg.)* No, no. I got it, man. It's no problem! I'm sure you've got a lot to unpack too, so when I get back we can start to get to know each other better!

GREG: All right. That sounds like a deal!

(Charlie exits.)

GREG: Wow, what a freak.

(Greg continues to unpack, but grows curious as to what is in his roommate's box across the room, by his roommate's bed. He slowly crosses to the box, opens it, and peers inside. At first, Greg pulls out simple, everyday items like a hairbrush, some books, a small lamp, then makes a huge discovery. Shocked at what he has found, he holds it up. It is a large, extremely sharp knife. Greg is worried and shocked.)

GREG: Holy sh…!!! What is this? Is this guy gonna kill me in my sleep?

(Their neighbor, Jeff enters.)

JEFF: Hey, neighbor! I was just walking down the hall and saw that your door was open so I thought I would drop in and introduce myself! My name is Jeff, and… *(Finally notices what Greg is holding up.)* Holy mother of Excalibur, that is a large knife.

GREG: Oh, no! This isn't my knife! It's my roommate's knife.

JEFF: Oh, thank God! Or are you just saying that because you don't want me to predict the fact that you're a psycho knife murderer?

GREG: What?! Are you kidding me? No, not at all! I've never even seen a knife this big in person. I swear this is my roommate's.

JEFF: Okay, okay, I believe you! Who is your roommate? *(Immediately answers his own question.)* Wait a second. Is your roommate…Charlie Peterson?

GREG: Uh, yeah? How did you know that? Do you know Charlie?

JEFF: What, are you kiddin' me? You think that I'd associate myself with Charlie Peterson? Greg, first rule of college, don't ever do random roommate selection.

GREG: What's so bad about him?

JEFF: Oh, man. Well, I'll just be on my way then. I'm gonna go back to my room and lock the door. I've got a lot of unpacking to do myself. *(Exits.)*

GREG: No! Wait! You didn't even answer my question! Come on, Jeff!

(Greg grows more worried with each passing second. He doesn't know what to do about the knife. After a few seconds of looking at it, he puts the knife back in the box along with Charlie's other belongings and closes the box, leaving it exactly how he found it.)

CHARLIE: *(Enters carrying two boxes.)* Hey, roomie! Could you help me with this top box?

GREG: *(Still startled.)* Um, yeah, sure! No problem!

(Greg takes the top box and sets it on the ground beside Charlie's bed.)

CHARLIE: Ah, thanks dude! So, how about we get to know each other a little better? I feel so bad for going off on you earlier. I feel like I really kinda messed things up between us, so we should start all over. Deal?

GREG: *(Scared.)* Yeah, yeah, of course! You've got a good *point*… I mean *idea*.

That is a *good idea.*

CHARLIE: *(Confused.)* Um, all right... Actually, first, you're gonna have to let me go leak the lizard.

GREG: Um... *(Confused.)* What?

CHARLIE: Leak the lizard? You know, like "break the seal."

GREG: *(Confused.)* On...what?

CHARLIE: I'm gonna go number one, Greg. I'm gonna "pay the water bill," "drain the main vein," "take a whiz..." Ya know – PEE!

GREG: *(Finally understanding.)* OH!!! You're going to go pee! Ah, yeah! Please, go ahead. And when you get back, we'll start cuttin' up! I mean, you know, laughing and being friends and stuff.

CHARLIE: *(Suspicious of Greg.)* All right, I'll be back. *(Exits.)*

JEFF: *(Enters.)* Greg?! Are you dead???

GREG: No! I'm not dead. *(Confused.)* Why would I be dead?!

JEFF: *(Looking around for Charlie.)* Because of you-know-who...

GREG: Charlie? My new roommate?

JEFF: *(Reassuringly.)* Ah, that's right. You still know him as Charlie. You know, it's probably nothing to worry about.

GREG: *(Grabs Jeff by shirt collar.)* Listen to me! Either you tell me what is wrong with my roommate or I swear I will find a use for that knife! *(Beat.)* The way I see it is, if my roommate is a cold-blooded murderer, or some kind of psychopath, he's not only a threat to me, his roommate, but also you, the nosey neighbor who lives down the hall and for some reason only speaks in some sort of ambiguous warning code. And let me tell you, I'll make Charlie my best friend. Oh, yeah, I'll help him with his homework, I'll remind him to brush his teeth at night, I'll be the best wingman to girls – or guys, if that's his thing, I don't know yet – either way, I'll show him my worth. I'll win his trust, and I'll make you the target. I'll make sure that Charlie associates the name "Jeff" with the word "death." I'll get a copy of your room key, even, from the R.A. – who I will also befriend because he is undoubtedly a stereotypical R.A., meaning he is an avid Star Wars fan. And, after a night of staying up, talking about the "brilliant" depth of Star Wars' epic storyline, and watching whichever movie it is where Darth Vader says he's Luke's father, he'll accidentally doze off and I'll take his master key. So watch your back, little piggy. *(Greg is breathing viciously.)*

JEFF: *(Scared, but blunt.)* Greg, you're a sociopath. *(Beat, before Greg can speak.)* And, Darth Vader actually never said that he was Luke's father. It's actually one of the most misquoted lines in cinematic —

GREG: WHO CARES?! Look, I'm not gonna be the target of a psychopath before I know what sex feels like.

JEFF: So, if I get you laid, you won't make me the target and you'll let Charlie kill you?

GREG: No, that's not the point at all. The point is that if my roommate is a psychopath, I deserve to know. Now, tell me, what's his deal?

JEFF: *(Easing up.)* Well, let's just say Charlie has been known to have anger problems. You see, we went to the same high school, but I never really saw him in a good mood because usually the football guys were pickin' on him. So, one day he snapped.

GREG: *(Shocked.)* What'd he do?

JEFF: I don't think I should say.

GREG: *(Anxious.)* What did he do?!

JEFF: *(Noticing Charlie's approach.)* Oh, shoot! Here he comes! See ya later, Greg! Just don't piss him off!

(Jeff crosses to exit, and walks by Charlie just as Charlie's entering.)

JEFF: Hey, Charlie! Lookin' *sharp*! *(Jeff winks at Greg, then exits.)*

GREG: *(Frustrated.)* What?! Jeff, please! Wait!

CHARLIE: Um... Who's Jeff? What?! *(Confused.)*

GREG: *(Scared, but regains composure.)* Oh, Jeff. Yeah, he's our neighbor... Anyway, let's, uh, re-introduce ourselves!

CHARLIE: Um, all right. *(Enthusiastic.)* Well, how are ya! My name is Charlie Peterson. *(They shake hands.)*

GREG: *(Nervously.)* Hi! My name is Greg Stabbings – Stevens. Greg Stevens, nice to meet you.

CHARLIE: What'd you say?

GREG: What? I said my name. Greg Stevens.

CHARLIE: I'm pretty sure I heard you say, Greg "Stabbings."

(Greg looks nervously to the box with the large knife in it.)

GREG: What? That's crazy. I definitely said Stevens.

CHARLIE: Hm... Okay, if you say so.

(Charlie returns to unpacking, while Greg grows even more anxious. Jeff enters, and careful to not be seen by Charlie, Jeff makes a cutting motion across his throat. Greg motions for Jeff to go away. Jeff ducks out. Charlie turns to Greg.)

CHARLIE: Did you say something?

GREG: Huh? No, I didn't say anything.

CHARLIE: Hm... Okay.

(A brief moment of silence, then both return to unpacking their boxes. After a few

Lisa Soland

moments, Greg is unable to take the tension any longer, and breaks down.)
GREG: Okay, man. I gotta ask. What the hell is in that box?
CHARLIE: The one by my bed?
GREG: Yes! The one by your bed! What's in it?
CHARLIE: Well, I think that one has some books in it. Why?
GREG: Books? That's it?
CHARLIE: Yes! BOOKS! Why do you ask?!
(Greg crosses to the box and begins to unload it. After removing the nonlethal objects, Greg pulls out the large knife.)
GREG: I'm asking because of this!
(Charlie laughs hysterically.)
GREG: What is so funny?! Oh God, you're a psycho knife murderer aren't you?! Are you going to kill me? Because you shouldn't! My parents are gonna be calling me soon to make sure I'm all unpacked and settled in! And, I'm a great wingman. So, we could go out cruisin' for chicks – or dudes – you know, whatever your preference is...just don't kill me in my sleep, all right?
CHARLIE: *(Stops laughing.)* WHAT?! Are you kidding me? Do you seriously think I am a psycho knife murderer? Of all the things in the world you could assume, you automatically assume the worst?!
GREG: *(Somewhat relieved.)* Wait, so you're not going to kill me in my sleep?
CHARLIE: *(Over-dramatic and sarcastic.)* Yes. I am going to kill you. I am going to take this knife and gut you like a fish. There is nothing more that I hate in this world than a new, non-conversationalist roommate that peruses my boxes of murdering weapons. For your actions, you must pay me with your life...
(Long pause. Greg looks to Charlie, unsure of whether or not what he just heard was true.)
CHARLIE: No, Greg, I'm not going to kill you. Are you crazy?
GREG: Then why the hell do you have that big of a knife? At college?!
CHARLIE: Greg, this knife has been passed down in my family for many generations. My great-great-grandfather gave this knife to my great-grand father after serving in the military, and my great-grand-father just decided to keep the tradition going. So, my dad gave me the knife when I left to come to college.
GREG: *(Thoroughly relieved.)* Oh, thank God.
CHARLIE: Wait, why were you going through my stuff, though?
GREG: *(Bluntly.)* You know, I think we should start over. I feel bad for going off on you earlier...

CHARLIE: *(Laughing.)* You know what? Oddly, I don't even care about you going through my stuff. Let's start over.

GREG: *(Relieved.)* All right, deal.

(They shake hands, then both continue to unpack. After a moment of silence, Charlie looks around the room.)

CHARLIE: Hey, have you seen my tarantula? He was in a box by my bed.

GREG: *(Laughing.)* Yeah, good one.

CHARLIE: No, seriously.

(Greg jumps on his bed and screams.)

(Blackout.)

END OF PLAY

Biography

Craig Pospisil is an award-winning playwright and filmmaker. He is the author of *Months on End*, *Somewhere In Between*, *The Dunes*, *Life is Short* and *Choosing Sides*, all published by Dramatists Play Service. His plays have been produced in New York, Los Angeles, and around the United States, in more than a dozen countries on six continents, and translated into Cantonese, Dutch, French, Greek and Spanish. His short film *January* has been accepted into sixteen festivals, including the Adirondack, Bahamas, Berkshire, Big Apple, Cayman Island, Hollywood Sky and Roma Cinema international film festivals. He has also written the musicals *Drift* and *Dot Comet*, and over 60 short plays, including *It's Not You* (theAtrainplays, Vol. 1), *On The Edge* (Best Ten-Minute Plays: 2005), *Dissonance* (Best American Short Plays 2010-2011), and *There's No Here Here* (Best American Short Plays 2014-2015). www.CraigPospisil.com

Perchance

Craig Pospisil

Perchance was originally written for and produced by the 24 Hour Plays (Tina Fallon, Kurt Gardner, Lindsay Bowen and Philip Naude, producers) at the Atlantic Theatre in New York City. It was directed by Mark Lonergan, and the cast was as follows: Robbie – Scott Wood, Cass – Liz Elkins, Antonio – Matt Saldivar, and Cynthia / Ticket Agent / Gate Agent – Carla Rzeszewski.

CHARACTERS

> ROBBIE: a man in his 20s, 30s, or 40s.
> CASS: his girlfriend.
> ANTONIO: Cass' new boyfriend.
> CYNTHIA: Robbie's sister.
> TICKET AGENT: airport worker, can be played by actress playing Cynthia.
> GATE AGENT: airport worker, can be played by actressa playing Cynthia.

SETTING

> Open stage, various locations.

TIME

> The present, more or less.

• • • • • • • • • • • •

The actors enter and take positions around the stage. Cass, Antonio and Cynthia face away from the audience. Robbie, however, faces the audience.

ROBBIE: It's kind of hazy, but what I remember is: Cass and I are in love. It's not perfect. I'm not going to lie and tell you that. But it was good, and I was happy. I didn't always know I was happy. In fact, sometimes I was downright miserable. And I don't just mean a little blue. I mean really depressed. And I'm not much fun to be around when I'm like that. I get pretty negative, call myself a failure. Things like that. I'm not suicidal or anything. Just depressed. A lot. Like everybody else, really. Just your average New Yorker, who was on Paxil for a while, but didn't like the sexual side effects, so tried Celexa, but that was worse, so then went on Wellbutrin for a couple years, and that was fine, but now is off the medication. *(Slight pause.)* Anyway Cass and I are in love. We live together. We've got a great life, good friends, terrific sex. Cass and me. With each other, not with the friends. As far as I know. *(Slight pause.)* Anyway, one morning —
 (Cass turns and faces inward, entering the scene.)
CASS: I think I'm in love with someone else and I'm moving to San Diego.
ROBBIE: What?!
CASS: Robbie, it just isn't working between the two of us.

ROBBIE: How can you say that?

CASS: Because I think I'm in love with someone else, and I'm moving to San Diego.

ROBBIE: You can't be serious. When did this happen?

CASS: Well, I bought the plane ticket online last night.

ROBBIE: Last night?! You mean, before we went to Chez Josephine for our anniversary?

CASS: No, after that.

ROBBIE: We fell into bed and had sex right after dinner.

CASS: Yeah, it was after that too. I waited until you fell asleep, then I went online and got a really cheap ticket on Last Minute Travel.com. Then I called Antonio.

ROBBIE: Antonio?

CASS: He's this amazing guy I met at that publishing conference in Denver last month.

(Antonio turns and faces the scene. He is suave and self-assured.)

ANTONIO: Hello.

ROBBIE: Then she tells me about Denver.

(Robbie steps back and watches the scene.)

ANTONIO: You have the look of someone whose life has stagnated and who now longs for a fresh stream in which to swim.

CASS: Oh my god! How did you know?

ANTONIO: It is my gift. So, why does someone so beautiful look so sad?

CASS: I don't know if I can talk about this.

ANTONIO: Very well. I don't mean to intrude.

CASS: *(In a rush.)* You see, the thing is I've been living with my boyfriend, who I love, for four years, and things are great…but they're exactly the same as they were at the beginning.

ANTONIO: And you long for change.

CASS: I don't know. Maybe. I mean, things are good. Sort of. But things should change, right?

ANTONIO: Change is the essence of life. To deny change is to deny life itself.

CASS: Exactly. I mean, it's not like I'm one of those women who needs to be married, but after this much time shouldn't we be moving that way?

(Robbie steps forward, addressing Cass.)

ROBBIE: Wait! I've been thinking about asking you to marry me.

CASS: *(To Robbie.)* Well, how do I know that?

ANTONIO: I would marry you today.

CASS: What?

ROBBIE: You have got to be kidding me.

ANTONIO: You have to be bold when you feel a connection like this with another person. I have missed enough chances in my life to know I would rather take a chance than not.

CASS: *(To Robbie.)* I'm going to San Diego.

(Cass and Antonio turn upstage. Robbie turns to the audience again.)

ROBBIE: And she goes into the bedroom and starts packing. And I...I don't know what to do. My life's just exploded in my face and...and I leave. I walk out the door and just start walking. Until I find myself at my sister's home.

(Cynthia, wearing a robe or dressing gown, turns and faces Robbie.)

CYNTHIA: The kids were a nightmare this morning. Brandie insisted she's going to school in her Cinderella costume from last Halloween, and Andrew couldn't find his English homework. And Joel didn't lift a finger to help me get the kids ready. I mean, I've got work to do too. Maybe it's not a 9 to 5 job like Mr. Advertising, but I've got to turn on the computer and start tapping away. You want some coffee?

ROBBIE: Cass is leaving me.

CYNTHIA: Oh my god. What did you do?

ROBBIE: Me?!

CYNTHIA: Have you been ignoring her?

ROBBIE: No!

CYNTHIA: Have you been all, "Oh, I'm so depressed, and I'm such a failure. Why is everything in my life so terrible?"

ROBBIE: *(Unconvincingly.)* No.

CYNTHIA: Oh, Robbie. What are you going to do?

ROBBIE: What can I do? She's leaving me for this impulsive jerk, who asked her to marry him the same night he met her. *(Slight pause.)* What kills me is I went shopping for an engagement ring while she was in Denver. I was going to propose to her last night.

CYNTHIA: Why didn't you?

ROBBIE: I didn't find a ring I liked.

CYNTHIA: Oh, my god! If you wanted to propose, you should've just proposed! All right, look, if you want her, you've got to do some serious groveling. Where is she?

ROBBIE: On her way to Kennedy.

CYNTHIA: Then you better haul ass. And bring a gift. Something romantic.

(Cynthia turns away. She ditches her robe and quickly ties a colorful scarf around her neck, morphing into Ticket Agent, as Robbie faces the audience again.)

ROBBIE: So I run out and flag down a cab to the airport, which takes
forever and costs me 80 bucks but I finally get there. Her flight for
San Diego leaves from gate 15 but, I can't get there without a ticket.

TICKET AGENT: Can I help you?

ROBBIE: Yeah, I'd like a ticket please.

TICKET AGENT: *(Pause, waiting.)* ...for what destination?

ROBBIE: Anywhere.

TICKET AGENT: I'm sorry. I don't understand, sir.

ROBBIE: What's your cheapest ticket to anywhere?

TICKET AGENT: I need a destination, sir.

ROBBIE: Okay, ah, how about Newark?

TICKET AGENT: Newark?

ROBBIE: Fine, ah, Washington. Is there a shuttle to Washington?

TICKET AGENT: Yes.

ROBBIE: Great. One ticket. One way.

TICKET AGENT: Just one way?

ROBBIE: Look, I'm not really flying anywhere. I need to get to one of the
gates.

(Ticket Agent stares at him like he's insane or a terrorist or both.)

TICKET AGENT: So, you want a ticket just so you can get through
security, is that right?

ROBBIE: No, no, I'm kidding. Don't worry, I'm not a terrorist. I swear.
Forget I even said the word "terrorist." Make that ticket round trip.
And first class.

(Robbie holds out a credit card, which Ticket Agent takes, giving him a ticket.)

ROBBIE: Somehow I get through security in time.

(Cass turns around. She carries a small overnight bag.)

CASS: Robbie, what are you doing here?

ROBBIE: You can't go.

CASS: Don't do this.

ROBBIE: Please. I love you.

(Antonio turns around and moves to Cass.)

ANTONIO: My darling. I couldn't wait for your plane to arrive in San Diego,
so I flew here overnight so we could begin our new adventure
together right away.

ROBBIE: This cannot be happening.

ANTONIO: Who is this?

CASS: This is Robbie.

ANTONIO: *(Suppressing a laugh.)* Yes, I understand your desire for change.

(Turning back to Cass.) I brought you a gift. This bottle is full of sand I found on the beaches of Ipanema. Some day I will take you there.

ROBBIE: Hey, I got you a gift too.

(He takes a deck of playing cards out of his pocket. Cass takes them and looks at them, clearly unimpressed.)

CASS: A deck of cards?

ROBBIE: It was all they had at the gift shop.

(Ticket Agent now turns back around as Gate Agent.)

GATE AGENT: Ladies and gentlemen, flight 819 for San Diego is ready for boarding. We will begin seating passengers in rows 20 and above.

ANTONIO: Shall we go?

CASS: I'm sorry, Robbie. I love you, but I have to go.

ROBBIE: Marry me.

CASS: What?

ROBBIE: Marry me. I don't have a ring for you or a bottle of sand, but I love you and I want to spend my life with you. I just want to make you happy.

(Antonio begins pulling Cass away, toward Gate Agent and the door to the plane.)

CASS: Robbie, I…

GATE AGENT: Now, boarding all rows. Final boarding call.

ROBBIE: He doesn't love you. He doesn't know you. He doesn't know you like to sleep with that orange teddy bear or that you're always exactly ten minutes late to everything.

ANTONIO: *(To Cass.)* I know the real you.

(Antonio leads Cass away, but she looks back. Robbie follows, handing his ticket to Gate Agent.)

GATE AGENT: This ticket is for Washington, DC, sir.

ROBBIE: I just need to talk to her.

GATE AGENT: I'm sorry, sir. You can't get on this plane.

ROBBIE: Cass!

GATE AGENT: Sir, please step back or I'll have to call security!

ROBBIE: Please don't go!

(Robbie tries to get on the plane, but Gate Agent wrestles him away from the door. Cass tries to move towards Robbie, but Antonio still pulls her away.)

CASS: Robbie!

ROBBIE: Cass! Marry me!

CASS: Yes! Yes, I'll marry you!

(Robbie and Cass reach for each other. The scene shifts into slow motion as Robbie and Cass break free from Gate Agent and Antonio, who are slowly spun away,

Lisa Soland

before finally facing upstage in the original positions. Robbie and Cass run towards each other. They do not touch, but spin around each other, somehow missing with Cass turning away, upstage to her original position, and Robbie coming back downstage to face the audience again.)

ROBBIE: And then I woke up. *(Slight pause.)* It took me a minute, because I'd been in a deep sleep, and you know how it can take a while to get your bearings. What's real, what was the dream. *(Slight pause.)* But then I remember. I never went to the airport or tried to stop her. I never proposed. And she never came back.

(The lights fade on Robbie and the others.)

END OF PLAY

Biography

Leonard Lively is a Theatre and Religion double major at Maryville College. He has performed as "The Cat in the Hat" in *Seussical* (Maryville College), "Whitney" in *The Stonewater Rapture* (Maryville College), and has performed in many local professional productions at The Cumberland County Playhouse.

Priscilla: The Tap Dancing Donkey
A Cautionary "Tail"

Leonard Lively

Priscilla: The Tap Dancing Donkey was written as part of the playwriting course at Maryville College in spring of 2016. *Priscilla* was then given a public reading in "Splattered Ink, Neatly Arranged," the playwriting performance that presented the work of the Maryville College playwrights.

CHARACTERS

> REPORTER: A documentarian between 20 and 30. Any gender.
> PRISCILLA: Either gender, but must be able to tap dance.
> VETERINARIAN: Either gender between 30 and 50.
> MARY-SUE: A young country bumpkin. 8-15.
> STANLEY: A middle-aged dad.
> BRITTANY: A new mom with a good heart. 20-40.
> FARMER JIM: A rough but well-meaning man. Middle age to 60s.

SETTING

> A blank stage, signifying various locations, with a platform upstage.

• • • • • • • • • • • •

Reporter, in a tailored suit (think Matt Lauer), stands downstage right, in the process of filming a documentary. Priscilla, the tap dancing donkey, stands on the upstage platform, motionless.

REPORTER: *(Speaking into a cord-less microphone.)* Priscilla was this country's first and foremost Donkey tap dancer. Some consider her the creator, innovator, and designer of the single, greatest breakthrough of the twentieth century: the tap-dancing donkey. Yes. You heard me correctly. A tap-dancing Ass. *(Beat.)* She tap-danced like no donkey has ever done and will ever do again.

(Priscilla does a dapper soft-shoe. Reporter pulls out an encyclopedia and reads.)

REPORTER: "Equus asinus. A tawdry beast of burden, the donkey has worked together with humanity for millennia. The American West was won by the donkey, and the Industrial Revolution was built on their backs. Donkeys built the railroads and dug the mines, and even George Washington bred donkeys in his spare time."

(Priscilla stomps on her platform stage and stares dumbly at the audience.)

REPORTER: "The domesticated ass is often noted for its stubborn, quiet, and humble nature. This exquisite creature is often characterized as stupid. This is an extreme mistake."

(Reporter directs the audience's attention to Priscilla.)

PRISCILLA: Hee-haw!

Lisa Soland

REPORTER: What a marvel! *(Puts encyclopedia away.)* Priscilla was purchased from the local band of traveling gypsies by a local hickseed named Farmer Jim. Smart he was not, but it didn't take him long to recognize Priscilla's talents. When asked about his discovery, he said, "She was in the barn and I noticed she was tap dancing. That's how I learned that she could tap dance."

(Priscilla taps, then brays.)

REPORTER: Initially Farmer Jim was scared for Priscilla's well-being. He asked himself, "Is it healthy for a donkey to tap dance?" Then he called the local Veterinarian.

(Veterinarian enters and Reporter crosses to meet him.)

VETERINARIAN: Farmer Jim called me on the phone and said he had this donkey with a "special talent" but he wouldn't tell me what it was over the phone. I drove out to the farm and met Priscilla standing out in the field. She was a nice animal – rusty grey, barrel-chested with pretty ears, nine inches long. She chomped on a mouthful of grass, kind of like a bored teenager chewing gum. But there was something about her. I couldn't take my eyes off of her. I could have watched her chew hay for five hours.

(Priscilla chews hay while the Veterinarian watches her for almost too long.)

VETERINARIAN: Then, all of a sudden, she started moving her feet real funny. I thought she was trying to kick flies away but soon I realized that it had a rhythm to it. She was dancing! As sure as I'm standing in front of you, this donkey broke out into a tap dance that would put Gene Kelly to shame. She was jumping up and down and chassé-ing around the field. I swear that at one point she picked up a stick with her mouth and danced with it like it was a cane.

(Priscilla tap dances.)

REPORTER: How did you react when you saw the tap dancing donkey for the first time?

VETERINARIAN: I thought, "Farmer Jim is sitting on a cash cow." Or I mean donkey. If he markets Priscilla correctly, he could be a very rich man. Actually, I'm the one who first suggested that Priscilla could be a star. Then Farmer Jim asked me if I would really pay to see a tap dancing donkey. Well, I personally wouldn't but then again I don't think comedy is funny. *(Exits.)*

REPORTER: From then on Farmer Jim put all his efforts into making Priscilla the most famous tap dancing donkey the world has ever seen, and in turn filled his pockets with more cash than an ass.

(Priscilla turns away, grunts, and chews hay.)

REPORTER: Priscilla never failed to charm everyone she encountered –
women, children, the misunderstood.

(Mary-Sue, a young country bumpkin, enters and the Reporter approaches her.)

MARY-SUE: *(In a hyperbole of a southern drawl; think Honey Boo-Boo.)* I
remember the first time I saw her. My daddy took me to the state
fair to ride the rides and eat the funn-uhl cakes and visit with the pigs.
I loved them piggies. I jumped in to the piggy cage to hug and play
with them cute, little porkers. And as I was frolicin' in the mud, the
most captivatin' creature walked up on me. This grey donkey, about
as tall as I am, just starin' at me with the most intense look in her
eyes.

*(Mary-Sue turns to face Priscilla in utter fixation and wonder. Priscilla stares
blankly into the audience, then bends down to eat some grass.)*

MARY-SUE: Then this donkey started hoppin' around in the mud, splashing
me and the pigs with manure.

(Priscilla demonstrates the dance.)

MARY-SUE: It looked awful funny but then a bunch of people started
crowdin' around the donkey pen. They was shoutin'.

*(Brittany, Farmer Jim, and Stanley take on the characters of amazed, poorly
educated fair spectators.)*

BRITTANY: *(As Sara-Jane, the farmer's daughter.)* This donkey's amazin'!

FARMER JIM: *(As Ol' Man Jenkins, the creepy neighbor.)* This donkey's a marvel!

STANLEY: *(As Timmy, the village idiot.)* This donkey is spec-tack-u-lr!

MARY-SUE: Then this guy in fancy clothes came up to Farmer Jim with
some papers and judgin' by Farmer Jim's reaction, it said some pretty
nice things on it, 'cause he was a hoopin' and a hollerin' and such.

REPORTER: How did your encounter with Priscilla affect your life?

MARY-SUE: After my daddy fished me outta the mud and took me back
home to Momma, I couldn't stop thinkin' about that donkey. I didn't
even know her name but it was like my mind was stuck on her. So I
went into Momma's craft box and pulled out the paper maché and
made myself a donkey head, which I put on my bedside table, with
lots of candles all around it. And I'd just stare into them paper maché
donkey eyes for hours and hours. Eyes so blue you could drown in
'em, and not think about a thing. *(Beat.)* 'Cause that was the gift
Priscilla really gave me – the gift of not thinkin'. *(Exits.)*

REPORTER: These words have been used to describe Priscilla: Candid.
Integrious. American. Cantankerous. Hilarious. Talented. Average.

Lisa Soland

Complicated. Simple. Sexy. Wet. Exorcist. Not mean. Whatever she was, the public went nuts. Most cited Priscilla's unique, custom-made horse tap shoes as what originally caught their eyes. And her special, stubborn, intense, endearing way she stared into the side of her stall while chewing hay.

(Priscilla, standing, stares off right, dumbly chewing.)

REPORTER: Many people's lives were changed by a chance meeting with Priscilla. People of all colors and shapes. Sometimes those shapes were even fat people.

(Stanley, a fat, American, middle-aged father, enters and Reporter approaches him.)

STANLEY: Priscilla was like a rock-and-roll star for my daughter. For her seventh birthday, she begged us to take her to see Priscilla and I couldn't say no to my little princess. We were in the front row! Priscilla was so close we could almost touch her. Then suddenly Priscilla hoof-selected my daughter out of the crowd by kicking her right in the jaw. *(Beat.)* It shattered in nine places!

REPORTER: Did you attempt to sue Farmer Jim for damages?

STANLEY: Priscilla personally selected my daughter out of the entire audience to kick. Why would I want to sue? I don't know why Priscilla chose her. I'm figuring my daughter has potential that Priscilla recognized. Or maybe Priscilla liked her donkey face paint. Or maybe my daughter's face was just in the right place at the right time. *(Shrugs.)* Anyway, my daughter told me that she didn't want us to take her to the hospital. She wanted to keep her broken jaw just the way it was – broken. It's something that makes her unique. A present from Priscilla. *(Exits.)*

REPORTER: Farmer Jim invested all of his time and effort into expanding Priscilla's fame from a regional celebrity to a worldwide phenomenon. He spent every minute with her – brushing her mane, cleaning her hooves, and teaching her new, dapper routines. Some might say that Priscilla grew into an obsession for Farmer Jim. He was known to refer to himself as "Priscilla," and vice versa. Some might compare Farmer Jim to Michael Jackson's father. An unhealthy relationship it was. He kept her locked away in the barn, not allowed to frolic and graze with the other donkeys on the farm, for fear of disease. She was forced to practice her act for fourteen hours a day. Some might even say that Farmer Jim knew how to make dat ass dance.

(Reporter sighs. Priscilla practices her routine, obviously exhausted.)

30 Short Plays for Passionate Actors

REPORTER: Even though Priscilla suffered day and night, she meant so many things to so many people. Some of those people were stupid. Some of those stupid people were nice.

(Brittany enters. Reporter approaches.)

BRITTANY: My husband and I wanted to have a baby. We tried and tried but it seemed hopeless. The doctors told me I was infertile and the news destroyed us. All we wanted was to start our own family. *(Beat.)* I was so depressed that I didn't leave the house for two months. Then finally my best friend invited me to see Priscilla's show. She said it would be good for me to get dressed up and fix my hair and venture out into the world again. I didn't try to argue with her. So I went.

REPORTER: Please tell our at-home viewing audience about your personal encounter with Priscilla.

BRITTANY: After the show, my friend and I waited by the stage door. When Priscilla came out, she stared at me with an intense, blank stare and shuffled over to me. We looked eye-to-eye and then she nuzzled my belly with her snout. My belly started to feel kind of like a warm buttered roll. Then Priscilla just looked into my eyes again and brayed.

(Priscilla brays loudly towards the audience.)

BRITTANY: When I got home I said to my husband, "Hey. Let's go to bed and make a baby." And he started crying. He said, "It's no use. We've tried and tried and it's no use. It'll just make us sad." It was then I told him about my meeting with Priscilla and how I think I am now able to conceive a child. *(Beat.)* So I told him that I would wear these red high heels that he likes. Well, I put on my stilettos, walked on his face, and he up and nailed me like a railroad track. *(Beat.)* You're going to cut that, right?

REPORTER: No.

BRITTANY: Oh, okay. *(Beat.)*

REPORTER: How did you react when you learned that you were pregnant?

BRITTANY: Well, there was a lot of crying, like I said, but there was also a lot of joy. Joy mostly in the form of crying. *(Beat.)* We had a girl. We named her Priscilla. My husband and I are so grateful for Priscilla's blessing, more than you can imagine. It has changed our entire lives. Our daughter is going into fourth grade in the fall. She's really stubborn. And if we try to make her do her chores she just stares at us and starts kicking.

REPORTER: Like a donkey?

Lisa Soland

(Brittany takes a moment to think and reflect. She sighs.)

BRITTANY: Yes. Like a donkey. *(Looks upwards.)* Thank you.

REPORTER: Priscilla's glory came to an abrupt halt when she appeared on American Bandstand with Dick Clark. She came out to perform her number in front of millions of viewers all across the country but her loyal fans noticed that Priscilla was acting abnormally. Her music came on but Priscilla didn't budge, like she was stubborn or something. Farmer Jim rushed out on to the stage in front of the cameras and yelled at her.

(During the following line Priscilla looks around in panic and exits. Reporter reacts in utter horror.)

FARMER JIM: *(Ethereal, from offstage.)* Dance! Dance, bitch! Get away Dick, no, no, get away. Dance! *(Softly singing, crazy.)* "Bandstand, Bandstand..."

(Priscilla looks around in panic and exits. Reporter reacts in utter horror.)

REPORTER: *(Collects himself.)* The headline of the New York Post read, "Priscilla Makes an Ass of Herself." Then Priscilla vanished. For five years, she was nowhere to be found. Conspiracy theories sprang up like wild fire.

(Mary-Sue, Brittany, and Stanley take on the characters of devoted fans of Priscilla, the type of people who argue about every minutia of Priscilla's fabled existence.)

MARY-SUE: *(As Henrietta, a well-meaning fool.)* Priscilla had moved to India to join the Hare Krishna cult.

BRITTANY: *(As Tabby, the successful donkey breeder.)* No. Priscilla traveled to Vancouver and now works as a public librarian.

STANLEY: *(As Bruce, the president of the official Priscilla fan club.)* Nay! Priscilla moved to California to live inside of a tree and will come back again in fifty-five years when someone designs a gravy spoon that won't spill the gravy on the table cloth as you ladle it onto your mashed potatoes.

(Mary-Sue, Brittany, and Stanley exit.)

REPORTER: One Michigan teenager claimed that he was Priscilla reborn. *(Beat.)* And that teenager is obviously an asshole.

(Farmer Jim enters with his hoe and he hoes.)

REPORTER: *(Suddenly intense and excited.)* Ladies and gentlemen, we have been able to secure an interview with Farmer Jim himself.

(Reporter literally jumps on Farmer Jim and tackles him to the ground.)

FARMER JIM: *(Defeated.)* Shit. You got me.

REPORTER: Farmer Jim, could we ask you a few questions about Priscilla?

FARMER JIM: *(With growing anger.)* Why? What do you want to know about her? What questions could you possibly have? She's a has-been. The fame is over. Done. Capisce? *(Beat.)* Get off of me, you skunk.

REPORTER: *(Gets off of Farmer Jim and stares back at him, heartbroken and obviously offended.)* Priscilla was a gem and a half.

FARMER JIM: Fuck off. I'm working.

(Reporter doesn't move and continues filming the documentary. Farmer Jim resumes doing farm work.)

REPORTER: The bright lights of fame were too much for dear Priscilla. She longed for a simpler time. So Priscilla had run back to the traveling gypsies with whom she was raised...

(Priscilla enters and frolics upstage.)

REPORTER: She was finally living in peace; however, her peace would soon come to an end. Farmer Jim tracked Priscilla down and took her back to the farm where he forced her to continue tap dancing for fame, glory, and money. He booked her to perform at Madison Square Garden in an effort to return her to the spotlight.

(Priscilla is uneasy.)

REPORTER: Priscilla's handlers all said that they could tell something wasn't right. Before the show, she was pacing back and forth, kicking at the walls, and nervously twitching her front left hoof, which everyone knew was her least favorite hoof. One of her handlers noticed Priscilla blankly staring into the wall, like she was thinking. Maybe she was thinking about her gypsy home, far, far away. The handler asked Farmer Jim to not force Priscilla to perform. But Farmer Jim did anyway, and perform she did. With all her might and talent, Priscilla tapped like there was no tomorrow.

(Priscilla does an elaborate and extensive tap routine. Farmer watches her dance and reflects on his past mistreatment of her. Suddenly Priscilla trips and breaks her ankle.)

REPORTER: What's this, ladies and gentlemen? Could it be? Did Priscilla just break her leg?

(Priscilla hobbles off her platform, crosses between Reporter and Farmer Jim, brays in panic and pain, then freezes. Reporter looks at Farmer Jim in shock, disgust, and horror.)

REPORTER: *(Obviously hurt.)* Farmer Jim?

FARMER JIM: What?

REPORTER: How could you do a thing like that?

FARMER JIM: Screw you!

261

REPORTER: *(Sing-songy.)* "I know you are but what am I?"

FARMER JIM: *(A confused beat.)* What the hell?

REPORTER: *(To audience.)* Farmer Jim didn't know what to do. Priscilla was his source of income and he had just bought the entire Ken Burns documentary collection and now had no way to pay for them. People say they had never seen Farmer Jim so, emotional before.

(Reporter looks at Farmer Jim, who is crying.)

FARMER JIM: *(In tears.)* I hate you so much.

REPORTER: *(To Farmer Jim.)* And we hate you too. *(To audience.)* Well folks, you all know what happens to a horse with a broken leg, and a donkey is no exception. Farmer Jim took out his gun.

(Reporter hands the sobbing Farmer Jim the gun.)

REPORTER: And he shot Priscilla between her shoulder blades.

(Farmer Jim pulls the trigger and the gun "clicks." Priscilla dies a very dramatic, agonizingly painful death. She lays there as a testament to this travesty.)

FARMER JIM: *(In tears.)* Take that, you piece of shit.

REPORTER: I hate you.

FARMER JIM: Finally, something we can agree on.

(Farmer Jim takes off his hat, sits down, and cries, attempting to ignore what Reporter says.)

REPORTER: Did Farmer Jim shoot Priscilla out of compassion, to put her out of her misery? Or did he shoot her out of anger? The world may never know. But whenever I miss Priscilla I look at a picture of the wound Farmer Jim's buckshot made in her shoulder blade. If you look closely, you can see a pattern. It could be an ice cream cone or it could be the constellation Asellus Borealis, otherwise known as the Northern Donkey. Priscilla knew the Asellus Borealis was my favorite constellation, because I wrote about it in a letter to her when I was five years old.

(Farmer Jim takes a letter out of his pocket and gives it to Reporter.)

REPORTER: What's this?

FARMER JIM: It's your letter. I kept it all these years. Never in my life have I seen more life in a young boy. Such faith. Such love. It truly touched my heart that she meant so much to you... *(Beat.)* ...because she meant so much to me.

(Farmer Jim weeps. After an awkwardly long beat, Reporter crosses to comfort Farmer Jim. Reporter pulls a picture out of his pocket.)

REPORTER: This is the picture of Priscilla's fatal wound. I carry it in my wallet, in front of my kids' pictures. Do you want to see?

(It takes Farmer Jim a few moments to stop crying and then he looks at the picture.)

REPORTER: Now when I think of Priscilla, the most talented Donkey to ever live, the Asinine Astaire, I just close my eyes and look to the stars. *(Closes his eyes, softly.)* Asellus. Borealis. Asellus Borealis.

FARMER JIM: What the hell are you talking about?

REPORTER: Asellus. Borealis. Asellus Borealis.

FARMER JIM: *(With growing intrigue.)* Can you really see her? *(Looks up.)*

REPORTER: Asellus. Borealis. Asellus Borealis.

(Reporter holds out his hand; Farmer Jim takes it. They both look upwards.)

REPORTER and FARMER JIM: Asellus. Borealis. Asellus. Borealis. Asellus. Borealis.

(The voice of Priscilla is heard from the heavens, braying loudly. It echoes as the lights fade.)

END OF PLAY

Lisa Soland

RIGHTS AND PERMISSIONS

THE EDITOR

Lisa Soland received her BFA in acting from Florida State and her Actors' Equity card serving as an apprentice at the Burt Reynolds Jupiter Theatre in Florida. After moving to Los Angeles to pursue a career in acting, she began writing her first play while in acting class with Master Teacher Charles Nelson Reilly. With his support, and guidance from her mentor, playwright William Luce, she continued to write plays for the theatre.

With over 40 publications, her plays *Waiting, The Name Game, Truth be Told, Cabo San Lucas* and *The Man in the Gray Suit & Other Short Plays,* can be found through publisher Samuel French, Inc. *Thread Count, Spatial Disorientation, The Corporate Ladder,* as well as countless 10-minute plays, can be found in "best of" anthologies published by Smith & Kraus, Applause Books, and Dramatic Publishing.

Her newest works include full-lengths *The Ladder Plays, The Hand on the Plough, The Sniper's Nest,* and the one-man play *Sgt. Alvin York, WWI Hero,* scheduled to open in October of 2017 in Pall Mall, Tennessee, the home of Alvin York. The play will then tour during the 100th anniversary of WWI.

Ms. Soland created and has led The All Original Playwright Workshop in Los Angeles since 1999. During that time, AOPW awarded 19 Fellowship Awards, which included a cash stipend and public reading of the playwright's new work. She has directed and/or produced over 80 plays and play readings, 55 of which were original.

She has taught playwriting at Florida State University, Pellissippi State College, Lincoln Memorial University and Maryville College, and continues to lead workshops throughout the country. Ms. Soland also consults playwrights privately online. She is a member of the Dramatists Guild, as well as AEA, AFTRA and SAG.

Ms. Soland owns and is Senior Editor of the children's publishing company Climbing Angel Publishing, with titles *The Christmas Tree Angel, The Unmade Moose, Thump* and *Somebunny To Love.*